THE POLITICAL PHILOSOPHY
OF JAWAHARLAL NEHRU

THE POLITICAL PHILOSOPHY
OF
JAWAHARLAL NEHRU

M. N. DAS

M.A., Ph.D. (London)

Head of the Department of History
Utkal University, Orissa, India

THE JOHN DAY COMPANY

NEW YORK

PRINTED IN GREAT BRITAIN

To My Father
Sri Madhu Sudan Das

PREFACE

Though not a political philosopher in the conventional sense, Jawaharlal Nehru has nevertheless steered his political ideas between idealism and realism, thinking somewhat as a philosopher while working as a politician, and distinguishing himself more or less as a philosopher-politician. The problems of political thought today cannot be entirely based on speculative arguments or ethical doctrines, but have to be closely related to the real issues of human affairs. In other words, philosophy and factual questions supplement each other. While Nehru speculated considerably on political issues, practical politics gave him the singular advantage of understanding many of them stripped of illusion. Combined thought and action helped him in formulating his ideals and, in a sense, his political philosophy became embodied in his practical experiments.

The greater part of Nehru's life has been a dedication to politics, of which about thirty years were spent as an active revolutionary. During that period he underwent nine terms of imprisonment, amounting to nine years less twenty-three days. While prison provided leisure for deep thought and writing, life outside became enriched with varied experiences. When the revolution ended on August 15, 1947, years of greater responsibility awaited him in office. From revolutionary activities, conflicts with government and similar traditions straight to the seat of authority to deal with difficult problems required no easy adjustment. A greater problem was also evident. Not only was Nehru a revolutionary and an agitator, he was also 'bred up in a high tradition under a great man', Gandhi. This was an ethical and moral tradition, and at the same time was applied to practical politics. He could not set aside this background while in power. Instead, he carried on a continuous attempt to bridge the gulf between idealism and practice.

Nehru is a man of wide reading and of broad human outlook. With a scholarly approach to politics he formed his intellectual convictions, mostly in an individual way. The times he lives in have deeply influenced him, as have also the great ideas of the age, and events have imperceptibly served as lessons. Gandhi spiritualized him in a broad sense, while Marxism had a powerful effect on his mind. Despite external influences, however, he strove for individuality, and it is this which has always remained the key-note of his ideas.

The greater fundamentals of his political thought were considerably crystallized during the revolutionary phase of his career. They seemed to him, at that time, unalterable. He thought that his major decisions in public affairs would remain untouched, for they were stronger than himself, and a force beyond his control drove him to them. But did the acquisition of power mean compromise with former principles? Of late, he himself has wondered if he is very different from his earlier days, realizing that 'naturally, one tones down in a position of responsibility'. But it might be said regarding his broader ideals that essentially they remain the same as ever, and any apparent deviation or revision is due to changing circumstances, practical considerations, or expediency rather than to a lack of faith. He dislikes political dogmas, and views set ideas pragmatically with a critical mind. Democracy or socialism, most political doctrines in fact, are ever changing concepts, the mind progressing with the passage of time. Nehru's real concern has been to implement desired ideals from judgements of value and in accordance with moral principles.

The deeper political ideas of Nehru are primarily gathered from his basic writings. It was an attempt to discover the past in its relation to the present that led him to write *Glimpses of World History* in the form of letters to his daughter. 'I wrote rather superficially and as simply as I could,' he says, 'for I was writing for a girl in her early teens, but behind that writing lay that quest and voyage of discovery. A sense of adventure filled me and I lived successively different ages and periods and had for companions men and women who had lived long ago.' He had leisure while in prison to let his mind wander or take root for a while, keeping in tune with his mood, allowing impressions to sink in and fill the dry bones of the past with flesh and blood. The *Autobiography* is a narration of his own thoughts and moods and how they were affected by external happenings. 'I endeavoured to make this a truthful record of my own mental development.' The quest was still the same, and he wrote down his past feelings and experiences in the hope that this might bring him some peace and psychic satisfaction. *The Discovery of India* was again an attempt in the solitude and passivity of prison to fill the vacuum of life with memories of past living, of his own life, and of the long chain of history of human activity. In this work too the personal element has pushed itself forward almost against his will; 'often I checked it and held it back, but sometimes I loosened the reins and allowed it to flow out of my pen, and mirror, to some extent, my mind.'

These three works—a history of the world, a history of his own life, and a history of India—thus reveal sufficiently the inner thoughts of their author and, together with other aspects, they contain a vivid picture of his political mind.

There are also a number of essays and writings of a fundamental character written by Nehru which reveal his philosophy. Several of them have been written against a political background. Numerous speeches, addresses and sayings, ranging over a variety of subjects and covering the greater part of his life, supply valuable information regarding the trends of his thought. An outlet for ideas is also provided by debates, conversations, talks, statements and letters. Abundant material is available for an assessment of his political thought, with his practicala ctivities supplying corroborative evidence. At times there is a deliberate enunciation of certain principles, at others it is merely the ventilation of feelings.

Nehru has lived an eventful life. His is the many-sided role of a revolutionary and a nationalist, a democrat and a socialist, an internationalist and a pacifist, a head of government and, above all, a lone individual and a thinker. In the following chapters an attempt is made to co-ordinate his ideas in the above roles. These ideas, in essence, reflect his political philosophy.

I am grateful to my preceptor, Professor C. H. Philips, Director of the School of Oriental and African Studies, University of London, for the opportunity he kindly gave me of using the resources of the School where I was able to complete this work. I am greatly obliged to Professor A. L. Basham, Professor of the History of South Asia in the University of London, for his valuable advice and suggestions.

Thanks are due to my good friends R. Edwin Ellinson and P. Bryant and to my wife Rajasree Das for their assistance in comparing the manuscript, reading the proofs and preparing an index.

It has been my aim in this volume to present, as objectively as possible, the political ideas of Nehru in the light of his own words from the material available to me.

London, 1960 M. N. DAS

WH   *Glimpses of World History:* Being Further Letters to his daughter, written in prison, and containing a Rambling Account of History for young people, 2 Vols., by Jawaharlal Nehru, Kitabistan, Allahabad, 1934-35.

AB   Jawaharlal Nehru: *An Autobiography*, with Musings on Recent Events in India, The Bodley Head, London (First published in 1936), 1958 Edition.

DI   *The Discovery of India* by Jawaharlal Nehru, Meridian Books Limited, London (First published September, 1946), 1951 Edition.

Essays I   *Recent Essays and Writings:* On the Future of India, Communalism and other Subjects, by Jawaharlal Nehru, Kitabistan, Allahabad (First published April, 1934), May 1934 Edition.

Essays II   *India and the World:* Essays by Jawaharlal Nehru, George Allen and Unwin Ltd, London, First published 1936.

Essays III   *Eighteen Months in India 1936-1937:* Being Further Essays and Writings by Jawaharlal Nehru, Kitabistan, Allahabad (First published March 1938), June 1938 Edition.

Writings I   *Selected Writings of Jawaharlal Nehru 1916-1950:* Dealing with the Shape of Things to Come in India and the World, Edited by J. S. Bright, The Indian Printing Works, New Delhi.

Writings II   Jawaharlal Nehru: *The Unity of India:* Collected Writings 1937-1940, Lindsay Drummond, London, 1948 Edition.

Speeches I   *Independence and After:* A Collection of the more important Speeches of Jawaharlal Nehru from September, 1946, to May, 1949, Ministry of Information and Broadcasting—Government of India, 1949.

Speeches II   *Jawaharlal Nehru's Speeches 1949-1953*, Ministry of Information and Broadcasting—Government of India, 1954.

Speeches III   *Jawaharlal Nehru's Speeches:* Volume Three: March, 1953-August, 1957, Ministry of Information and Broadcasting—Government of India, 1958.

Debates C.A.   Constituent Assembly Debates.

Debates C.A.
(Legislative)   Constituent Assembly of India (Legislative) Debates.

Debates P.I.   Parliamentary Debates Parliament of India.

Debates H.P.   Parliamentary Debates House of the People.

Letters   *A Bunch of Old Letters:* Written mostly to Jawaharlal Nehru and some written by him, Asia Publishing House, Bombay, 1958.

Talks   *Talks with Nehru:* A discussion between Nehru and Norman Cousins, London, 1951.

Conversations   *Conversations with Mr Nehru* by Tibor Mende, Secker and Warburg, London, 1956.

On Gandhi   *Nehru on Gandhi:* A selection, arranged in the order of events, from the writings and speeches of Jawaharlal Nehru, The John Day Company, New York, 1948.

Birthday Book   *Nehru Abhinandan Granth:* A Birthday Book, New Delhi, 1949.

Biblio   *Jawaharlal Nehru: A Descriptive Bibliography* by J. S. Sharma, S. Chand & Co., Delhi, 1955.

Note: The *Autobiography* was published in the United States of America under the title *Toward Freedom*, by The John Day Company, New York. Other works published in America by John Day are *Glimpses of World History, The Discovery of India, The Unity of India, Independence and After, Talks With Nehru,* and *Nehru on Gandhi.*

CONTENTS

CHAPTER I

MIND AND PHILOSOPHY

The Worlds of Action and Ideas

A man of practical and positive nature, Jawaharlal Nehru is also a man of abstract ideas, thus living in two worlds—a world of action and a world of thought. The thought developed through intellectual curiosity and the search for knowledge, while action followed the sequence of external events. Man is a part of nature, and also a part of society; and therefore he has to be 'natural with nature and human with human society'. Between the two worlds a balance is needed, which Nehru tries to maintain. He does not want to lose himself 'in aimless and romantic quests unconnected with life's problems', for destiny marches on and does not wait for anyone's leisure; nor does he want to concern himself 'with externals only, forgetting the significance of the inner life of man'.* There is an innate desire to understand life by a frank and courageous approach to realities; at the same time, to look at it from the standpoint of thought and vision. In his life, he attempts a harmony between the two.

His Philosophical Mood

A philosophical mood through all stages of life from adolescence to old age is an apparent feature of Nehru's character. A childhood without companions, education in a different and distant country, a life in many prisons, and ultimately the office which placed him above others, helped him in varying degrees to live a

---

* Nehru believes in the saying of Spinoza that 'The greatest good is the knowledge of the union which the mind has with the whole of nature. . . . The more the mind knows the better it understands its forces and the order of nature; the more it understands its forces or strength, the better it will be able to direct itself and lay down rules for itself; and the more it understands the order of nature, the more easily it will be able to liberate itself from useless things; this is the whole method.' *DI*, X, 535.

detached life. How far a detached life accounts for a philosophical mood is difficult to say. But in the case of Nehru it is his contemplative mood that made him cultivate a certain detachment. Perhaps they were complementary in his life—detachment leading to contemplation and contemplation calling for detachment. Slowly he trained his mind not to attach a great deal of value to himself. He succeeded, though not to any large extent, as there were other factors which made real detachment impossible. But even the partial success which he achieved was 'very helpful', because, as he says:

'. . . in the midst of activity, I could separate myself from it and look at it as a thing apart. Sometimes, I would steal an hour or two, and forgetting my usual preoccupations, retire into that cloistered chamber of my mind and live, for a while, another life.'[1]

Nehru wants to believe that all people have some kind of philosophy of life, conscious or unconscious, and if not thought out then inherited or accepted from others and considered as self-evident. One may also seek refuge from the perils of thought in faith in some religious creed or dogma, or in national destiny, or in a vague and comforting humanitarianism. He further believes that often all these qualities and others are present together in the mind, and, having little to connect them, split personalities are developed.[2] Through his similar reflections, one may discern his own mind, a mind which is not prepared to keep itself away from the more remote thoughts.

There had been moments of great despair in his life when life seemed to be 'a dreary affair, a very wilderness of desolation'. He fought many a battle within himself and learned many a hard lesson. And, 'One must journey through life alone',[3] this is what he learnt, however painful. Such feelings made the sense of detachment more real, and the mind was conditioned accordingly.

His Imaginative and Poetic Nature
Politics wholly absorbed Nehru from a comparatively early age,

[1] *DI*, III, 52.
[2] *DI*, V, 159-60.
[3] *AB*, LXI, 507.

leaving him with little time for other interests. But politics could not suppress in him his inherent nature of being imaginative and poetic. With his pen he expressed his nature; and either in his basic writings or in casual letters, essays, or even talks, the flow of a sublime imagination is traced. That is an aspect of his inner self. His mind would like to peep into the wisdom of the ancients, the faith of the middle ages, the scepticism of the present and the glory that is to be. And out of them it is enchanting for the mind to think of 'a magic city, full of dream castles and flowering gardens and running brooks, where beauty and happiness dwell and the ills that this sorry world suffers from can gain no admittance'. And then that life would 'become one long and happy endeavour, a ceaseless adventure, to build the city of magic and drive away all the ugliness and misery around us'.[1]

Poetry and politics are seemingly different things, and the former cannot be the concern of a politician. But something akin to poetry remained in him, and the extreme worldliness of politics failed to dominate his inner personality. From childhood almost he had developed a liking for poetry, a liking which, according to Nehru himself, endured to some extent and survived the many other changes to which he was subject.[2] Regarding politics, even so late as 1944 he was prepared to say that he 'was not much of a politician', although politics had seized him and made him its 'victim'.[3] And, when really at the helm of political authority, he could confess to India's Constituent Assembly: 'I am afraid I am a bad bargainer. I am not used to the ways of the market place. I hope I am a good fighter and I hope I am a good friend. I am not anything in between and so when you have to bargain hard for anything, do not send me.'[4] When the burdens of state lay heavily on his shoulders, his mind could afford little time to rest imaginatively or to escape into a far away realm. Nevertheless, the fundamentals of his character hardly changed, however little the opportunity for expression.

[1] A Study of Nehru, p. 132, A Letter from Nehru to Krishna Hutheesing written in November 1930 from Naini Jail, Allahabad.
[2] AB, III, 14.
[3] DI, VII, 330.
[4] Debates C. A., VIII, No. 1, May 16, 1949.

His Complexity of Mind

The mind of Nehru appears to be a complex one, obsessed as it is with various conflicts. Often enough he is seen to be troubled by these conflicts, the age he lives in, the crisis in the spirit of man, and by the world situation. Clouds of thought appear, they clear away, but again reappear. Often, the dull and wearying public functions and the dust and tumble of politics would touch him only on the surface, while the inner conflict would be wrecking his mind.

'My real conflict lay within me, a conflict of ideas, desires and loyalties, of subconscious depths struggling with outer circumstances, of an inner hunger unsatisfied.'[1]

He would become a battleground for the struggle of various forces. He would seek escape, would try to find harmony and equilibrium, and in attempting this would rush into action, because the outer conflict relieved the strain of the inner struggle.

No less is the trouble from the spirit of the time. Looking back to the days of the past he finds them as the 'days of faith; blind, unquestioning faith'. He is thrilled at the amazing intensity of devotion which the various embodiments of that bygone age hold before him; but knows that the days of that faith are gone. Instead, the present age is a different one, 'it is an age of disillusion, of doubt and uncertainty and questioning'.

'We can no longer accept many of the ancient beliefs and customs; we have no more faith in them, in Asia or in Europe or America. So we search for new ways, new aspects of the truth more in harmony with our environment. And we question each other and debate and quarrel and evolve any number of "isms" and philosophies. As in the days of Socrates, we live in an age of questioning, but that questioning is not confined to a city like Athens; it is world-wide.'[2]

He respects his age as one of the great ages of mankind, but is conscious that one has to pay the price for the privilege of living in it. The great ages are always 'full of conflict and instability',[3] and there are attempts in them to change over from the old to something new. While he is anxious for the change and the new

[1] *AB*, XXVIII, 207.
[2] *Essays II*, 169, 'The Last Letter to Indira', August, 1933.
[3] *DI*, X, 534.

order of things to come, the mind is troubled by numerous questions as to how and in what way? Years pass by, but the spirit of 'a haunted age', as he calls it, does not cease to disturb his mind. The feeling of 'ghosts and apparitions surrounding us', of many things which men cannot grip, nevertheless which are dangerous, continue to remain. 'We live in this haunted age where vast numbers of people in various countries become frustrated because they see no light, because they see danger, the danger of a future war and the danger of a future break-up, before them.'[1]

His concern over the crisis in the very spirit of man is deep. Behind the last war he saw what appeared to be this internal conflict of the spirit of man. While he is enamoured of the 'something godlike in man', he is also wide awake to 'something of the devil in him'. The civilization itself appears in crises, with people talking and acting more and more 'in terms of might and the insolence of power'; and others, afraid of power, lining up behind that very thing. As a result, the good things of life suffer, the very basis of a decent approach to life, religious, spiritual, or scientific. 'They are submerged in this deluge of hatred and violence and fear. Fear and hatred and violence are the worst companions that an individual or a nation can have.'[2]

This obviously leads to the world's crises. The global wars have left a deep impression on his mind; and he has always wondered why in the sphere of politics and economics there should be a search for power and yet when the power has been attained, much else of value should have gone.

'Political trickery and intrigue take the place of idealism, and cowardice and selfishness the place of disinterested courage. Form prevails over substance, and power, so eagerly sought after, somehow fails to achieve what it aimed at. For power has its limitations, and force recoils on itself. Neither can control the spirit, though they may harden and coarsen it.'[3]

The mind, disturbed by such problems, develops complexity. Thoughts become manifold, and there is a continuous struggle to find answers. He himself is conscious of the fact that in each man

[1] *Debates* P. I., 1951, XII, Part II, May 29, 1951.
[2] *Speeches* III, 436, January 15, 1957.
[3] *DI*, X, 534.

there are many different human beings with their inconsistencies and contradictions, each pulling in a different direction. Be that as it may, Nehru consistently endeavours to resolve the conflicts of his mind into open and clear ideas. More or less, he can translate his complex mind into simple fundamentals, and while the crisis of his mind remains within himself, for the outside world his ideas are presented in a somewhat crystallized form. The crisis of the mind is often enough solved by giving free vent to the feelings, for one thing is certain; he does not believe in suppressing his emotions. Furthermore, without being dogmatic, but trying to be dynamic, and with a scientific approach to most matters, he is able to represent his mind in an easy way.

His Mind in Relation to Different Phases of Life

Nehru discovers at times some kind of changing mind within himself. As forceful events created different circumstances, the mind in order to adapt itself became supple. Varying moods thus became imperative and they were within his own perception. Changing moods were 'very apparent'[1] in the course of the letters which finally emerged as the *Glimpses of World History*. Opinions were often expressed rather aggressively, and his mind afterwards became aware of a different emphasis. He began his *Autobiography* 'in a mood of self-questioning', and attempted to trace in it his own 'mental development'.[2] He had continually had a feeling of growing up, and that feeling continued to be with him. Several years later the *Discovery of India* was being written, and Nehru noted a good deal of change in himself. He had grown more contemplative. There was perhaps a little more poise and equilibrium, some sense of detachment, a greater calmness of spirit. Tragedy did not overcome him to the same extent as before. The turmoil was less, and inclined to be more temporary, even though the tragedies were greater. He wondered if this was due to a spirit of resignation, or due to a toughening of the texture. Or, was it just age, a lessening of vitality, or the effect of prison?

'The tortured mind seeks some mechanism of escape, the senses get dulled from repeated shocks, and a feeling comes over one that

[1] *WH*, Preface.
[2] *AB*, Preface and Epilogue.

so much evil and misfortune shadow the world that a little more or less does not make much difference. There is only one thing that remains to us that cannot be taken away: to act with courage and dignity and to stick to the ideals that have given meaning to life; but that is not the politician's way.'[1]

From the fort prison of Ahmadnagar the prisoner would look back to the days of his youth when he lived for considerable periods 'in a state of emotional exaltation', wrapped up in the action which absorbed him. Those days would seem far away, with an ocean of experience and painful thought in between. The burden of thought he regarded as a hindrance, and in the mind where there was once certainty, he found doubts creeping in. 'Perhaps it is just age, or the common temper of our day.' In some earlier days, he thought, there was a definiteness about his thinking and objectives which faded away later; and no longer could he function as he did in his younger days, as an arrow flying automatically to the target of his choice, ignoring all else but that target. His whole attitude to life seemed to undergo a transformation.

But those were the morbid years of World War II, and he himself was a prisoner, tormented by a distressing present and faced with an uncertain future. Diffidence could cast its natural gloom over his mind. But that phase of life came to an end all too soon when he himself became free and his country independent. As he stood on the crossroads of time, he felt 'the weight of all manner of things crowding around' him. He was at the end of an era, looking forward to embark upon a new age. All the past gathered around him and exhilarated him, and at the same time, somewhat oppressed him when he thought if he was worthy of the great past of his country. Keeping the past in view, he turned to think of the future, the greater future, as he hoped.

'. . . standing on this sword's edge of the present between this mighty past and the mightier future, I tremble a little and feel overwhelmed by this mighty task. We have come here at a strange moment in India's history. I do not know but I do feel that there is some magic in this moment of transition from the old to the new, something of that magic which one sees when the night turns

[1] *DI*, I, 9.

into day and even though the day may be a cloudy one, it is day after all, for when the clouds move away, we can see the sun later on.'[1]

A new vista of thought opened itself, once again with a definiteness about his thinking and objectives. There was the inspiration to develop a dynamic mentality, and a daring spirit of adventure; and in the world of thought, to dare 'to pierce the heavens', and not be afraid of any idea.

Thus, some main phases of life are reflected in the mind through their different meanings, but all the same, the basic ideas seem to remain the same as ever. These basic ideas reflect the philosophy of his life.

His Attitude towards God

At the seventieth year of Nehru's life, one of his closest friends, Amrit Kaur, who knew him from a very early age, proceeded to say that 'by far the greatest lack in him is his inability to believe in God'; and that pious elderly lady continued to hope that 'for him some day faith will transcend reason and that belief in God will come to his rescue and be for him the anchor that it has been for so many great men during periods of storm and stress, whereby they were able to face and surmount crises'.[2] It puzzled some people how Gandhi, with his absolute faith in God, should have accepted the atheistic Nehru as his right-hand man and, in a very real sense, dearest to himself. But Gandhi had his answers. On one occasion, during the days of the individual *satyagraha* in 1940, when Nehru's arrest by the government was practically certain and a sense of sadness was in the air, he had come to Sevagram to see Gandhi. As he was taking leave, the wife of the Mahatma blessed him and said: 'God will look after you.' Thereupon Nehru turned to her with a smile and said: 'Where is God, Ba*? If He exists, He must be very fast asleep.' This evoked hearty laughter from Gandhi who knew and often used to say: 'While Jawaharlal always says he does not believe in God he is nearer God than many who profess to be His worshippers.'[3] A

* Kasturba, wife of Mahatma Gandhi, reverently called 'Ba'.
[1] *Debates* C. A., I, No. 5, Resolution re: Aims and Objects, December 13, 1946.
[2] *A Study of Nehru*, p. 155, Amrit Kaur, 'A Friend Without Friends'.
[3] *Birthday Book*, 139-40, Amrit Kaur, 'Wealth of Human Sympathy'.

strict adherence to Goodness and Truth was to Gandhi as good as
a sincere devotion to God, and when he found the former in
Nehru, he did not care to think if the latter were missing.

The Nature of His Agnosticism

A sense of mysteries and of unknown depths comes to Nehru at
times, and he creates an urge in himself to understand them or
even to experience them in their fullness. But the way to that
understanding is to him essentially the way of science, the
objective approach. He believes that there can be no such thing
as true objectiveness; but then, if the subjective element is
unavoidable and inevitable, he is prepared to consider it when it
is conditioned, as far as possible, by the scientific method. It is
this reliance on science which takes him away from the mysteries.

'What the mysterious is I do not know. I do not call it God
because God has come to mean much that I do not believe in. I
find myself incapable of thinking of a deity or of any unknown
supreme power in anthropomorphic terms, and the fact that many
people think so is continually a source of surprise to me. Any
idea of a personal God seems very odd to me.'[1]

He appreciates the conception of monism, the non-dualist
philosophy of the Hindu *Vedanta*, realizing at the same time that a
mere intellectual appreciation of such matters does not carry one
far. Rather, the *Vedanta* or similar approaches frighten him with
'their vague, formless incursions into infinity'.

Yet he thinks of a God. 'Even if God did not exist, it would
be necessary to invent Him,' said Voltaire, and Nehru would
agree with him. But at the same time he thinks of a reverse pro-
position—'even if God exists, it may be desirable not to look
up to Him or to rely upon Him. Too much dependence on
supernatural factors may lead, and has often led, to a loss of self-
reliance in man and to a blunting of his capacity and creative
ability.'[2] What Nehru thinks to be desirable is some faith in things
of the spirit which are beyond the scope of the physical world,
some reliance on moral, spiritual, and idealistic conceptions. Or
else, there will be no anchorage, no objectives or purpose in life.

[1] *DI*, I, 13.
[2] *DI*, X, 489.

'Whether we believe in God or not,' he says, 'it is impossible not to believe in something, whether we call it a creative life-giving force or vital energy inherent in matter which gives it its capacity for self-movement and change and growth, or by some other name, something that is as real, though elusive, as life is real when contrasted with death.'[1] Inside the orbit of this broad concept, he is even prepared to see some kind of ideal—personal, national or international, some distant objective, some vague conception of a perfect man or a better world—as the objects of belief.

His Attitude towards Religion

In his childhood Nehru listened to the stories from the Hindu mythology, and his knowledge on the subject became 'quite considerable'. But religion seemed to him 'to be a woman's affair', and the ceremonies and *pujas*, visits to temples and holy men, left little impression on his mind.[2] A little later he was under the influence of theosophy, gradually imbibing theosophical phraseology and ideas, and feeling at the same time that here was the key to the secrets of the universe. He began to think of religion and other worlds. At that time, the Hindu religion especially rose in his estimation. He did not like its ritual or ceremonial, but appreciated its *Upanishads* and the *Gita*. At the age of thirteen he decided to join the Theosophical Society, and when his father did not attach any importance to it, he was hurt, and felt that his father 'was lacking in spirituality'.[3] But in a short time he bade goodbye to Theosophy. For several years after, he had nothing to do with religion, until Gandhi began to influence him. He was too much under Gandhi's influence in political and other matters 'to remain wholly immune even in the sphere of religion'. 'I came nearer to a religious frame of mind in 1921 than at any other time since my early boyhood. Even so I did not come very near.'[4]

As for himself, at any time in his grown-up life he could have passed for any religious denomination, Christian, Buddhist, Hindu or Moslem, provided that by religion one means the innermost virtues of life. Religion means to him the very essence of charac-

[1] *Ibid.*
[2] *AB*, II, 8.
[3] *AB*, III, 15.
[4] *AB*, X, 73.

ter, truthfulness, love and the purity of mind. 'I was born a Hindu, but I do not know how far I am justified in calling myself one or in speaking on behalf of Hindus,' so he said at one time.[1] But he is still a Hindu provided he is not called upon to accept many of the outer forms of Hinduism.

The role which organized religion played in the history of India during Nehru's own time greatly provoked him against what religion stood for in its outer meaning.* 'There can be no doubt that the founders of the great religions have been among the greatest and noblest men that the world has produced,' he wrote. 'But their disciples and the people who have come after them have often been far from great or good. Often in history we see that religion, which was meant to raise us and make us better and nobler, has made people behave like beasts. Instead of bringing enlightenment to them, it has often tried to keep them in the dark; instead of broadening their minds, it has frequently made them narrow-minded and intolerant of others. In the name of religion many great and fine deeds have been performed. In the name of religion also thousands and millions have been killed, and every possible crime has been committed.'[2]

At times he felt that he had no use for either religion or philanthropy, since they often covered 'the rankest hypocrisy and selfishness'. He would believe in ethics and morality and truthfulness and other virtues, but his belief in them should not turn them into methods, though they could only be the attributes of a method.[3] On other occasions, his 'accumulated irritation' would turn to religion and the religious outlook. They were enemies to clearness of thought and fixity of purpose, because they were based on emotion and passion. Religion which presumes to be spiritual would appear to him as far from real spirituality. Moreover, thinking in terms of some other world, it had little conception of human values, social values and social justice. He found in

---

* 'India is supposed to be a religious country above everything else,' he says in the *Autobiography*, 'and Hindu and Moslem and Sikh and others take pride in their faiths and tesify to their truth by breaking heads. The spectacle of what is called religion, or at any rate organized religion, in India and elsewhere, has filled me with horror, and I have frequently condemned it and wished to make a clean sweep of it.' (XLVII, 374).

[1] *Writings* I, 41.
[2] *Writings* I, 37.
[3] *Essays* I, 33, 'Some Criticisms Considered'.

religion preconceived notions, because of which, he thought, it deliberately shut its eyes to reality for the fear that reality might not fit in with notions.[1]

The Element of Scepticism

Apart from other considerations, it was again his faith in science which made him sceptical towards religious doctrines. The Prophets have always had a great appeal for him, and he finds it difficult to analyse this appeal, but certainly it is not a religious appeal. It is the personality of a Buddha or Christ which attracts him greatly.[2] But as for other things:

'Religion as I saw it practised, and accepted even by thinking minds, whether it was Hinduism or Islam or Buddhism or Christianity, did not attract me. It seemed to be closely associated with superstitious practices and dogmatic beliefs, and behind it lay a method of approach to life's problems which was certainly not that of science. There was an element of magic about it, an uncritical credulousness, a reliance on the supernatural.'[3]

Of course, it is obvious to him that religion has supplied some deeply felt inner need of human nature, and that the vast majority of people all over the world could not do without some form of religious belief. Also, there is something beyond the scientific positive knowledge of the day, and no thinking person can ignore it. In thinking to balance religion and science, the unknown and the known, Nehru hopes that science may widen its boundaries and may invade the so-called invisible world and help men to understand the purpose of life in its widest sense. He hopes for the application of the scientific method to emotional and religious experiences.

Mysticism, in its narrow sense, irritates him. He is not attracted towards metaphysics. 'And yet,' he says, 'I have sometimes found a certain intellectual fascination in trying to follow the rigid lines of metaphysical and philosophic thought of the ancients or the moderns. But I have never felt at ease there and have escaped from their spell with a feeling of relief.'[4] The theories regarding some

[1] *AB*, LXI, 507.
[2] *AB*, XXXVI, 271.
[3] *DI*, I, 11.
[4] *DI*, I, 12.

other world or a future life, regarding the soul or reincarnation, the theory of cause and effect governing life's actions and similar ones arouse in him merely intellectual speculation, without affecting in any way his life or belief. Here again, the dominating factor in his mind is, while the thoughts based on some premises are presumed to be self-evident, in reality they may or may not be true. In the same context, spiritualism with its seances and its so-called manifestations of spirits seems to him 'a rather absurd and impertinent way of investigating psychic phenomena and the mysteries of the after-life'.

Reliance on Truth and Science

Opposed to narrowness and intolerance, credulity and superstition, emotionalism and irrationalism, Nehru finds peace in conforming to ethics and the principles of the good life. To that life and to this phenomenal world he wants to apply reason and knowledge and experience. A reliance on truth and science has been consciously developed in the mind, and a mental satisfaction in him is perceptible on account of that. Truth as ultimate reality, he believes, must be eternal, imperishable and unchanging. But that perhaps cannot be apprehended in its fullness by the finite mind of man which can only grasp some small aspect of it. But as the mind develops and enlarges its scope, new aspects of it come to light, though the core of it may yet be the same.

'And so, truth has ever to be sought and renewed, reshaped, and developed, so that, as understood by man, it might keep in line with the growth of his thought and the development of human life. Only then does it become a living truth for humanity, supplying the essential need for which it craves, and offering guidance in the present and for the future.'[1]

If any aspect of the truth has been petrified by dogma in a past age, it ceases to grow, and therefore cannot answer the questions of a succeeding age. Nehru's concept of truth therefore is something dynamic and not static; it is a life-giving impulse, but not a dead thought and ceremonial, or a hindrance to the growth of the mind and of humanity.

Science has its limitations in spite of its achievements, yet he

[1] *DI*, X, 486.

wants to hold on to it, and with it to reason, to attain truth or reality. It is better, according to him, to understand a part of truth and apply it to life, than to understand nothing at all and flounder helplessly in a vain attempt to pierce the mystery of existence. For all peoples of all countries the applications of science are inevitable today, and even something more is necessary.

'It is the scientific approach, the adventurous and yet critical temper of science, the search for truth and new knowledge, the refusal to accept anything without testing and trial, the capacity to change previous conclusions in the face of new evidence, the reliance on observed fact and not on pre-conceived theory, the hard discipline of the mind—all this is necessary, not merely for the application of science but for life itself and the solution of its many problems.'[1]

His Opposition to Obscurantism

The spirit of dogma, Nehru says, has badly affected the religious quest of man. Ideas which assert in effect that 'I am in possession of the truth, and nobody outside the pale has it', make men's minds narrow, and shut the door against a tolerant and objective approach, 'where men not only look up at the heavens without fear but are also prepared to look down into the pit of hell without fear'. He makes a case for a tolerant view of life so that one may hold one opinion while respecting the opinions of others in consideration that there may be truth in the others' opinions, too. Truth is too big to be grasped all at once, and however much one may know there is always much else to be known.[2]

Here again Nehru turns to science, because the scientist is supposed to be an objective seeker after truth. But he thinks that no man today, not even a scientist, can live in a world of his own. Science, as he sees it, has begun to cross the borders of morals and ethics, but if it gets divorced from the realm of morality and ethics, then its power may be used for evil purposes. The scientific spirit, therefore, ought to be essentially one of tolerance and humility.

'Scientists should note that they do not have a monopoly of

[1] *DI*, X, 488.
[2] *Speeches* III, 433, January 14, 1957.

the truth; that nobody has a monopoly, no country, no people, no book. Truth is too vast to be contained in the minds of human beings, or in books, however sacred.'[1]

His Faith in Man

By far the greater part of the philosophy of Nehru centres round man—human nature, human affairs and human interests. However difficult it is for him to retain unqualified faith in man, to lose this faith is even more difficult.

'God we may deny, but what hope is there for us if we deny man and thus reduce everything to futility?'[2]

With an unbounded sympathy for man he has looked to him with almost the devotion of a faith. He looks upon the past history of man 'with the eye of sympathy'. The dry bones fill up before his eyes with flesh and blood, and he finds 'a mighty procession of living men and women and children in every age and every clime, different from us and yet very like us, with much the same human virtues and human failings'.[3] A kind of understanding is established, and to understand men who lived long ago, he understands their environment, the conditions under which they lived, and the ideas that filled their minds. It seems absurd for him to judge past people as if they lived now and thought as we do.

What perhaps attracts him most in man is his spirit. The gallant fight of man against the elements, his courage that conquers nature itself, his limitless endurance, his high endeavour and loyalty to comrades and forgetfulness of self, and his good humour in the face of every conceivable misfortune, would create in Nehru's mind, in some lone moments of life, a deep sympathy for man. Why should such be the nature of man, he would wonder. It is not for any advantage to man himself, nor even for the public good. 'Why, then? Simply because of the daring that is in man, the spirit that will not submit but always seeks to mount higher and higher, the call that comes from the stars.' Most men may be deaf to that call, but it is well that a few should hear it.

'To them life is a continual challenge, a long adventure, a testing of their worth:

[1] *Ibid.*
[2] *DI*, IX, 445.
[3] *Essays* II, 166, 'The Last Letter to Indira', August, 1933.

C

"I count life just a stuff
To try the soul's strength on. . . ." [1]

The puny body of man has a mind that recognizes no bounds, and a spirit that knows no defeat. Adventure is always there for the adventurous, and the wide world beckons to those who have courage and spirit, and the stars hurl their challenge across the skies. With such faith in the strength of man, he nevertheless becomes aware at times of the weakness of man to misuse that strength. While he is attracted by the spirit that conquers nature or brings about great human convulsions like the French or Russian Revolutions, he feels disturbed over that aspect of human nature which points to violence and deceit. Even the very progress of science, isolated from moral discipline, might lead to the concentration of power in the hands of selfish men, inviting the destruction of its own achievements. Yet, his faith does not desert him, and he remembers that nothing can happen that is likely to overcome the spirit of man; and also life, for all its ills, has joy and beauty.

'How amazing is this spirit of man! In spite of innumerable failings, man, throughout the ages, has sacrificed his life and all he held dear for an ideal, for truth, for faith, for country and honour. That ideal may change, but that capacity for self-sacrifice continues, and, because of that, much may be forgiven to man, and it is impossible to lose hope for him. In the midst of disaster, he has not lost his dignity or his faith in the values he cherished. Plaything of nature's mighty forces, less than a speck of dust in this vast universe, he has hurled defiance at the elemental powers, and with his mind, cradle of revolution, sought to master them.' [2]

His Scientific Humanism

Nehru defines the better type of modern mind as practical and pragmatic, ethical and social, altruistic and humanitarian. 'It is governed by a practical idealism for social betterment.' The ideals which move the mind, according to him, represent the spirit of the age, or, as he calls it, the *Yugadharma*.* 'It has discarded,' he

* The Zeitgeist.
[1] *Essays* III, 4, 'In a Train'.
[2] *DI*, I , 18.

says, 'to a large extent the philosophic approach of the ancients, their search for ultimate reality, as well as the devotionalism and mysticism of the medieval period. Humanity is its god and social service its religion.'[1] From such ideals he evolves his concept of 'scientific humanism', which may be described as representing an aspect of his own philosophy.

In the field of action, to promote human happiness, human co-operation and human progress, what he considers as essential is the human approach. Whatever one's job is, one has, after all, to deal with humanity. In this respect, one cannot be rigid or dog-matic, since it is difficult to lay down any rule embracing all human beings. The approach therefore has to be 'a knowledge-able approach and an open-minded approach and always a human approach'. 'The moment we forget the human approach, somehow the foundation of our thinking is removed.'[2] He directs his human-ism against the orthodoxies of the modern state or government, which aim to subordinate man to the abstract concepts of political theories.

An Inner Consideration for Man

While believing in the welfare of the human race as a whole, he puts his faith in the welfare and freedom of the individual. His humanism and liberality are fostered by an inner respect for the individual self. The mild temper of the humanist prevails all through, and the relation with other individuals is often enough based on a tender human touch. Emotional feelings in personal life are not infrequently marked, and human feeling from others is appreciated with emotion. 'Even my gaolers and the policemen,' he would write, 'who have arrested me or escorted me as a prisoner from place to place, have been kind to me, and much of the bitter-ness of conflict and the sting of gaol life has been toned down because of this human touch.'[3] A small incident at times would move him and remain fresh in his memory. Under the cover of darkness one night when Nehru was being transferred from one prison to another the superintendent of police, who was an

[1] *DI*, X, 532.
[2] *Speeches* III, 86, April 14, 1956.
[3] *AB*, XLIV, 347.

Englishman, handed him rather shyly a packet of illustrated magazines for his use. 'I had never met him before, nor have I seen him since. I do not even know his name. This spontaneous act of courtesy and the kindly thought that prompted it touched me and I felt very grateful to him,' he wrote in his *Autobiography*.[1] The behaviour of a person acting as an individual while obeying his own impulses appears to him as something nobler.

'The soldier, stiffening to attention, drops his humanity, and, acting as an automaton, shoots and kills inoffensive and harmless persons who have done him no ill. So also . . . the police officer who would hesitate to do an unkindness to an individual would, the day after, direct a *lathi* charge on innocent people. He would not think of himself as an individual then, nor will he consider as individuals those crowds whom he beats down or shoots.'[2]

To Nehru, the human link seems to disappear as soon as one begins to think of others as a mass or a crowd. What it is therefore necessary to bear in mind, according to him, is that crowds also consist of individuals, of men and women and children, who love and hate and suffer. Emotion towards man as such often prompts him to place the individual even above the abstract ideas of justice and punishment. Thinking of the mind of a judge, he could proceed to ask if the thoughts of the judges ever went beyond the set ideas of law and took human shape, 'considering the miserable offender as a human being with parents, wife, children, friends?'[3]

This kind of humane attitude manifests itself both in smaller and higher activities of his life. In a strictly personal sense, his respect for man is so apparent that when Prime Minister he would not think of disturbing the untimely sleep of a humble attendant. The incident occurred when Nehru invited a foreign visitor who was on a special visit to India. In the course of an interview at the Prime Minister's house, he took the guest into the dining-room to show a Chinese painting. While groping about for the light, Nehru stumbled over the body of a man asleep on the floor. 'Someone is asleep here,' he said, and proceeded to carry on the rest of the conversation in whispers![4]

[1] *AB*, XLIV, 346.
[2] *AB*, XLIV, 346-47.
[3] *Essays* II, 136, 'The Mind of a Judge', September, 1935.
[4] Campbell-Johnson, *Mission with Mountbatten*, 271-72.

The Lesson of Life

Nehru's ideas on life are related to realities. He is not interested in the after life, and in what happens after death. 'I find the problems of this life sufficiently absorbing to fill my mind.'[1] How to understand life, not to reject it but to accept it, how to conform to it and to improve it—these are his problems. The injustice, the unhappiness, and the brutality of the world may sometimes oppress men and darken their minds, but if one takes a dismal view, he has not learnt aright the lesson of life. History teaches the growth, the progress and the possibility of an infinite advance for man, and therefore,

'. . . life is rich and varied, and though it has many swamps and marshes and muddy places, it has also the great sea, and the mountains, and snow, and glaciers, and wonderful star-lit nights, and the love of family and friends, and the comradeship of workers in a common cause, and music, and books, and the Empire of ideas. So that each one of us may well say:

Lord, though I lived on earth, the child of earth,
Yet was I fathered by the starry sky.'[2]

Life and Action

He admires the beauties of the universe, and feels it easy to live in a world of thought and imagination. But at the same time he does not want to escape in this way from the unhappiness of others. He is no escapist. To escape is no sign of courage or fellow-feeling. 'Thought,' he says, 'in order to justify itself, must lead to action.'[3] Any vital action, according to him, springs from the depths of the being. The urge to action and the desire to experience life through action, influenced all his thought and activity. 'Even sustained thinking, apart from being itself a kind of action, becomes part of the action to come. It is not something entirely abstract, in the void, unrelated to action and life. The past becomes something that leads up to the present, the moment of action, the

---

[1] *AB*, XLVII, 377.
[2] *Essays* II, 170, 'The Last Letter to Indira', August, 1933.
[3] *Ibid.* (Nehru greatly appreciates the words of Romain Rolland: 'Action is the end of thought. All thought which does not look towards action is an abortion and a treachery. If then we are the servants of thought we must be the servants of action.')

future something that flows from it; and all three are inextricably intertwined and interrelated.'[1]

People often avoid action, feels Nehru, because they are afraid of the consequences, for action means risk and danger. But to him, danger seems terrible only from a distance; but it is not so bad if one has a close look at it. 'And often it is a pleasant companion, adding to the zest and delight of life.' To him, the ordinary course of life becomes dull at times, and one takes too many things for granted, finding no joy in them. And yet one appreciates those very common things when one has lived without them for a while.

'Many people go up high mountains and risk life and limb for the joy of the climb and the exhilaration that comes from a difficulty surmounted, a danger overcome; and because of the danger that hovers all around them, their perceptions get keener, their joy of the life which hangs by a thread, the more intense.

'All of us have our choice of living in the valleys below with their unhealthy mists and fogs, but giving a measure of bodily security; or of climbing the high mountains, with risk and danger for companions, to breathe the pure air above, and take joy in the distant views, and welcome the rising sun.'[2]

The problems of the day are enough for Nehru, and he does not care what happens to him or to his reputation once he is gone.[3] But while living, he wants to work in a way that may lead in the future to a better way. 'Thus, in the final analysis, one just works.' In his thought, there is no place for the negation of or abstention from life. He loves it, and in his own way seeks to experience it. Many invisible barriers may grow up to surround him, but the desire to play with life, to peep over its edges, continues. In one of the critical moments of his life, when surrounded by despair, he said:

'Perhaps I ought to have been an aviator, so that when the slowness and dullness of life overcame me I could have rushed into the tumult of the clouds and said to myself:—

"I balanced all, brought all to mind,
The years to come seemed waste of breath,

[1] *DI*, I, 8.
[2] *Essays* II, 170-71, 'The Last Letter to Indira', August, 1933.
[3] *Conversations*, 144.

> A waste of breath the years behind,
> In balance with this life, this death." '[1]

His Pagan View of Life

In order to live a life of vigour, Nehru is attracted towards some kind of old pagan feeling. For him there seems to have been an inner call to 'have sight of Proteus rising from the sea'; or 'hear old Triton blow his wreathed horn'. From a very early stage, the aesthetic side of life had an appeal for him. The idea of going through life worthily, not indulging it in the vulgar way, but still making the most of it and living a full and many-sided life held great attraction, and at the same time, risk and adventure fascinated him. 'I was always, like my father, a bit of a gambler, at first with money and then for higher stakes, with the bigger issues of life.' This is how he described in the *Autobiography* the days of his youth.[2] When fifty-five, he was writing: 'I was, somewhere at the back of my mind, a pagan with a pagan's liking for the exuberance of life and nature, and not very much averse to the conflicts that life provides.'[3] And, when approaching seventy, he was still a pagan, looking though at some other aspects of paganism. '. . . there might be something worthwhile in the pagan view of life, because it is a tolerant view of life. . . . It looks at the universe and the mysteries of the universe and tries to fathom them in a spirit of humility. . . . While the pagan view of life worships its own gods, it also does honour to unknown gods.'[4]

His paganism made him both daring and jovial. Gandhi is once reported to have said: 'Believe me if Jawaharlal is not in gaol today, it is not because he is afraid of it. He is quite capable of mounting the gallows with a smile on his lips.'[5] Once, when inside the prison, he got the news that his mother had been knocked down and hit repeatedly by the police while at the head of a procession. The thought of his frail old mother lying bleeding on the dusty road obsessed him so much that he wondered how he would have behaved if he had been there.

---

[1] *DI*, I, 8.
[2] *AB*, IV, 20.
[3] *DI*, IV, 112.
[4] *Speeches* III, 433, January 14, 1957.
[5] John Gunther, *Inside Asia*, 450.

'How far would my non-violence have carried me? Not very far, I fear, for that sight would have made me forget the long lesson I had tried to learn for more than a dozen years; and I would have recked little of the consequences, personal or national.'[1]

It is again the same paganism in him that would inspire him to jump out with a stick, in the pose of a medieval knight, to fight with a little child, absolutely forgetting the burden of age on his shoulders. With youth, 'he shakes off fifty years of his age', and would 'scale barriers, even climb lamp-posts, run and jump and skip'.[2] And, even as Prime Minister, he would dance with the primitive dwellers of India or the folk dancers in their colourful costumes.

His Liking for the Light Touch

Life should possess some capacity for humour and laughter, and Nehru presumes that life certainly would have been almost intolerable for him but for the humour and light touches which some people have given to it.[3] At times he would enjoy a joke at his own expense. 'I am not a literary man, and I am not a historian; what indeed am I?' so he would ask before proceeding to reply, 'I have been a dabbler in many things; I began with science at college and then took to the law, and after developing various other interests in life, finally adopted the popular and widely practised profession of gaol-going in India!'[4] Amidst the political activities of his early revolutionary career, when people everywhere showered on him extravagant adjectives, he would feel greatly relieved when his wife, sisters and others inside the family circle, including his little daughter, would poke fun at him by applying those very adjectives, such as *Bharat Bhusan*—'Jewel of India', *Tyagamurti*—'O Embodiment of Sacrifice'. This kind of light-hearted response would soothe him, and the tension from the solemn public gatherings would gradually ease.

At some other time, in sorrowful moments also, he would fancy a joke and enjoy himself. Lonely and depressed in the prison,

[1] *AB*, XLII, 335.
[2] *A Study of Nehru*, 143.
[3] *AB*, XXVIII, 207.
[4] *Essays* II, 164, 'The Last Letter to Indira', August, 1933.

when he once saw his bed being heavily chained in the narrow space between his cell and the prison wall where he was allowed to sleep at night in the open, he discovered the motive of the gaol-officers—'lest I might take it up and walk away, or, more probably, to avoid the bed being used as a kind of scaling ladder to climb the wall of the enclosure'.[1] Even on other occasions, he would enjoy a joke at the cost of his powerful adversaries. Once, in the days of struggle, while the British House of Commons met to consider the protection of animals in India, Nehru in his prison was prompt enough to say: 'A very laudable object. But it is worth remembering that the two-legged animal, *homo sapiens*, in India is also worthy of care and protection—especially those who undergo the long physical and mental torture of prison life and come out with an impaired capacity for normal life.'[2] And, in the heated days of the national movement, he would turn in disgust to the Indian Liberals and ask: 'Is it my fancy merely that takes me back through the ages and makes me listen to that famous cry: "Scribes and Pharisees. . . . Ye blind guides, which strain at a gnat and swallow a camel!" '[3]

His Adoration of Nature

Nehru is attracted to nature almost with a poet's mind. His writings at various times give ample evidence of the influences which nature has cast on him. His description of nature is inspired, and a sympathetic adoration of it is invariably marked. Some strange satisfaction always awaited him in the wild and desolate haunts of nature, and the snow covered mountains, the narrow and lonely valleys high up in the world, and the little glaciers, would give him exciting experiences. The higher valleys and mountains of Kashmir fascinated him a great deal, and after visiting them he would resolve to return again. The very thought of a visit to Manasarovar, the wonder lake of the Himalayas, and the snow covered Kailas nearby, would fill him with delight. But entangled as he was in the coils of politics and public affairs, he had often to satisfy himself with a mere longing for them. 'Instead of going up

---

[1] *AB*, XXX, 217.
[2] *Essays* II, 128-29, 'Prison Land', 1934.
[3] *AB*, LI, 415.

mountains or crossing the seas I have to satisfy my wanderlust by coming to prison. But still I plan, for that is a joy that no one can deny even in prison, and besides what else can one do in prison?' And so in prison he would dream with satisfaction of the day when he would be able to wander about the Himalayas, recalling the lines of Walter de la Mare:

> 'Yea, in my mind these mountains rise,
> Their perils dyed with evening's rose;
> And still my ghost sits at my eyes
> And thirsts for their untroubled snows.'[1]

Inside the prison, lying there in the open outside the barracks, he would watch the skies and the clouds and enjoy their changing hues.

> 'To watch the changing clouds, like clime in clime;
> Oh! sweet to lie and bless the luxury of time.'

Time was not a luxury for him; it was a burden. But the time he spent in watching the ever-shifting monsoon clouds was filled with delight and a sense of relief. He could even feel a sense of escape from confinement.

'. . . when the monsoon clouds sailed gaily by, assuming fantastic shapes, and playing in a riot of colour, I gasped in surprised delight and watched them almost as if I was in a trance. Sometimes the clouds would break, and one saw through an opening in them that wonderful monsoon phenomenon, a dark blue of an amazing depth, which seemed to be a portion of infinity.'[2]

On another occasion, in another prison, he would follow the year's cycle, the winter, the spring, the summer and the rainy

---

[1] *AB*, VI, 38-9.
[2] *AB*, XIII, 94.
The sky had a tremendous appeal for him, especially in prison. 'With a wistful eye' he looked

> 'Upon that little tent of blue
> Which prisoners call the sky,
> And at every drifting cloud that went
> With sails of silver by.' (*AB* ,XXX, 218).

season. He would sit, write and think, and watch the seasons go by, and listen to the pit-a-pat of the rain on his barrack roof:—

'O soft sound of rain
On earth and on the roofs
For a heart that is pining
Oh! the song of the rain.'[1]

And again, in some other gaol or gaols, he would be lost in deep thought looking at the moon.

'The moon, ever a companion to me in prison, has grown more friendly with closer acquaintance, a reminder of the loveliness of this world, of the waxing and waning of life, of light following darkness, of death and resurrection following each other in interminable succession. Ever changing, yet ever the same, I have watched it in its different phases and its many moods in the evening, as the shadows lengthen, in the still hours of the night, and when the breath and whisper of dawn bring promise of the coming day.'[2]

'A secret intimacy' was established with nature. The mountain, with its solidity and imperturbability, would look down upon him 'with the wisdom of a million years', and mock at his varying humours and soothe his fevered mind; and the cool tropical jungle with its abundant life would look at him 'with a thousand eyes'. The loveliness of nature, enjoyed in some distant place or country, would leave its impress on the mind, and he would 'love to think' of what he had seen—of the graceful areca tree, slender and straight and true, of the innumerable coconuts, the palm-fringed seashore where the emerald green of the island meets the blue of the sea and the sky, of the sea water glistening and playing on the surf, and the wind rustling through the palm leaves.[3]

More observant of nature's ways, he would even be fascinated by the teeming life around him which constituted the animal or insect world. In the various prisons where he lived—Dehra Dun, Lucknow, Almora, Naini, Bareilly, Alipore, or others—he could find time to take an interest in the life of the creatures that lived

[1] *Essays* II, 163, 'The Last Letter to Indira', August, 1933.
[2] *DI*, I, 1.
[3] *WH*, 84, Nehru to Indira, March 26, 1932.

around and about. There was more often a feeling of kindliness, a love for creation in the kingdom of nature.

Faith in the Unity of Nature

In the thoughts of Nehru, there is an evident tendency which points to an ultimate faith in the unity of nature. 'Man no longer sees nature as something apart and distinct from himself,' he says. 'Human destiny appears to become a part of nature's rhythmic energy.'[1] The latest developments in physics, according to him, have gone a long way to demonstrate a fundamental unity in nature. As a belief it is very old; but in the present-day world, it is a principle of science based on proof.

'The human mind appears to have a passion for finding out some kind of unity in life, in nature and the universe. That desire, whether it is justified or not, must fulfil some essential need of the mind. The old philosophers were ever seeking this, and even modern scientists are impelled by this urge. All our schemes and planning, our ideas of education and social and political organization, have at their back the search for unity and harmony.'[2]

Some able thinkers and philosophers may say that this basic concept is false and that there is no such thing as order or unity in this accidental universe. That may be so, but to Nehru, there can be little doubt that even this mistaken belief, if such it is, yielded positive results and produced a harmony, a balance, and a richness in life.

[1] *DI*, I, 17.
[2] *DI*, V, 136.

CHAPTER II

REVOLUTION IN THEORY AND PRACTICE

―――――◆―――――

Revolution an Inevitable Factor of History

Jawaharlal Nehru takes a broad view of 'Revolution' both in the subjective and objective sense. To him revolution is one of the fundamental forces which shape history. Revolution and change, in his thoughts, seem at times in a sense as co-extensive, and they are interpreted not only as natural but also as necessary symptoms in the national body politic.

'Nothing in the world that is alive remains unchanging. All nature changes from day to day and minute to minute. Only the dead stop growing and are quiescent. Fresh water runs on, and if you stop it, it becomes stagnant. So also the life of man and the life of a nation.'[1]

This is what he thinks when he wants to answer—why should men want revolution and change? The inherent cause of revolution lies in the fact that some people refuse to admit that the world changes. Against the change that time calls for they 'keep their minds closed and locked up and will not permit any new ideas to come into them'. They are frightened at the idea of thinking, but since change leads to the growth of mankind, the world moves on in spite of them. Such contradictory forces cause revolution. It is the physical manifestation of the conflict between growth that is natural and stagnation that is unhealthy. When the unthinking minds do not adapt themselves to changing conditions, there is revolution. The purpose of revolution is 'to clear out all the stagnant pools and let in clean fresh water everywhere.' 'There are periods in history,' he says again, 'when the processes and tempo of change are more in evidence. At other times, the

[1] *WH*, Vol. I, 8-9, Nehru to Indira, January 7, 1931.

appearance is much more static. The static period in the life of a nation is a period of gradual deterioration and weakness, leading to the decay of the creative arts and tendencies and often to political subjection.'[1] Such decay or subjection is again followed by upsurge or revolution and thus the cycle goes on.

A Harbinger of Greater Security

Instinctively human beings desire some measure of security and stability. According to Nehru, without security and stability there could be no society or social life. But when this security and stability are enjoyed by some and are denied to vast majorities of people, society stands on imperfect foundations. So long as the masses do not share in them, there can be no stable society. 'And so you see in the history of the world revolution after revolution,' explains Nehru, 'not because any group or person is a lover of bloodshed and anarchy and disorder but because of this desire for greater security for larger number of persons.'[2] Thus, revolutions aim at the well-being of the vast majority of the people, and become means to an end, namely, social security and stability. Until that end is reached, society continues to struggle towards it, sometimes even a little blindly. The greater the struggle, and the greater the urge to that end, the healthier and more vital the society. Without this urge, society becomes static and lifeless and gradually withers away.

'So long, therefore, as the world is not perfect, a healthy society must have the seeds of revolt in it. It must alternate between revolution and consolidation.'[3]

Costs of Revolution Nominal

Revolution, ultimately leading to the well-being of a society, does not cost the society a great deal. The French Revolution was a terrible thing. But yet, according to Nehru, it was a flea-bite compared to the chronic evils of poverty and unemployment. This leads him to suggest that the costs of social revolution, however great they might be, are less than the social evils, and less than the

---

[1] *Speeches* III, 414, September 30, 1955.
[2] *Writings* I, 71, December ,1928.
[3] *Ibid.*

costs of wars which occur from time to time under defective political and social systems. Referring to the famous French Revolution, he says:

'The Terror of the French Revolution looms large because many titled and aristocratic persons were its victims, and we are so used to honouring the privileged classes that our sympathies go out to them when they are in trouble. It is well to sympathize with them as with others. But it is also well to remember that they are just a few. We may wish them well. But those who really matter are the masses, and we cannot sacrifice the many to a few.'[1]

Nehru proceeds to agree with Rousseau that it is the people who compose the human race. What is not the people is so small a concern that it is not worth the trouble of counting.

Desirability of Dissatisfaction

Desire for a better and healthier order in society leads to discontent against existing order of things. This discontent seems to Nehru desirable. Discontent may lead to revolution which for the time may disturb security. But since greater security follows the change, discontent and dissatisfaction, judged by their ultimate result, are good. If people are not dissatisfied with existing conditions, if they do not feel the urge which makes them restless and drives and lashes them to action, then there is no revolution, and society becomes static. 'It is not those who are continually seeking security and have made a god of discretion who reform the world. It is not the sleek and shiny people having more than their share of this world's goods who are the apostles of change. The world changes and progresses because of those who are disaffected and dissatisfied and who are not prepared to tolerate the evils and injustice of things as they are or have them.'[2] Those who are satisfied have no desire to change, but those who are not supply the dynamic element in society; to be the standard-bearers of revolt against all that is evil and to prevent other people from suppressing all social progress and movement by the mere force of their inertia.

[1] WH, Vol. I, 594, Nehru to Indira, October 27, 1932.
[2] Writings I, 71, December, 1928.

Need for Radicalism

Revolution at times needs to be radical. When revolutionary changes are required, they cannot be brought about by reformist tactics and methods. To Nehru, the reformer who is afraid of radical change or of overthrowing an oppressive regime, and who seeks merely to eliminate some of its abuses, becomes in reality one of its defenders.[1] At times, therefore, when it is necessary, people should cultivate a revolutionary outlook, one that devises a radical and far-reaching change, and not merely that halting outlook of the half-hearted reformer. The degree of radicalism depends on the nature of the suffering of the people. If the suffering is great the fire of revolution burns within the people and demands immediate remedies. Unless the suffering is removed, the fire burns. 'Leaders and individuals may come and go; they may get tired and slacken off; they may compromise or betray; but the exploited and suffering masses must carry on the struggle, for their drill-sergeant is hunger.' At the face of the suffering, revolution cannot be postponed, nor can mere sermons prevent its coming. Freedom from exploitation for the people is not a problem of the hereafter. It is a question of the here and now, of immediate relief.

'Roast lamb and mint sauce may be a tasty dish for those who eat it, but the poor lamb is not likely to appreciate the force of the best of arguments which point out the beauty of sacrifice for the good of the elect and the joys of close communion, even though dead, with mint sauce.'[2]

Nehru does not find sanctity behind the political systems or orders which do not stand for the unqualified and unconditional welfare of the people. If institutions or systems grew up or were established without popular sanction behind them, revolution is perfectly justified in abolishing them. To him, it appeared fantastic to expect the people to keep on their chains of slavery, imposed upon them by force and fraud, and to submit to a system which crushes the life-blood out of them. 'The only final authority and paramount power that we recognize is the will of the people, and the only thing that counts ultimately is the good of

[1] *Writings* I, 104.
[2] *Essays* II, 59-60, 'Whither India', 1933.

the people,' so he said on one occasion while challenging the validity of certain emblems of reaction and autocracy.[1]

Revolution against Foreign Rule Unavoidable

Revolution is justified in history for liberation of men from foreign rule.* According to Nehru, 'No living nation under alien rule can ever be at peace with its conqueror. For peace means submission and submission means the death of all that is vital in the nation.'[2] Great empires of history, based on subject populations, contained in them germs of revolution. The Roman empire of ancient times and the British empire of recent times, and in fact all empires, so thinks Nehru, are more or less similar. The inherent defect in them is that 'They fatten on the exploitation of the many'.[3] The rulers of empires, especially the Romans and the English, thought Nehru, were singularly devoid of imagination. 'Smug and self-satisfied, and convinced that the world was made specially for their benefit, they go through life untroubled by doubt or difficulty.'[4]

Such empires are not merely problems for subject populations, but, in the interpretation of Nehru, they create problems in a much wider sphere. Thinking of the British Indian empire, he considered it as 'one of the major problems of the world'. India was the typical and classical country of imperialist domination. The whole structure of British imperialism rested on it, but, what is more, other countries were lured on to the paths of imperialist adventure by the successful British example.[5]

Whatever the virtues or vices of foreign rule, it is not in the nature of things that the people in a subject country should give preference to slavery. In Nehru's study of the British Empire in

---

* The Congress under the presidentship of Jawaharlal Nehru at Lahore and at the instance of Mahatma Gandhi prepared an independence manifesto (January, 1930) which began:

'We believe that it is the inalienable right of the Indian people as of any other people, to have freedom and to enjoy the fruits of their toil and have the necessities of life so that they may have full opportunities of growth. We believe also that if any Government deprives the people of these rights and oppresses them, the people have a further right to alter it or to abolish it.'

[1] *Writings* II, Part I, Ch. 2, 31-32, February ,1939.
[2] *Writings* I, 150, October, 1928.
[3] *WH*, Vol. I, 150-51, Nehru to Indira, April 25, 1932.
[4] *Ibid.*
[5] *WH*, Vol. II, 1115, Nehru to Indira, May 11, 1933.

India he finds that from the day that his country fell under an alien rule, there had always been people who had dreamed of the struggle for independence and had worked for it and sacrificed their all for it. As generation succeeded generation there was no lack of men and women who refused to bow their heads and bend their knees before the alien rulers. For that disobedience they paid a very heavy price, but the gallant stream went on and increased in volume. A country can show her vitality when her sons and daughters make endless sacrifices to free her from foreigners. He discovers also in the psychology of a nation a feeling of shame at its long submission to an alien rule that degrades and humiliates people, and consequently a desire to submit no longer whatever the consequences. Revolution, thus, becomes obvious, and it comes sooner or later. Its coming is imperative on another account. There can be no end to a foreign rule except by revolution. As he puts it:

'Ruling powers and ruling classes have not been known in history to abdicate willingly.'[1]

Revolution, an Expression of Creative Energy

According to Nehru, a nation, like an individual, has many personalities and many approaches to life. In its normal existence, he finds a continuous process of adjustment going on and some kind of an equilibrium established. A foreign rule arrests this normal development. Society, in order to become both stable and progressive, needs a certain more or less fixed foundation of principles as well as a dynamic outlook. When the foundation is disturbed and the dynamic outlook is suppressed, the society degenerates. Foreign rule, being cut off from the creative energies of the people it dominates, and generally possessing its own economic and cultural centre far from the subject country, helps the developing spiritual and cultural starvation of the subject peoples. To him it appears that in such circumstances the only real scope that the nation's creative energy finds is in some kind of opposition to that rule. He says:

'That opposition represents the conscious or unconscious effort of the living and growing forces to break through the shell

[1] *Essays* II, 185, 'A Letter to an Englishman', January, 1936.

that confines them and is thus a progressive and inevitable tendency.'[1]

Its Permanency in Some Form

Revolution against foreign government is unavoidable, but after the freedom is achieved revolution does not cease. Struggle for political liberty is only one phase of revolution, but there are other phases of it which ought to manifest themselves after liberty is attained. To Nehru, political freedom must be followed by the struggle to eradicate the many ills that a country suffers from. Years after the independence of India, he considered himself and his compatriots in struggle as the children of the Indian Revolution, and felt the urge to work in the same revolutionary spirit in eliminating poverty and raising the standards of the people, and giving them full and equal opportunities of growth and advancement.[2] 'Remember this, that we are still the children of the Indian Revolution,' he said in 1955. 'We have not ceased to be revolutionaries.'[3] While he thinks of revolution in this context, obviously he means by it progress and change. 'History shows us,' he says, 'two principles at work, the principle of continuity and the principle of change. They appear to be opposed to each other and, yet, each has something of the other. We notice that we consider sudden changes in the shape of violent revolutions or an earthquake. Yet, every geologist knows that the major changes in the earth's surface are gradual, and earthquakes are trivial in comparison to them. So also revolutions are merely the outward evidence of a long process of change and subtle erosion. Thus, change itself is a continuous process, and even a static continuity must yield to gradual change so long as it is not overcome by complete stagnation and death.'[4]

Revolution not Necessarily Destructive

While revolution cannot be dispensed with in the greater interest of society, Nehru does not believe in the theory of random

[1] *DI*, X, 484.
[2] *Speeches* III, 47-8, December 18, 1956.
[3] *Ibid*, 134, December 26, 1955.
[4] *Speeches* III, 414, September 30, 1955.

destruction of something old to achieve something new. Revolution for political freedom of a subject population may be of one nature, but revolution for social or economic changes may be of a different nature. 'I am a great believer in being aggressive,' he once said in reference to his relation with the British authorities.[1] Some amount of aggressiveness perhaps always remained in him, and while this aggressiveness was great in the political sphere, it was also present in other spheres of his activity, especially when the activity was connected with change. But aggressiveness does not seem to have prompted him to give up faith in moderation in every case of change. Revolutions and upheavals are products of history, but at times violence, defeat and civil war govern the subsequent events. Conscious of this, Nehru does not accept the theory that in order to have progress one must destroy. The idea that by increasing conflict and bitterness one can have a clean slate to write upon did not appear to him sound.

'No country has ever had a clean slate to write upon, not even after the biggest of revolutions. No one should deliberately destroy something which is worthwhile in order to build something which may be good in certain circumstances.'[2]

It is clear that while Nehru believes in radicalism in the case of revolutions for political liberty from alien rule, or for freedom from autocratic governments, he accepts prudence in the case of social or economic or other similar changes in society, however necessary or urgent they may seem to be. Moreover, he believes that in a free country revolutionary changes can be brought about without actual revolution by constitutional methods. Further, the word revolution is misapplied if for any minor matter one wants a revolution. A country's reputation is based on some fundamental characteristics. It requires a certain amount of stability, a certain amount of peace, and a certain measure of progress. According to him, if people enter the region of violent explosions simply because they dislike this thing or that, then they lose not only their reputation but even things much more important than that.[3] To him, in a free and stable country it is better to

[1] *Birthday Book*, 194.
[2] *Speeches* III, 8, December 21, 1954.
[3] *Ibid*, 188, February 23, 1956.

develop the idea of measured or ordered progress. He does not understand the purpose of revolution in the type of country 'where every other month one hears of some kind of a violent revolution'. Revolution in violent forms in a free country—if it is not for a great cause supported by the vast majority of people— runs a great risk. 'Once you enter the region of trying to settle problems by violent methods,' he says, 'you go towards something that is perilously near to civil war.'[1]

Revolution in Practice

For the major part of his life Nehru had been a revolutionary in the most practical sense, fighting against one of the greatest imperialist powers of modern times. His approach to revolution and his ideas and thoughts on revolution are sometimes better known from his work as a revolutionary. Whilst working as a practical revolutionary he was greatly influenced by the Gandhian philosophy of revolution, and many fundamentals of that philosophy are, therefore, to be traced in him. But in many circumstances his approach was different. On the whole, he worked as a revolutionary with the philosophy of Gandhi mixed up with that of his own.

The End and Means

One of the basic principles which Nehru accepted like Gandhi in regard to revolution was the justification of means to justify the end. He admired the moral and ethical side of the national movement and of the *satyagraha* on which Gandhi laid supreme emphasis; and the spiritualization of politics—not in its narrow religious sense—appealed to his mind. The goal before India was national freedom, and, as Nehru added to it, also the ending of the exploitation of the people. The doctrines of non-co-operation which were accepted during the first phase of the Gandhian revolution were the means which satisfied Nehru's moral sense, and he could thereafter be a firm believer in the virtues of righteous means. He explains:

'A worthy end should have worthy means leading up to it. That seemed not only a good ethical doctrine but sound, practical

[1] *Ibid.*

politics, for the means that are not good often defeat the end in view and raise new problems and difficulties.'[1]

It is degrading to the self-respect of an individual or a nation to submit to such means which are ignoble. He believed in marching ahead swiftly and with dignity and for this he wanted the revolution to depend on such tactics and technique which were far from being unbecoming. He was proud of his leader and of the unique methods he had evolved, and while in action he came under an agreeable sense of moral superiority over his opponents, both in regard to the goal as well as the methods.

Faith in Open Revolution

Since the means were regarded as even more important than the end, some definite revolutionary methods were invented to justify that principle. One of them was that the revolution was made open. No scope was kept for underground activities or secret methods, and everything was made clear to the opponents against whom the revolution was aimed. 'The innumerable spies and secret-service men,' says Nehru, 'who used to surround us and follow us about became rather pitiable individuals as there was nothing secret for them to discover. All our cards were always on the table.'[2]

But this kind of open revolution was always exposed to grave dangers as far as its own cause was concerned. Some secrecy is always necessary for any revolutionary body to function. Nehru realized how the Congress had to face situations when it became impossible for it to function normally because of the open method policy. When the Congress would be declared an unlawful organization by the government, and its committees could not meet for consultation or any action openly, secret meetings could be considered as the only way out. The experiences of 1930 and 1932 showed that it was easily possible for the Congress to organize a secret network of information all over India. As Nehru saw, without much effort and in spite of some opposition, good results were produced. But the feeling was there that secrecy did not fit in with the spirit of civil disobedience movement, and

[1] *AB*, X, 73.
[2] *Ibid*, 69.

that it produced a damping effect on the mass consciousness. In July, 1933, Gandhi condemned all secrecy in Indian revolution. Nehru agreed with this when he said to Gandhi:

'I think that most of us agree, and certainly I am of that opinion, that our movement is essentially an open one and secret methods do not fit in with it. Such methods, if indulged in to any large extent, are likely to change the whole character of the movement, as it has been conceived, and produce a certain amount of demoralization. Agreeing with this, some of us feel that, to some extent, as for instance in communicating with each other or sending directions or keeping contacts, a measure of secrecy may be necessary. Perhaps secrecy is hardly the word for these activities and privacy would suit them better. Privacy of course is always open to all groups and individuals. Secrecy, or the avoidance of it, as you said, cannot be made into a fetish.'[1]

At the same time, he pointed out that under certain exceptional circumstances it might be desirable for local or provincial committees or groups to issue bulletins of directions, etc., secretly. Of course, 'This must not be encouraged; indeed it should be discouraged, but a certain latitude in exceptional circumstances might be permitted.' To this Gandhi replied:

'There may be exceptional circumstances that may warrant secret methods. I would forego that advantage, for the sake of the masses whom we want to educate in fearlessness. I will not confuse their minds by leading them to think that under certain circumstances, they may resort to secret methods. Secrecy is inimical to the growth of the spirit of civil resistance. If Congressmen will realize that all property is liable to be confiscated at any moment, they will learn to be utterly independent of it.'[2]

Philosophy of Self-suffering
In an attempt to combine morality with revolutionary politics, in order to justify further the theory of good means, the Gandhian revolution adopted the philosophy of self-suffering. It was Gandhi's way that the people should refuse to submit to the policy of the government and show their resentment and determination

---

[1] *Writings* I, 189, Nehru to Gandhi, September 13, 1933.
[2] *Ibid*, 192, Gandhi to Nehru, September 14, 1933.

by voluntarily inviting suffering for themselves, yet without the object of creating trouble. Furthermore, apart from political, some kind of personal suffering was demanded of the revolutionary. Nehru was a convert to these ideals from an early stage. From the personal point of view he invited self-suffering by living on parched rice and roasted gram, and by travelling in third class railway compartments in the burning summer. Such ways of living once led his father to complain before Gandhi: '. . . this is more than I can stand. I appreciate sacrifice and endurance, but this is just primitiveness; it hurts me. . . .'[1] On the political front, the suffering was considerable, and Nehru had to invite imprisonment on a number of occasions. The whole country was called upon to believe in the philosophy of self-suffering, and that became a basic faith with the people. The morale of this aspect of the revolution was that scores of thousands of people refused 'to bend before the physical might of a proud empire, and preferred to see their bodies crushed, their homes broken, their dear ones suffer, rather than yield their souls'. 'We put on a brave face in gaol or outside,' writes Nehru, 'and smiled and laughed, but we smiled often through our tears, and our laughter was sometimes near to crying.'[2] The invitation of suffering by people in the hands of the government exposed, according to him, the real character of the rule, both to the people coerced and to the world at large. Coercion was an expensive affair for the rulers. Nothing was more irritating and, in the final analysis, harmful to a government than to have to deal with people who would not bend to its will, whatever the consequences. As for the people, suffering seemed better than non-suffering, because, says Nehru:

'For us the choice is: abject submission to the power of the State, spiritual degradation, the denial of the truth that is in us, and our moral prostitution for purposes that we consider base—or opposition with all the consequences thereof. No one likes to go to gaol or to invite trouble. But often gaol is preferable to the other alternative.'[3]

---

[1] *Birthday Book*, 187-88.
[2] *AB*, XLVIII, 392.
[3] *AB*, XLVIII, 394.

Non-violence and Truth

The most remarkable technique of the Indian revolution was however the acceptance of non-violence and truth as the means of the revolution. The non-co-operation, *satyagraha*, mass or individual civil disobedience, all rested on non-violence and truth. A non-violent revolution was necessarily peaceful, and Gandhi in his novel way tried to identify non-violence with truth and goodness. Such principles of revolution were somewhat unique and in fact difficult for operation. The doctrine of non-violence became the key to revolution, but, as Nehru saw, vast numbers of people repeated it unthinkingly but with approval, some wrestled with it and then accepted it, with or without reservation, and some openly jeered at it.[1] Yet it played a vital part in the political and social life of India, and attracted a good deal of attention in the outside world. 'Those who have to bring about radical changes in human conditions and surroundings,' said Gandhi, 'can not do it except by raising a ferment in society. There are only two methods of doing this, violent and non-violent. Violent pressure is felt on the physical being and it degrades him who uses it as it depresses the victim, but non-violent pressure exerted through self-suffering, as by fasting, works in an entirely different way.'[2]

Nehru and Non-violence

Such Gandhian philosophy, though it was followed by Nehru in practice, nevertheless created gave doubts in his mind. The doctrine of non-violence absorbed much of his thought, and perhaps at length he found himself in a difficult position to solve the riddles which thought provoked in him. He wondered if national and social groups could imbibe sufficiently the individual creed of non-violence, for it involved a tremendous rise of mankind in the mass to a high level of love and goodness. It was true, he thought, that the only really desirable ultimate ideal was to raise humanity to that level and to abolish hatred and ugliness and selfishness. But, to attain that ideal, were men to work for it directly by preaching those virtues, regardless of the obstructions

[1] *AB*, LXIII, 537.
[2] Gandhi quoted in *AB*, LXIII 537.

which made it impossible of achievement; or must they not remove those obstructions first and create a more suitable and more favourable environment for the growth of love, beauty and goodness? Or, could the two processes be combined?

'I dislike violence intensely,' he stated regarding himself, 'and yet I am full of violence myself, and consciously or unconsciously, I am often attempting to coerce others.'[1] He thought it difficult to draw the line between violence and non-violence, and considered that often enough moral force was a far more terrible coercive factor than physical violence. As regards non-violence being synonymous with truth, he found himself in similar difficulty. 'What is truth is an ancient question to which a thousand answers have been given, and yet the question remains.' Whatever it might be, he was not prepared to wholly identify truth with non-violence. About violence, though it was bad, Nehru did not consider it as intrinsically immoral. 'There are shades and grades of it and often it may be preferable to something that is worse. Gandhiji himself has said that it is better than cowardice, fear, and slavery, and a host of other evils might be added to this list.'[2]

On the more practical side of the revolution itself, Nehru did not want to carry the doctrine of non-violence to its extreme end. When Gandhi suspended the non-co-operation movement on account of a little violence committed by a mob of villagers at Chauri Chaura, Nehru became 'angry'. 'Chauri Chaura may have been and was a deplorable occurrence and wholly opposed to the spirit of the non-violent movement; but were a remote village and a mob of excited peasants in an out-of-the-way place going to put an end, for some time at least, to our national struggle for freedom?' he asked in resentment.[3] To him, if that was the inevitable consequence of a sporadic act of violence, then surely there was something lacking in the philosophy and technique of a non-violent struggle. Nobody could guarantee against the occurrence of some such incident in future, and it was impossible to train the three hundred and odd millions of India in the theory and practice of non-violent action before the revolution could go

[1] *AB*, LXIII, 539.
[2] *Ibid.*
[3] *AB*, XII, 82.

forward. Moreover, even if the people were trained, the police could provoke them to violence; or else, the *agents provocateurs* could induce them to it. Considering such possibilities, Nehru felt that the non-violent method of resistance was bound to fail. But Gandhi said to him:

'I assure you that if the thing had not been suspended we would have been leading not a non-violent struggle but essentially a violent struggle. It is undoubtedly true that non-violence is spreading like the scent of the otto of roses throughout the length and breadth of the land, but the foetid smell of violence is still powerful and it would be unwise to ignore or underrate it. The cause will prosper by this retreat. The movement had unconsciously drifted from the right path. We have come back to our moorings, and we can again go straight ahead.'[1]

Nehru knew all that Gandhi meant by non-violence. In spite of its negative name it was a dynamic method and it was not a coward's refuge from action, but the brave man's defiance of evil and national subjection. He knew that to Gandhi when there was only a choice between cowardice and violence he would advise violence, and that Gandhi would rather have India resort to arms in order to defend her honour than that she should, in a cowardly manner, become or remain a helpless victim to her own dishonour; and that the non-violence of Gandhi did not mean meek submission to the will of the evil-doer, but it meant the putting of one's whole soul against the will of the tyrant. But knowing even the inner meaning of Gandhian non-violence, Nehru could not accept it in its entirety because of its high idealism. Considering it from practical angles, he said:

'We were moved by these arguments (Gandhiji's arguments), but for us and for the National Congress as a whole the non-violent method was not, and could not be, a religion or an unchallengeable creed or dogma. It could only be a policy and a method promising certain results, and by those results it would have to be finally judged. Individuals might make of it a religion or incontrovertible creed. But no political organization, so long as it remained political, could do so.'[2]

---

[1] *Letters*, 24, Gandhi to Nehru, February 19, 1922.
[2] *AB*, XII, 84.

Non-violence, a Practical Necessity

It appears certain that while Gandhi regarded non-violence as a highly ethical or religious principle, Nehru accepted it as a practical instrument to fight the British. 'Armed rebellion seemed out of the question for the Indian people,' he said. 'We are disarmed, and most of us did not even know the use of arms. Besides, in a contest of violence, the organized power of the British Government, or any state, was far greater than anything that could be raised against it. Armies might mutiny, but unarmed people could not rebel and face armed forces.'[1] Nehru knew that people could be taught both violent and non-violent revolution, but realized that the latter could lead to greater results. Somewhere at a people's gathering, in the early days of the revolution, he roused the people to fury against the British Government, and got them to vote for its destruction by armed insurrection if arms could be available. Then, pointing out the lack of arms and explaining Gandhiji's technique of non-violence, he persuaded them to vote against their own opinion, and in favour of the declaration that, even if arms were available, they would eschew them and attain independence through non-violent struggle.[2]

In the non-violent revolution Nehru further saw what may be termed 'legitimate' methods. 'Legitimate I hope they will always be, for we must not sully the great cause for which we stand by any deed that will bring dishonour to it and that we may ourselves regret later.' Legitimate and peaceful methods were more desirable and more enduring than those of violence. He advised the Congress to accept non-violent methods as a practical necessity thus:

'Violence too often brings reaction and demoralization in its train, and in our country specially it may lead to disruption. It is perfectly true that organized violence rules the world today, and it may be that we could profit by its use. But we have not the material or the training for organized violence, and individual or sporadic violence is a confession of despair. The great majority of us, I take it, judge the issue not on moral but on practical grounds,

---

[1] *On Gandhi*, 10-11.
[2] *Birthday Book*, 187-88.

and if we reject the way of violence it is because it promises no substantial results.'[1]

Non-violence Not a Creed

As the non-violent revolution made progress, Nehru's faith in it increased. But it can be said that he did not proceed to develop a rigid and dogmatic attitude towards non-violence, nor did he accept it as a creed. '. . . if this Congress or the nation at any future time comes to the conclusion that methods of violence will rid us of slavery then I have no doubt that it will adopt them. Violence is bad, but slavery is far worse.'[2] He made it clear on many occasions that non-violence is no infallible creed with him; and although he greatly preferred it to violence, he said, 'I prefer freedom with violence to subjection with non-violence.'[3] When the civil disobedience movement began, he worked on the principle that the movement should not be abandoned because of the occurrence of sporadic acts of violence.* On the other hand the non-violent revolution in its broader implications was regarded by him as potential a force as any other revolution could be. William James, the psychologist, thought that war encouraged some virtues in men, namely fidelity, cohesiveness, tenacity, heroism, conscience, education, inventiveness, economy, and physical health and vigour. Because of this, the psychologist sought for a moral equivalent of war which, without the horror of war, would encourage the above virtues in a community. According to Nehru, if the psychologist had known of non-co-operation and civil disobedience he would have found something after his own heart, a moral and peaceful equivalent of war.[4] In spite of the abundance of 'nons' in the Indian revolution, such as non-violence, non-co-operation, etc., it was not a negative or passive affair. It was an active, dynamic, energizing drive which lifted a whole nation out of a morass of demoralization and helplessness,

---

* Of course he knew that if the principal movement is a peaceful one, contemporaneous attempts at sporadic violence can only distract attention and weaken it. It is not possible to carry on at one and the same time the two movements side by side.

[1] *Essays* II, 33, 'Presidential Address', December, 1929.
[2] *Ibid.*
[3] *Essays* I, 35, 'Some criticisms considered'.
[4] *AB*, LIV, 436.

the inevitable result of a long period of subjection.[1] Nehru never regarded it as 'a kind of pious and static pacifism', but always as a 'forceful method of enforcing the mass will'.[2]

With such faith in the efficacy and virtues of non-violent methods, Nehru held on to it till the end of the revolution. Non-violent revolution, he believed, required training for the masses in some simple kinds of activity, and, more so, training to abstain from certain other kinds of activity. Such training, as the years went on, made the revolution a very powerful and organized affair. The country became more and more disciplined and there was a clear appreciation of the nature of the struggle. People understood the technique of the revolution and fully realized that there was absolute earnestness about non-violence. As the revolution headed towards culmination, and external factors like World War II added fuel to the fire, excitement and tension rapidly grew. There was the possibility of young men turning to violence, but yet the Congress went on reminding the country of the basic policy of non-violence and warned it against any breach of it. The people were taught to believe that '*satyagraha* means goodwill towards all, especially towards opponents'. During the last phase of the revolution, when the 'Quit India' movement was launched in 1942, all the prominent, the less prominent, and other numerous local leaders all over India were suddenly removed to prisons. The revolution then virtually fell into the hands of the leaderless people everywhere. No time to give instructions or directions was had by the Congress. The arrests of the leaders, followed by frequent firings, roused the people to anger, and a spontaneous mass upheaval took place. Before the determination of the government to crush the revolution with all its force and by means of violence, it became difficult for the people to remain absolutely non-violent. Yet the doctrine of non-violence pervaded the atmosphere. As Nehru put it, 'The people forgot the lesson of non-violence which had been dinned into their ears for more than twenty years, and yet they were wholly unprepared, mentally or otherwise, for any effective violence. That very teaching of non-violent methods produced doubt and hesitation

---

[1] *Essays* II, 223-24, 'The Way to Peace', 1936.
[2] *Essays* I, 35, 'Some criticisms considered'.

and came in the way of violent action.'[1] The long training of the people under non-violent techniques had one notable result, so felt Nehru, that 'in spite of the passions aroused there was very little, if any, racial feeling, and, on the whole, there was a deliberate attempt on the part of the people to avoid causing bodily injury to their opponents. There was a great deal of destruction of communications and governmental property, but even in the midst of this destruction care was taken to avoid loss of life.'[2] The 1942 Revolution was the last great Indian upheaval against the British. It is rather surprising that, considering the area and population, the damage which the revolution caused was insignificant.*

Terrorism No Revolution

The non-violent revolution did not connect itself with violence, secret intrigue, and conspiracy, which are the usual accompaniments of revolutionary activity, and yet did not become less revolutionary thereby. In its own way it required 'cold-blooded courage and endurance of a high order'. According to Nehru, perhaps it was easier to indulge in short violent spurts of courage, even unto death, than to give up, under the sole compulsion of one's own mind, almost everything that life offered and carry on in that way day after day, month after month, year after year.[3] Action was to be the basis and objective of the revolutionary organization, but under the doctrine of non-violence this action was to be based on peaceful methods. Before the coming of Gandhi, the alternatives had been 'just talking and passing resolutions, or terroristic activity'. Both of these were set aside and especially terrorism was condemned in the strongest terms. As early as May, 1923, Nehru declared individual terrorism and the killing by bomb or pistol of individual officers as 'a bankrupt's creed'. 'It was demoralizing for the people,' he said, 'and it was

---

* According to official reports, so far as Nehru himself was able to find, about 100 persons were killed by mobs in the course of the disturbances all over India. On the other hand, official estimates of the number of people killed and wounded by police and military firing in the 1942 disturbances were: 1,028 killed and 3,200 wounded. Popular estimates place the number of deaths at 25,000, but Nehru thinks perhaps 10,000 may be nearer the mark.
[1] *DI*, X, 463.
[2] *Ibid*, 464.
[3] *DI*, VIII, 347.

ridiculous to think that it could shake a powerfully organized government, however much it might frighten individuals.' He went on to point out that that kind of individual violence was even given up by the Russian revolutionaries.[1]

In the opinion of Nehru, terrorism usually represents the infancy of a revolutionary urge in a country. That stage passes, and with it passes terrorism as an important phenomenon.[2] In India terrorists flourished from almost the beginning of consciousness among the people of the struggle against foreign rule. As the national movement advanced and its non-violent phase appeared, the philosophy behind terrorism quickly vanished. The people not only became, in course of time, much more indifferent to, but hostile to, the idea of terrorism as a method of political action. The doctrine of non-violence powerfully affected even the classes from which the terrorists were usually drawn, namely, 'the lower middle-classes and intelligentsia'. To Nehru, it was not the government coercion which killed terrorism—which could only suppress and not eradicate—but other basic causes and world events which did. He, on his part, exerted to impress upon others that terrorism was an outworn and profitless method which hindered real revolutionary action.

While terrorism as a political method was dying down, the terrorists faced the difficulty of what they were to do. One of the most aggressive among the Indian terrorists* once met Nehru to say that he and many of his associates were convinced that purely terrorist methods were futile. Nehru was glad to learn this, and tried to explain to him his philosophy of political action in order to convert him to his own viewpoint. But the basic question for the terrorist was: what was he to do? They were treated as outlaws, were hunted from place to place with a price on their heads, and with the prospect of the gallows ever before them. They had to resort to terroristic acts in self-defence. All Nehru could suggest was that the terrorist 'should use his influence to prevent the occurrence of terrorist acts in the future, for these could only injure the larger cause as well as his own group'.[3] By

[1] *Writings* I, 147, May 11, 1923.
[2] *AB*, XXIV, 175.
[3] *AB*, XXXV, 262.
* Chandra Shekhar Azad.

1930-31 terrorism as some kind of group activity was practically dead. Yet individual action in that direction was not altogether lacking. Towards the close of 1931, Nehru discussed the question of terrorism in a number of public meetings in Bengal, trying to show how 'wrong and futile and harmful' it was for Indian freedom. The terrorists were very angry with him because of his propaganda; and even one or two of them came to warn him finally that if he continued in the future they would deal with him as they had dealt with others.

Appreciation of Individual Valour

However much Nehru disliked terrorism as a political faith and the terrorist actions resulting therefrom, there seems to be little doubt that there was some kind of humane feeling in him towards the courage of the individuals who sacrificed their lives for the motherland. Moreover, terrorism was not always the last word in perversity. In the history of the Indian revolution there were activities a great deal more damnable than that. For example, between political terrorism and communal violence the latter appeared to him as much worse. He says:

'When people murder in the name of religion, or to reserve a place for themselves in Paradise, it is a dangerous thing to accustom them to the idea of terroristic violence. Political murder is bad. And yet the political terrorist can be reasoned with and won over to the other ways, because presumably the end he is striving for is an earthly one, not personal but national. Religious murder is worse, for it deals with things of the other world, and one cannot even attempt to reason about such matters.'[1]

Nehru, in his own words, did not abuse the terrorists, nor did he call them 'dastardly' or 'cowardly' after the fashion of some who themselves rarely yielded to the temptation of doing anything brave or involving risk. 'It has always seemed to me a singularly stupid thing to call a man or woman, who is constantly risking life, a coward.' Moreover, it appeared to him that it was very easy to condemn persons or acts without seeking to understand the springs of action, the causes that underlie them. In the

[1] *AB*, XL, 315.

E

case of Bhagat Singh,* Nehru discovered behind his act of
terrorism an attempt to vindicate, for the moment, the honour of
Lala Lajpat Rai, who was assaulted and beaten by a young
English police officer despite his being one of the greatest of
national leaders, and through him the honour of the nation. In
this case he even thought it justifiable to challenge the Viceroy,
when the latter referred to the subject of violence and non-
violence, by saying:

'. . . my heart is full of admiration for the courage and self-
sacrifice of a man like Bhagat Singh. Courage of the Bhagat Singh
type is exceedingly rare. If the Viceroy expects us to refrain from
admiring this wonderful courage and the high purpose behind it,
he is mistaken. Let him ask his own heart what he would have
felt if Bhagat Singh had been an Englishman and acted for
England.'[1]

Peaceful Revolution in Every Sphere

It is more or less through the non-violent techniques of the
Indian revolution that Nehru came to realize the real efficacy of
peace and peaceful methods in bringing about all kinds of change,
political, social or economic. Revolution can be peaceful and yet a
revolution. The freedom of India was won by peaceful and yet
effective action on a mass scale, and Nehru prided himself that it
was 'a bloodless revolution in conditions of honour and dignity'.[2]
In social and economic sphere he wanted to work with the same
revolutionary spirit conditioned by peace. He began to lay
emphasis on the 'peaceful and co-operative method' of approach
in regard to social and economic changes.[3]

* Bhagat Singh was among the accused in the famous Lahore Conspiracy case. That
case arose out of the murder of the Superintendent of Police at Lahore, Mr Saunders, on
September 17, 1928. The revolutionaries believed that Mr Saunders was responsible for
the attack on Lala Lajpat Rai at the time of the anti-Simon demonstration in Lahore in
1928, which ultimately resulted in his death. The assassination of Mr Saunders was thus an
act of reprisal.

Bhagat Singh and his comrades were executed. The Karachi Congress which met under
the gloom cast by the news of this execution passed the following resolution:—

'This Congress, while dissociating itself from and disapproving of political violence in
any shape or form, places on record its admiration of the bravery and sacrifice of the late
Sirdar Bhagat Singh and his comrades . . . and mourns with the bereaved families the
loss of these lives.'

[1] Writings I, 257.
[2] Speeches III, 47, December 18, 1956.
[3] Ibid, 8.

As Nehru viewed the world after the end of the political revolution in his own country, and while settling down to implement socio-economic changes on a peaceful basis, the spirit in other countries appeared to him as opposed to any kind of domination, whether it was national, economic, class or racial. 'There is a strong urge to resist this kind of domination,' he felt.[1] There was nationalism, which resisted foreign domination on the political level; and economic domination was equally resisted. Racialism was bitterly resented. Then there was class conflict on the economic level. Taking all this into consideration Nehru said:

'. . . the question arises whether in the political sphere, or in the economic, in the racial or in any other sphere, whether these changes can be made peacefully or not?'[2]

As a believer in the success of peaceful revolution, he began to advocate that much of the conflict could be removed without violence and forcible methods. 'In fact,' he says, 'we seem to have arrived at a stage where any big-scale violence—whether on the political or on the economic level—results not only in upsets and disequilibrium, but in trails of conflict and bitterness which are even worse than the preceding state of affairs.'[3] Yet, according to him, these great differences must be resolved.

Revolution and the Element of Time
Nehru believes that the process of change should not be delayed. One has to achieve results within a certain period of time, otherwise there is the danger of all attempts at healthy progress being upset by disruption or other forces. Progress must be rapid 'to maintain hope'. His impression is that once the people realize that you are going in a certain direction, they are optimistic. They are prepared to put up with delay; a little delay, because they know that they are going towards something. It is only when they feel that they are not going anywhere that they become angry.

Legislative Revolution Not Enough
Since the element of time is indispensable with consideration for progress, mere legislative process may not lead to desired goals.

[1] *Conversations*, 44.
[2] *Ibid.*
[3] *Ibid*, 45

All changes cannot come merely by legislation, and in fact people themselves change without it. External forces and new ideas bring about changes. Political revolution in India was achieved irrespective of legislative background. Nehru believes, therefore, that in making the people accept changes, both the legislative influence and the influence of a direct approach to them should be taken into account. For revolutionary changes in a society, 'surgical operations' are certainly necessary, and according to Nehru they can be carried out democratically both on the political and on the economic level. Removal of the Indian princes he considers as a 'surgical operation', and also in the case of the landlord system. 'The point is not whether you should have a "surgical operation" or not,' he says, 'but what method you adopt for this operation. A majority in a democratic Assembly, by passing a law—a very advanced law—performs an operation like that.'[1] A law can be passed against social evils which can bring revolutionary change, but it also seems true to him that is is more difficult to deal with the ingrained customs and beliefs of the people. Sometimes legislative revolution may lead only to a partial success. There are things like accumulated weight of tradition, custom and inertia. In such circumstances Nehru advises other methods—peaceful of course—to effect change. Modern conditions should be brought to bear on social evils. Propaganda, persuasion, and the changing conditions of life, side by side with law, should all be brought together to affect the social forces.

Ultimate Objective of All Revolutions

It seems that through his revolutionary outlook Nehru has developed in himself some ideas regarding an ultimate objective of all revolutions. That objective may be described as a state of perfection encompassing the entire globe. During his struggle for the freedom of India, he developed the thought that the great aim before him was the 'human freedom' which included the freedom of his own people as well as other peoples. For long he thought that countries, or continents, were but geographical expressions, and that the problems which faced men were really world problems, or problems of humanity.

Ibid, 56.

'And unless we solve them for the whole world, there will continue to be trouble. Such a solution can only mean the ending of poverty and misery everywhere. This may take a long time but we must aim at this and at nothing less than this. Only then can we have real culture and civilization based on equality, where there is no exploitation of any country or class. Such a society will be a creative and a progressive society, adapting itself to changing circumstances, and basing itself on the co-operation of its members. And ultimately it must spread all over the world.'[1]

A world order such as this for which humanity will struggle will uphold a new civilization, and, in the vision of Nehru, there will be no danger of such a civilization collapsing or decaying as the old civilizations did. The emancipation of mankind in its absolute reality seems to be what he thinks as the final goal of world revolutions. His time he always regarded as 'an age of mighty transition'. Many countries were struggling for their rightful place in the human family. Many others were passing through trials and tribulation. He advised not to be disheartened by this, because there was new vitality and powerful creative impulses in the people and the masses were awake, demanding their heritage. With faith in new forces and ultimately in the human spirit, he said:

'The freedom that we envisage is not to be confined to this nation or that or to a particular people, but must spread out over the whole human race. That universal human freedom also cannot be based on the supremacy of any particular class. It must be the freedom of the common man everywhere and full opportunities for him to develop.'[2]

If the urge for freedom from injustice can be regarded as the cause of revolutions, abolition of all injustice may lead to the desired goal. However utopian the ideal may appear, Nehru seems to entertain in his political thought some optimism for this ideal, and there appears to be a great deal of consistency in this respect at different times.

---

[1] *WH*, Vol. I, 284-85, Nehru to Indira, June 12, 1932.
[2] *Speeches* I, 300, Speech at Asian Conference, March 23, 1947.

CHAPTER III

CONCEPTION OF NATIONALISM

His Life vis-à-vis World Nationalism

The life of Jawaharlal Nehru coincides with some instructive phases in the development of nationalism. Nationalism, in its modern connotation, is said to have been born towards the end of the eighteenth century, when its force was felt in Western Europe and North America. In the course of the nineteenth century no western nation could exist without feeling the urge towards nationalism. The close of the century saw in many ways the fruition of nationalism in Europe; it also marked the beginning of nationalism in Asia. Nehru was born in the twilight of a politically awakening East.*

In the later part of the nineteenth century, western nationalism was moving on two different planes. An emotional attachment towards the land, belief in the past and its traditions, a feeling of oneness among the people, an urge to fight against foreign domination or despotic governments, faith in the individual liberty and rights of men, aspirations for greater liberty, equality and happiness of all, and similar noble instincts led to a kind of nationalism which is described as liberal humanitarian nationalism. This nationalism aimed to identify itself with political democracy, laying stress on popular sovereignty, general will and national government. This kind of liberal democratic nationalism

---

* Nehru was born in 1889 when the Indian National Congress was four years old. In his childhood he often listened to grown-up talk relating to 'the overbearing character and insulting manners of the English people, as well as Eurasians, towards Indians, and how it was the duty of every Indian to stand up to this and not to tolerate it'. In the opening years of the twentieth century, the Japanese victories stirred up his enthusiasm. 'Nationalistic ideas filled my mind. I mused of Indian freedom and Asiatic freedom from the thraldom of Europe. I dreamt of brave deeds, of how, sword in hand, I would fight for India and help in freeing her.' (AB, III, 16).

proceeded on the lines of the rational interpretation of things. Distinct from this there developed another kind of nationalism, which laid emphasis on the past and the traditions of each national entity. Universality of human desire for freedom and equality was pushed aside, and instead the specialities and peculiarities of individual nations were paid greater attention, together with their distinct aspirations and outlooks. This nationalism leaned on irrationalism and began to lay stress on instinct as opposed to reason. It was seen to have been based on a conservative and authoritarian foundation. Racial superiority, strength of the state, and other allied doctrines became its prominent features.

In India, nationalism at the end of the nineteenth century and the beginning of the twentieth began to stabilize itself on liberal humanitarian principles. It aimed at struggle against foreign rule, as well as at the freedom of men and democratic institutions.

Nehru's entry into active politics coincided with the struggle between the two different kinds of western nationalism in World War I. To the Indian nationalists, the crisis brought mixed feelings. Since they were up against the British, the latter deserved little sympathy, and therefore German victories brought satisfaction both to the moderate and extremist elements in India. According to Nehru, there was no love for Germany, but only the desire to see the British humbled. 'It was the weak and helpless man's idea of vicarious revenge.' In that conflict of ideologies, Nehru's mind sided with the liberal camp of nationalism.

'Of all the nations involved my sympathies were probably most with France.'[1]

Liberal humanitarian nationalism came out victorious from the war and it became more universal. National self-determination became one of the accepted principles which also meant individual freedom, democratic constitutions and representative governments. In India, the nationalist movement took concrete shape from this period onwards. Gandhi made it a mass movement based on the urge for independence, national unity and the rights of men. Added to these, Indian nationalism began to manifest itself through peace and non-violence. This had a much deeper significance not only with regard to the national struggle but also

[1] *AB*, V, 31.

to the growth of Indian nationalism after independence. Nationalism in the West is said to have been born in violence, and the bitterness of violent struggles against dominating powers preserved hateful memories in the history of nations. In its subsequent growth, nationalism found it difficult to emancipate itself from an antipathy towards enemy states or rivals. It may be said that nationalism in India did not suffer from the above defect, and consequently could develop a more liberal and tolerant outlook. Nehru began to appreciate from the beginning the desirability of freedom from hatred of alien rulers against whom the battle was fought. Referring to the national struggle in India after World War I, he says:

'Nationalism is essentially an anti-feeling, and it feeds and fattens on hatred and anger against other national groups, and especially against the foreign rulers of a subject country. There was certainly this hatred and anger in India in 1921 against the British but, in comparison with other countries similarly situated, it was extraordinarily little.'[1]

As the movement in India grew, the feeling of hatred towards the British began to lessen, but nationalism as a factor came to have greater appeal for the people at large. It became more widespread, and at the same time it learnt to be 'generous'.

While a peaceful revolution in India progressed, nationalism in some western countries began to adopt a different form again. Fascism and nazism, representing this kind of extreme nationalism, emerged. Whatever the reason for the rise of this tendency, the consequences were fraught with danger. In its own way, it pretended to develop a new culture, which banished every liberal thought. It stood for the very negation of pacifism and humanitarianism.

In World War II, the fascist and nazi nationalism met its doom. The end of the war also saw the triumph of Indian nationalism which, from the end of World War I to the end of World War II, had proceeded on the broad basis of nationalism with faith in the universal virtues of pacifism, liberalism and rationalism. When the fascist type of nationalism was at its height in Europe, and the national struggle was almost at its climax in India, Nehru

[1] *AB*, XI, 75.

drew a sharp dividing line between the two ideologies, and declared in April, 1936:

'Nationalism in the East, it must be remembered, was essentially different from the new and terribly narrow nationalism of Fascist countries; the former was the historical urge to freedom, the latter the last refuge of reaction.'[1]

Faith in Nationalism as a Living Force

Nehru as a nationalist regarded nationalism as a living force in the history of modern nations. Nationalism had its weaknesses; ideas began to percolate that the days of nationalism were over, and that internationalism in the shape of socialist or proletarian movements seemed to condemn nationalism. But such developments did not make him pessimistic regarding the present or the future of nationalism at any time. He saw in his conception of nationalism not a narrow and fanatical urge but a healthy force. It was an emotional attachment to the motherland 'conditioned and limited in many ways'. Only when the conditioning and limiting factors were absent nationalism might prove different. In the days of foreign domination, nationalism meant to him an inevitable factor, conditioned into a natural and healthy growth. 'For any subject country,' he said, 'national freedom must be the first and dominant urge; for India, with her intense sense of individuality and a past heritage, it was doubly so.'[2]

During the War, according to Nehru, events all over the world proved that the idea that nationalism was fading away before the impact of internationalism and proletarian movements had little truth. In spite of the ideas of proletarian internationalism and the like, the coming of War 'swept everybody everywhere into the net of nationalism'. This was due to the very nature of nationalism —being one of the most powerful urges that move a people, with their sentiments, traditions, and sense of common being and common purpose. In the historic developments during the war years, Nehru saw what he described as a 'remarkable resurgence of nationalism, or rather a re-discovery of it and a new realization of its vital significance'. This led him to say in 1944:

[1] Essays II, 70, 'Presidential Address to the National Congress, Lucknow', April, 1936.
[2] DI, III, 36.

'Old established traditions cannot be easily scrapped or dispensed with; in moments of crisis they rise and dominate the minds of men, and often, as we have seen, a deliberate attempt is made to use those traditions to rouse a people to a high pitch of effort and sacrifice. Traditions have to be accepted to a large extent and adapted and transformed to meet new conditions and ways of thought, and at the same time new traditions have to be built up. The nationalist ideal is deep and strong; it is not a thing of the past with no future significance.'[1]

He was also aware of the resurgence of internationalism at the end of World War II, and thought of an equilibrium between the different forces. But the abiding appeal of nationalism to the spirit of man, he felt, required to be recognized and provided for, though with its sway limited to a narrow sphere.

Nationalism not an Antiquated Cult

During the war years, Indian nationalism had to face attacks from various quarters. An Indian intellectual of repute, M. N. Roy, suggested that nationalism in India be discarded 'as an antiquated cult.'* He 'began to advocate unconditional co-operation with the British Government'.[2] The nationalists were reminded from some other quarters that their nationalism was a sign of their backwardness and that even the demand for independence indicated narrowmindedness. 'Those who tell us so,' remarked Nehru, 'seem to imagine that true internationalism would triumph if we agreed to remain as junior partners in the British Empire or Commonwealth of Nations. They do not appear to realize that this particular type of so-called internationalism is only an extension of a narrow British nationalism. . . .'[3] He, however, thought that India, in spite of her intense nationalistic fervour, was

---

* He said in August, 1941: 'For two generations, nationalism has been the dominating doctrine of the public life of India. Even today, it holds the centre of the stage, although other doctrines have appeared on the scene. While India has been making not too rapid a progress towards the vague and diversely defined goal of free nationhood, the world as a whole was the scene of events which rendered traditional values worthless, and cherished ideals devoid of any meaning. India cannot possibly escape the impact of those events. Under that impact, she also must learn to revaluate values.' M. N. Roy, *Nationalism: An Antiquated Cult*, p. 1, August 17, 1941.

[1] *DI*, III, 37.
[2] Subhas Chandra Bose, *The Indian Struggle* 1935-1942, p. 25.
[3] *DI*, III, 37.

prepared to go further than many nations in accepting real internationalism and co-ordination.

A Vital Force after Independence

Nationalism, according to Nehru, continues to be a vital force in the life of a people, even after their freedom from foreign domination. In a country struggling against her foreign rulers, one knows exactly what nationalism means. It is, in this case, merely an anti-foreign feeling. But at times he wondered, 'What is nationalism in a free country?' He was alive to the problems which faced nationalism after its main urge was satisfied. It is a healthy force in a country striving for its freedom, but it may become, after the country has been liberated, unhealthy and even reactionary. 'It may seek to promote its interests at the expense of other countries and it may repeat the very errors against which it had to contend.' Is it possible, then, to draw the line between what is good and what is bad in nationalism? In spite of such doubts, he finds in it 'a constructive force' for progress. Three years after the independence of India, he said:

'We have just won our freedom but the nationalist sentiments that inspired our struggle still warm our hearts; they warm the heart of every Asian because the memories of past colonialism are still vivid in his mind. So, nationalism is still a live force in every part of Asia. A movement must define itself in terms of nationalism, if it has to become real to the people. In any Asian country, a movement will succeed or fail in the measure that it associates itself with the deep-seated urge of nationalism.'[1]

Nehru's faith in nationalism, both in a country's subjugation and in its freedom, is apparent. The fundamentals on which this faith rests are many.

His Faith in the Greatness of India and Her History

Nationalism being a state of mind in its attachment to the motherland, its intensity is determined by one's intellectual faith in the greatness of a country, besides the common emotional appeal. Nehru understood India both through an intellectual and an emotional mind. He had no blind reverence for the past, but the

[1] *Speeches* II, 163, October 3, 1950.

past greatness of the country stirred his imagination so deeply that he wondered, 'What is my inheritance? To what am I an heir?' And he thought that he was the heir

'To all that humanity has achieved during tens of thousands of years, to all that it has thought and felt and suffered and taken pleasure in, to its cries of triumph and its bitter agony of defeat, to that astonishing adventure of man which began so long ago and yet continues and beckons to us. To all this and more, in common with all men. But there is a special heritage for those of us of India, not an exclusive one, for none is exclusive and all are common to the race of man, one more especially applicable to us, something that is in our flesh and blood and bones, that has gone to make us what we are and what we are likely to be.'[1]

His *Discovery of India* helps in a sense to discover the real nationalist in him. It was in fact the result of an intellectual revolt against the traditional representation of India by the forces which he regarded as hostile, and which kept her in subjugation. There were distinguished exceptions, but in general, so felt Nehru, the history of India was written mainly from the British imperialist view point, laying stress on her 'numerous failings in the past and present and the virtues and high destiny of the British'.[2] India accepted to some extent this kind of interpretation, and, even when people resisted it, they were instinctively influenced by it. As time passed, the Indians gradually suspected and examined critically the old versions of their history. Critical researches by western and Indian scholars revealed brilliant and highly civilized periods in the remote past, and this led to a challenge of the old interpretation of events. It seemed quite extraordinary to Nehru how the English people, apart from some experts and others, remained ignorant about India. 'If facts elude them, how much more is the spirit of India beyond their reach?' he would ask. 'They seized her body and possessed her, but it was the possession of violence. They did not know her or try to know her. They never looked into her eyes, for theirs were averted and hers downcast through shame and humiliation.'[3]

Behind and within India's battered body Nehru would glimpse

[1] *DI*, I, 21.
[2] *AB*, LIII, 426.
[3] *AB*, LIII, 429.

a majesty of soul. He undertook the mission to discover his country. Like a pilgrim he journeyed and like a scholar he studied. He would stand on the mound of Mahenjo-daro in the Indus Valley in the north-west of India to understand the civilization which existed over five thousand years ago; he would visit old monuments and ruins and ancient sculptures and frescoes—Ajanta, Ellora, the Elephanta Caves, and other places—and also see the lovely buildings of a later age in Agra and Delhi, 'where every stone told its story of India's past'. At Sarnath, near Benares, he would almost see the Buddha preaching his first sermon, and his words would come like a distant echo to him through two thousand five hundred years. Asoka's stone pillars spoke to him of a man who, though an emperor, was greater than any king or emperor. So also he would see Akbar at Fatehpur-Sikri, forgetful of his empire, conversing and debating with the learned of all faiths.

The mighty rivers of India attracted him and reminded him of innumerable phases of her history. The mountains and plains all had their tales to tell. While his travels brought such penetrating vision, his studies stirred the imagination deeper still.

'I read her history and read also a part of her abundant ancient literature, and was powerfully impressed by the vigour of the thought, the clarity of the language, and the richness of the mind that lay behind it. I journeyed through India in the company of mighty travellers from China and Western and Central Asia who came here in the remote past and left records of their travels. I thought of what India had accomplished in Eastern Asia, in Angkor, Borobudur, and many other places.'[1]

The journeys, the visits and study gave him a searching insight into the past. 'To a somewhat bare intellectual understanding,' he says, 'was added an emotional appreciation, and gradually a sense of reality began to creep into my mental picture of India, and the land of my forefathers became peopled with living beings, who laughed and wept, loved and suffered; and among them were men who seemed to know life and understand it, and out of their wisdom they had built a structure which gave India a cultural stability which lasted for thousands of years.'[2]

[1] *DI*, III, 34.
[2] *DI*, III, 35.

There seemed to Nehru to be something unique about the continuity of a cultural tradition through five thousand years of Indian history, a tradition which, according to him, was widespread among the masses and which powerfully influenced them. That vision of five thousand years gave him a new perspective, making the burden of foreign rule lighter, and bringing a confidence that India 'would find herself again'. His attitude to India became emotional. 'It took the form of nationalism.'[1]

History supplied him with a moral conviction that he was fighting for the emancipation of a great country whose dependence was unnatural. He found the impress of his country's greatness not merely within her own frontiers, but far across lands and seas. One had only to go back in time and travel in mind to find out the immortal testimony of her spirit, her power, and her love of beauty in various countries of Asia. Few realized, he felt, the significance of those achievements, and few realized that if India was great in thought and philosophy she was equally great in action. To him, the history which Indian men and women made far away from their homeland is yet to be written. With such national pride he could say:

'Most westerners still imagine that ancient history is largely concerned with the Mediterranean countries, and medieval and modern history is dominated by the quarrelsome little continent of Europe. And still they make plans for the future as if Europe only counted and the rest could be fitted in anywhere.'[2]

Revival of Past History a Modern Trend

Nationalism to Nehru is 'essentially a group memory of past achievements, traditions, and experiences'. A blind reverence for the past is as bad as a contempt for it. 'The present and the future inevitably grow out of the past and bear its stamp, and to forget this is to build without foundations and to cut off the roots of national growth.' To him, one of the remarkable developments of the present age has been the rediscovery of the past and of the nation. That has been the tendency everywhere. Even among the ranks of labour and proletarian elements, who are supposed to

[1] *DI*, III, 36.
[2] *DI*, V, 179.

be the foremost champions of international action, this going back to national traditions is most marked. 'War or similar crisis dissolves their internationalism and they become subject to nationalist hates and fears even more than other groups,' he says. The most striking example of this he saw in the Soviet Union during the war. Without giving up its essential social and economic structure, the Soviet Union became more nationalist-minded, and the appeal of the fatherland grew much greater than the appeal of the international proletariat. Famous figures in national history were again revived and again became heroes of the Soviet people. Besides other potential factors, the revival of national memories and traditions and a new awareness of the past added strength to the Soviet people in their growth. Nehru did not believe that the nationalist outlook of Russia was just a reversion to old-style nationalism. It was not. The revolution and all that followed it remained. Even the new social structure led inevitably to a certain international outlook. 'Nevertheless,' said Nehru in 1944, 'nationalism has reappeared in such a way as to fit in with the new environment and add to the strength of the people.'[1] Thus, people everywhere sought comfort and strength in their old traditions. This, to Nehru, was a main trend in modern nationalism.

Nationalism not Revivalism

But nationalism to Nehru should not mean revivalism. The past is a source of inspiration to the nationalist in a broader sense. It contains the picture of a country's greatness to create confidence in his mind for the present and for the future. Nehru meant by history the history of the whole country in which the nation in its entirety is depicted. It is not the history of a sect or a religion, or a class. Moreover, a study of the past should not develop a narrow and reactionary outlook for a retreat to the institutions of the past. That would be the very negation of nationalism. For long in India he was cautious against any diversion towards narrow-mindedness in the name of nationalism. Referring to the religious sentiment which was beginning to develop during the non-co-operation days of the national struggle, he had said:

[1] DI, X, 491.

'I used to be troubled sometimes at the growth of this religious element in our politics, both on the Hindu and the Muslim side. I did not like it at all. Much that Moulvies and Maulanas and Swamis and the like said in their public addresses seemed to me most unfortunate. Their history and sociology and economics appeared to me all wrong, and the religious twist that was given to everything prevented all clear thinking.'[1]

Obviously, therefore, nationalism through a common past and common traditions should not stop on the frontiers of religion or religions inside any particular country. The people need cultural roots to cling to, to gain assurance of their own worth, but these roots should be all-embracing and not narrow or conflicting. Iran, to Nehru, without in any way weakening its religious faith, could deliberately go back to its pre-Islamic days of greatness, and utilize that memory to strengthen its nationalism. The past of India, with all its cultural variety and greatness, was a common heritage of all the Indian people, Hindu, Moslem, Christian, and others. To establish this he argued:

'The fact of subsequent conversion to other faiths did not deprive them of this heritage; just as the Greeks, after their conversion to Christianity, did not lose their pride in the mighty achievements of their ancestors, or the Italians in the great days of the Roman Republic and early empire. If all the people of India had been converted to Islam or Christianity, her cultural heritage would still have remained to inspire them and give them that poise and dignity, which a long record of civilized existence with all its mental struggles with the problems of life gives a people.'[2]

A Rational Approach to the Past

The approach to the past, thus, ought to be rational. Also, nationalism should not lead to an uncritical examination of the past. India was in Nehru's blood and there was much in her that instinctively thrilled him. Yet, from the first, he approached her almost as an alien critic, full of dislike for the present as well as for many of the relics of the past that he saw. 'To some extent I came to her via the West, and looked at her as a friendly westerner

[1] *AB*, X, 72.
[2] *DI*, VII, 319.

might have done.'[1] He wanted to change her outlook and appearance and give her the garb of modernity. Doubts, of course, arose within him. 'Did I know India?—I who presumed to scrap much of her past heritage?'[2] He had the conviction that India could not have continued a cultured existence for thousands of years if she had not possessed something very vital and enduring, yet he thought that there was a great deal that had to be scrapped, that must be scrapped.

While Nehru believed in distinguishing good from bad in the national life through observation of the past, he was aware of the evil aspect of too much attraction towards the past. There were peoples or nations who lived a fevered life in the present only, and almost forgot the past. For them, thought Nehru, a little humility towards the wisdom of the past, which, after all, is the accumulated experience of the human race, would be of gain. But for countries which had too much of the past and which ignored the present, a different emphasis was necessary. In the case of India he wanted to get rid of the cramped religious outlook, the obsession with the supernatural and metaphysical speculation, and the loosening of the mind's discipline in religious ceremonial and mystical emotionalism which obstructed people's understanding of each other and of the world. He wanted the people to come to grips with the present. 'Some Hindus talk of going back to the Vedas; some Moslems dream of an Islamic theocracy. Idle fancies, for there is no going back to the past; there is no turning back even if this was thought desirable. There is only one-way traffic in Time.'[3]

Nationalism Inspired by Foreign Rule

The past, history, traditions and heritage, inspire nationalism among different peoples in varying degrees. Whether dependent or independent, a country comes under this force readily. Among other fundamentals, foreign rule has been a potential force in inspiring nationalism in any country. In India, it took shape through the struggle against the British. The struggle brought home to the nationalist the real implications of nationalism,

[1] *DI*, II, 34.
[2] *Ibid.*
[3] *DI*, X, 495.

F

and the latter feeling gave the struggle a sense of purpose. As Nehru became engaged in activities which promised to lead to India's freedom, he 'became obsessed with the thought of India' which in turn created an urge in him for further work in that direction. Behind this interaction remained the basic factor, viz., foreign rule. As he says:

'The initial urge came to me, I suppose, through pride, both individual and national, and the desire, common to all men, to resist another's domination and have freedom to live the life of our choice. It seemed monstrous to me that a great country like India, with a rich and immemorial past, should be bound hand and foot to a far-away island which imposed its will upon her.'[1]

Patriotism Demands Action

Resentment against alien rule calls for patriotic action. What action, it might not be clear, but to Nehru the idea became absolute from the beginning that the people must not tamely submit to existing conditions. Successful action might not at all seem to be easy, but he felt that the honour of a people demanded a more aggressive and fighting attitude to foreign rule. When the non-co-operation movement was started, patriotism found a channel in which to flow. 'We were full of excitement and optimism,' he said, 'and a buoyant enthusiasm. We sensed the happiness of a person crusading for a cause. We were not troubled with doubts or hesitation; our path seemed to lie clear in front of us and we marched ahead, lifted up by the enthusiasm of others, and helping to push on others.'[2]

Patriotic action brought a sense of freedom to him and a pride in that freedom. To a nation in action the old feeling of oppression and frustration began to disappear. As the national struggle continued, the morale of the people grew. Side by side, the nation could know the main obstacles which stood in its way, as well as the evils and vices which made the national life impure. The period of struggle was in fact the formative stage of nationalism, and in India it is during that period that Nehru learnt much about his nation.

[1] *DI*, III, 33.
[2] *AB*, X, 69.

Evils of Foreign Rule

Two things which appeared to Nehru as the most lamentable features of foreign rule were imperialism and racialism. They led to the degradation of all concerned. Imperialism which meant the domination of one people over another was bad. And so also was racialism. The whole ideology of British rule, according to Nehru, was that of the master race, and the structure of government was based upon it. 'Biologists tell us,' he said, 'that racialism is a myth and there is no such thing as a master race. But we in India have known racialism in all its forms ever since the commencement of British rule.'[1] The theory of the master race subjected India as a nation and Indians as individuals to insult, humiliation, and contemptuous treatment. To the nationalist it was difficult to tolerate.

'. . . what hurts still more is the fact that we submitted for so long to this degradation. I would have preferred any kind of resistance to this, whatever the consequences, rather than that our people should endure this treatment.'[2]

The feeling of sympathy for one's own race becomes deep while one resents the racial superiority of others. This, in a way, strengthens the spirit of nationalism. Foreign rule also fosters other evils which degrade a subject people. The British brought about the political unification of India. They also let loose new dynamic forces which fostered that unity and created a desire for freedom. But the British tried to disrupt that very unity which they helped to create. They wanted to weaken the nationalist elements so that British rule might continue. They encouraged reactionary elements and looked to them for support, promoted divisions and encouraged one group against another, encouraged fissiparous tendencies due to religion or province, and organized classes which were afraid of a change that might engulf them. All this was natural for a foreign power to pursue. But through it nationalism learnt to harden itself. Pointing to efforts 'to encourage the disruptive, obscurantist, reactionary, sectarian and opportunist elements in the country', Nehru said:

'Perhaps that too is a needed test and challenge for us, and

[1] *DI*, VII, 304.
[2] *Ibid.*

before India is reborn it will have to go through again and again the fire that cleanses and tempers and burns up the weak, the impure and the corrupt.'[1]

His Sentimental Feelings during Struggle

Foreign domination not merely presented hard realities, but it also made Nehru sentimental in his thought. He often let himself be swayed by deeper emotions of nationalism, finding inspiration from various heroic deeds of others either in India or elsewhere, and inspiring others through his own emotion. 'Brick by brick has our national movement been built up,' he would say to his listeners, 'and often on the prostrate bodies of her martyred sons has India advanced. The giants of old may not be with us, but the courage of old is with us still, and India can yet produce martyrs like Jatindas and Wizaya.'[2]

Often in his historical writings one comes across lines which speak of a mood typical of the man. Leonidas and his 1,400 comrades lay dead at Thermopylae before the Persians could go forward. This occurred in the year 480 BC. To Nehru, even today one's heart thrills to think of this unconquerable courage; even today the traveller to Thermopylae might see with tear-dimmed eyes the message, engraved in stone, of Leonidas and his colleagues:

'Go tell to Sparta, thou that passest by,
That here obedient to their words we lie.'

And next Nehru would go on to say:

'Wonderful is the courage that conquers death! Leonidas and Thermopylae live for evermore, and even we in distant India feel a thrill when we think of them. What then shall we say or feel of our own people, our own forebears, men and women of Hindustan, who right through our long history, have smiled and mocked at death, who have preferred death to dishonour or slavery, and who have preferred to break rather than bow down to tyranny? Think of Chittor and its peerless story, of the amazing heroism

---

[1] *AB*, LIV, 449.
[2] *Essays* II, 14, 'Presidential Address to the National Congress', Lahore, December, 1929.

of its Rajput men and women! Think also of our present day, of our comrades, warm-blooded like us, who have not flinched at death for India's freedom.'[1]

Revitalization of the Nation as Aim of Nationalism

It was through patriotic struggle and emotional vision that Nehru developed his nationalism. During the fight for freedom he felt that the people of India had vast stores of suppressed energy and ability which he should try to release to make them feel young and vital again. 'India, constituted as she is,' he said, 'cannot play a secondary part in the world. She will either count for a great deal or not count at all. No middle position attracted me. Nor did I think any intermediate position feasible.'[2] Behind his many years of struggle lay the desire to revitalize India. He thought that through action and self-imposed suffering and sacrifice, through voluntarily facing risk and danger, through refusal to submit to what people considered evil and wrong, the battery of India's spirit would be recharged, and that she would be awakened from her long slumber. In building up a nation he wanted to aim high and look far. Nationalism appeared to him as something much bigger than what mere politics could make of it. Conflict with an alien government was not everything; the real factor was the people. With higher objectives, Nehru and his compatriots frequently acted as no politician, moving in the narrow sphere of politics only, would have done. These compatriots, according to him, erred at times from the point of view of opportunist politics, but they always aimed to raise the whole level of the Indian people, psychologically and spiritually, as well as politically and economically. 'It was the building up of that real inner strength of the people that we were after, knowing that the rest would inevitably follow.'[3]

Unity of India the Supreme Concern

Perhaps the supreme concern of Nehru during the later part of the freedom movement was to achieve the unity of India as a nation. For him the unity of India was not merely an intellectual

[1] *WH*, Vol. I, 64, Nehru to Indira, January 21, 1931.
[2] *DI*, III, 40.
[3] *DI*, III, 40-41.

conception, but was an emotional experience which overpowered him. That essential unity, he felt, had been so powerful that no political division, no disaster or catastrophe, had been able to overcome it. He knew that the diversity of India was tremendous. It lay on the surface and anybody could see it. It concerned itself with physical appearances as well as with certain mental habits and traits. But he was more convinced of the fact that though outwardly there was diversity and infinite variety among the people, yet everywhere there was the tremendous impress of oneness, which held people together for ages past. He wrote in the *Discovery*:

'There is little in common, to outward seeming, between the Pathan of the North-West and the Tamil in the far South. Their racial stocks are not the same, though there may be common strands running through them; they differ in face and figure, food and clothing, and, of course, language. In the North-Western Frontier Province there is already the breath of Central Asia, and many a custom there, as in Kashmir, reminds one of the countries on the other side of the Himalayas. Pathan popular dances are singularly like Russian Cossack dancing. Yet, with all these differences, there is no mistaking the impress of India on the Pathan, as this is obvious on the Tamil.'[1]

Nehru held the thesis that India, like ancient China, was a world in itself, with a culture and a civilization which gave shape to all things. Outside influences poured in and often influenced that culture and were absorbed. Disruptive tendencies gave rise immediately to an attempt to find a synthesis. Some kind of a dream of unity occupied the mind of the country since the dawn of civilization. That unity was not conceived as something imposed from outside, a standardization of externals or even of beliefs. It was something deeper and, within its fold, the widest tolerance of belief and custom was practised, and every variety was acknowledged and even encouraged.

On the question of the unity of his country, besides the theories which he advanced to prove and establish it, Nehru at times also felt emotional. Once again, in his historical writings, one often comes across a touching faith in a one-India ideal. In the life of

[1] *DI*, III, 44-45.

Shankara, that ancient sage of India, he would find a man 'who looked upon the whole of India from Cape Comorin to the Himalayas as his field of action,' striving hard 'to synthesize the diverse currents that were troubling the mind of India of his day and to build a unity of outlook out of that diversity'.

'There is a significance about these long journeys of Shankara throughout this vast land at a time when travel was difficult and the means of transport very slow and primitive. The very conception of these journeys, and his meeting kindred souls everywhere and speaking to them in Sanskrit, the common language of the learned throughout India, brings out the essential unity of India even in those far-off days.'[1]

And in a similar mood, he would find Vivekananda, the modern sage, thundering 'from Cape Comorin on the southern tip of India to the Himalayas' wearing himself out in that process.

Coming to the national movement, he found in the National Congress, apart from its fundamental objective, namely the freedom of India, its basic faith in the principle of national unity with the proper solution of minority problems. The British had long given political unity to India. It became more and more comprehensive owing to the development of communications and transport. To Nehru, the above external forces only began to operate on the basis of the traditional unity of India. 'It was a unity of a common subjection,' he said in 1938, 'but it gave rise to the unity of common nationalism. The idea of a united and a free India gripped the people. It was not a superficial idea imposed from above, but the natural outcome of that fundamental unity which has been the background of Indian life for thousands of years.'[2]

Nationalism and Language

With a deep faith in one-Indian nationalism, Nehru discounted all possible superficial distinctions which existed among the people in the shape of languages or religions. He never considered for a moment that differences in language might hinder the growth of nationalism. 'One of the legends about India which our

[1] *DI*, V, 169.
[2] *Writings* II, Part I, Ch. 1, 19, 'Essay in Foreign Affairs', USA, January, 1938.

English rulers have persistently circulated all over the world is that India has several hundred languages—I forget the exact number,' he would ridicule.[1] He exploded the oft-repeated story of five hundred or more languages as 'a fiction of the mind of the philologist and the census commissioner, who note down every variation in dialect and every petty hill-tongue . . . as a separate language, although sometimes it is spoken only by a few hundred or a few thousand persons'.[2] If the census talks about the hundreds of languages in India, it also points out, says Nehru, that Germany has about fifty or sixty languages. But 'I do not remember anyone pointing out this fact in proof of the disunity or disparity of Germany.'[3] India would seem to him to have surprisingly few languages, considering its area; and compared to the same area in Europe it was far more closely allied with regard to language. Fifteen languages covered the whole of undivided India, and of those Hindi, with its variation Urdu, was by far the most wide-spread and was understood even where it was not spoken.* Whatever the number, Nehru was confident of the coming of one *lingua franca* for the whole of India. Thus nationalism to him had no danger from that quarter.

Nationalism and Religion

The greatest problem, however, which Indian nationalism had to face was religion. To Nehru there was no such thing as a Hindu nationalism, or a Muslim nationalism; there was only one nationalism—Indian nationalism. The minorities in India were not racial or national minorities as in Europe, but were religious minorities. Racially, though India is a patchwork and a curious mixture, yet, according to him, no racial questions had arisen or could arise in India. 'Religion transcends these racial differences, which fade into one another and are often hard to distinguish. Religious barriers are obviously not permanent, as conversions can take

---

* The modern Indian languages descended from Sanskrit, and therefore called Indo-Aryan languages, are: Hindi-Urdu, Bengali, Marathi, Gujrati, Oriya, Assamese, Rajasthani, Punjabi, Sindhi, Pushtu, and Kashmiri. The Dravidian languages are: Tamil, Telugu, Kanarese, and Malayalam.

[1] *AB*, LV, 452.
[2] *DI*, V, 148.
[3] *AB*, LV, 453.

place from one religion to another, and a person changing his religion does not thereby lose his racial background or his cultural and linguistic inheritance.'[1]

In spite of Nehru, the trend of events moved fast in a different direction. As the national struggle entered its final phase, there also developed what is known as communal strife. Hindus and Muslims came to be regarded as different nations altogether, and Muhammad Ali Jinnah became an uncompromising advocate of the so-called two-nation theory. These developments gave the greatest shock to Nehru, whose concept of Indian nationalism was as uncompromising as Jinnah's Muslim nationalism. Nehru argued that if nationality was based on religion, then there were not only two but many nations in India. The entire concept of religious nationalism seemed to him absurd.

'Of two brothers one may be a Hindu, another a Moslem; they would belong to two different nations. These two nations existed in varying proportions in most of the villages of India. They were nations which had no boundaries; they overlapped. A Bengali Moslem and a Bengali Hindu living together, speaking the same language, and having much the same traditions and customs, belonged to different nations. All this was very difficult to grasp; it seemed a reversion to some medieval theory.'[2]

What a nation is may be difficult to define, but possibly the essential characteristic of national consciousness, according to Nehru, is a sense of belonging together and facing the rest of mankind. These hopes of his with reference to India were disturbed, and finally, inside India, Pakistan was created as a home for the Muslim nation. How far Pakistan is justified is another matter; but the fact remained that there were almost as many Muslims inside the Indian nation as in the Muslim national state of Pakistan.*

---

* After the partition of India, Nehru had to face one of the most difficult situations in his life in attempting to remove communalism. He always regarded it as the most danger-ous manifestation of a narrow type of nationalism. '. . . nationalism often covers a multi-tude of sins and a multitude of throw-backs on something that is dead and gone. What is communalism? In its very essence it is a throw-back to some medieval age, to a medieval state of mind and medieval habits and medieval slogans', he said in the Parliament of India. *Debates*, P.I., 1950, Part II, Vol. I, February 3, 1950.
[1] *DI*, VIII, 359.
[2] *DI*, VIII, 369.

Emotional Integration of the People: The Purpose of Nationalism
Independence brought a new spirit of nationalism to Nehru.
India continued to remain the 'much-loved motherland, the
ancient, the eternal', to whom he paid his usual reverent homage,
but with independence he had to bind himself 'afresh to her
service'.[1] Hereafter, nationalism meant to him an emotional
integration of the entire people. 'We all belong to Mother India,'
he declared after independence, 'and have to live and die here. We
all are equal partners in the freedom that we have won. Every one
of our three or four hundred million people must have an equal
right to the opportunities and blessings that free India has to
offer.'[2]

To Nehru, the lessons of the past and history concerning the
national unity or disunity were many. His long experiences of
life, also, were meaningful to him. In a subcontinent like India,
disruptive tendencies were quite apparent. There was communalism, or religion misapplied to politics; there was provincialism
or 'stateism' as it was called; there was also casteism which seemed
to him as perhaps the most insidious and dangerous of all in the
country. The caste system weakened India nationally and socially.
It divided people into small groups separating them into hier-
archies, some calling themselves high caste, some middle caste,
some low caste and some no caste at all. Conscious of these
factors, and of the reasons for India's weakness and downfall in
the past in spite of her many virtues and abilities, he went on
laying stress everywhere on the unity of India, and on the need to
fight communalism, provincialism, separatism and casteism. He
went on reminding the people that there were no divisions between the north and south and east and west of India, but there
was only one India of which all the people were inheritors. The
whole of India, he pointed out, was the common heritage of every
Indian, as also was all India's history, down thousands and
thousands of years to the present day. He reminded the nation of
its great future which was also going to be a common future.
Trying to make the nation conscious of its mission, he called the
people to stand up straight, and look up at the skies, keeping their

---

[1] *Speeches* I, August 15, 1947 (Biblio, 153).
[2] *On Gandhi*, 146, February 12, 1948.

feet firmly planted on the ground, and to bring about a synthesis, namely the integration of the Indian people.

'Political integration has already taken place to some extent, but what I am after is something much deeper than that—an emotional integration of the Indian people so that we might be welded into one, and made into one strong national unit, maintaining at the same time all our wonderful diversity.'[1]

Service to Country as a Religion

Religious differences which did a good deal of harm to India before independence could not be in any way tolerated in the secular national state which the free India declared herself to be. Nehru wanted to make nationalism itself a kind of common religion for all and said: 'The time has come when we have to consider the service of India as our first religion whatever religion each one of us might profess. In the same way, we hope all to consider ourselves Indians first, whatever caste or community we might represent.'[2]

Nationalism based on Greater Ideals and Actions

A great nation must believe in greater ideals as well as in greater actions. It is through both that Nehru wanted to develop the spirit of nationalism in the people. Keeping a few big schemes before his country, he at times would feel exhilarated and excited, and think, 'Where is she going? Where have we to lead her, which way have we to walk and what mighty tasks have we to undertake?' He began to believe more and more that the continuous progress of a living nation was possible only through big works, executed with a large heart and a large mind. 'Small minds or small-minded nations cannot undertake big works. When we see big works our stature grows with them, and our minds open out a little.' With these words he opened the Bhakra Nangal.[3]

The ideals which he kept before him in trying to make nationalism a strong force were broad and true, in the line of liberal humanitarian nationalism.

'We have served India not just because she is a geographical

---

[1] *Speeches* III, 35, October 6, 1955.
[2] *Biblio*, 77, April 6, 1955.
[3] *Speeches* III, 4, July 8, 1954.

entity and the land of our birth, but because we thought that she represented certain ideals and objectives, the material and spiritual growth of man, and the unity of mankind.'[1]

His Opposition to National Irrationalism

Much as he devoted himself to the development of Indian nationalism, he never allowed his nationalistic ideas to tend towards any kind of irrationalism. 'I generally do not encourage the idea,' he declared in the Constituent Assembly of India during the legislative debates, 'which is a peculiar product of intensive nationalism, of each person thinking his country as a chosen country of God—normally the people of each country think that they are the chosen people; whether it is in America or Europe or Asia we all tend to think that we are the chosen race—I do not wish to encourage that idea. I am proud enough of my people, my country, my heritage, but it is a narrow-minded view to think that we are the chosen people and all the others are outside the pale.'[2]

Fundamentally, he realized that India is a country with a basic unity, but of great variety in religion, in cultural traditions and in ways of living. It is through mutual forbearance and respect that he wanted to see a strong, stable and co-operative community grow up. Any other extreme nationalist approach would appear to him as dangerous. 'Some people talk of one nation, one culture, one language. That cry reminds me of some of the Fascist and Nazi slogans of old. We are one nation of course, but to try to regiment it in one way will mean discord and conflict and bitterness. It will put an end to the richness and variety of India and confine and limit the creative spirit and the joy in life of our people.'[3] His stand against any kind of irrational approach made him a relentless enemy of the communal organizations. To him, they were guilty of the narrow outlook which kills the spirit and the mind, and weakens the nation. They represented some kind of medieval mentality, and stood for reaction in the political and economic fields. To him they appeared as nothing less than the replicas of fascism and nazism in Europe.[4]

---

[1] Presidential Address, Indian National Congress, 57th Session, October 18, 1951.
[2] Debates C. A. (Legislative), 1949, Vol. II, March 8, 1949.
[3] Presidential Address, Indian National Congress, 58th Session, January 17, 1953.
[4] Ibid.

In a rational way he lays great emphasis on national solidarity which means to him equally the development of the strength of a nation. This strength he does not want to derive from any external source. It is a strength which rests on the people and the people alone. 'We must seek,' he says, 'to build up our strength on ourselves and not by dependence on others. Dependence in one direction leads to dependence in another. Nations, it is said, by themselves are made. By self-reliance, we shall command respect and we shall make our country more and more our own, of each one of us.'[1]

Nationalism is a vital force and Nehru does not want to renounce any part of the genius of the people, or basic traditions, lest they lose a great deal thereby and become rootless.[2] But nationalism, in the present context of world history, is not an end in itself. For long he felt the necessity of nations making the whole world a field of study. Nations and individuals are required to grow out of the narrow grooves of thought and action, and lay emphasis on a world synthesis. Nehru kept his feet firmly planted on the ground of nationalism, but through nationalism he wanted to serve the cause of internationalism.

'We have to build up this great country into a mighty nation, mighty not in the ordinary sense of the word, that is, having great armies and all that, but mighty in thought, mighty in action, mighty in culture and mighty in its peaceful service of humanity.'[3]

---

[1] *Ibid*, 59th Session, January 23, 1954.
[2] *Debates* P.I., 1950, Part II, Vol. 1, February 3, 1950.
[3] *Speeches* III, 35, October 6, 1955.

CHAPTER IV

FAITH IN DEMOCRACY

An Experimentalist in the Democratic System

Jawaharlal Nehru has propounded no theories of democracy. It was James Bryce who said during the first quarter of this century that 'Novelties are not possible in a subject the literature of which began with Plato and Aristotle and has been enriched by thousands of pens since their day'.[1] This may be true, but one thing is also probable—that democracy in its working processes is continually changing, every epoch of time bringing new ideas as the result of new experiments. Those who experiment with democracy in the practical field may not necessarily be theorists, but they may, at times, through their work contribute something towards the evolution of novelties. Nehru is more of an experimentalist in the science of democracy. He does not merely want to talk about democracy, but wants to consider 'all kinds of aspects of it' in its actual working. 'An Englishman may think of democracy in terms of his system; an American in terms of his system. Russia talks about the people's democracy, which is completely different. They use the same word.'[2] Not worried very much by what others have said or thought about democracy, he seems to think of it in his own way and devotes himself to experiments. Democracy is not regarded as a fixed concept, and in fact he does not even want to define it in order to give it a universal meaning, because definitions seem to him difficult, and he feels that 'to define anything that is big is to limit it'. To him democracy 'is a dynamic, not a static, thing, and as it changes it may be that its domain will become wider and wider. Ultimately, it is a mental

[1] James Bryce, *Modern Democracies*, Preface, ix.
[2] *Talks*, 18.

94

approach applied to our political and economic problems.'[1] Thus he concerns himself more with the actual problems.

Nevertheless, today certain basic ideas about democracy have become almost universal. While Nehru's experiments in this field have raised many doubts in his mind, there has been little doubt regarding the virtues of the universally accepted democratic fundamentals.

His Esteem of the People

From ancient times to the present day, the meaning of democracy has been described in various ways as the liberty of the people, equality of the people, fraternity of the people, or the sovereignty of the people. Radical thinkers on democracy have, while suggesting the sovereign power of the people, subordinated everything else to this idea. Fascism, which eclipsed democracy for a time in recent history, invented a more popular concept than the concept of the sovereign power of the people—the myth of a motherland or fatherland, great and glorious, for which people are born to die. Through some mysterious process, fascism and nazism merged the ideas of nation and land and state into one, and raised it above the idea of the supremacy of the people. Nation and land appeared greater than the living people.* Fascism and nazism stood for a complete and uncompromising denial of the principles of liberalism and democracy. They based themselves upon the total subordination of the individual. The rights and freedom of man were denied in favour of the state. In spite of this, authoritarianism could flourish and it was popular at the expense of the people.

---

* Before the rise of Mussolini, the poet Gabriele d'Annunzio exalted the concept of a victorious Italy; and Mussolini declared in 1932, 'Today, with a fully tranquil conscience I say to you, that the twentieth century will be the century of fascism, the century of Italian power, the century during which Italy will become for the third time the leader of mankind.' The German Idealist school played no mean part in developing the absolutist philosophy. Whatever the degree of respect the idealist philosophers maintained for the dignity and rights of man as an individual, nearly all of them ascribed unlimited majesty and excellence to the State. Kant and Fichte gave the theory of the importance of political organization to the individual; eventually it came to suggest a cult of State and even of monarch *per se*. Hegel's glorification of the State was superb. State was the absolute spirit, consciously realizing itself in the world; its existence had no other explanation than that God so willed it. In fact, *it* was God. Under such a philosophy individual man had to wither. State in all its majesty manifested itself through the power of political authority, and the latter through its action only expressed the supreme moral will.

[1] *Ibid*, 19.

To Nehru, land and people appear almost as equals. In one of his great tours throughout India, he went on telling the people that it is they who happen to be India. As he wandered from gathering to gathering among the peasants, whom he considered as the real children of the soil, he would hold before them a picture of India from the Khyber in the far north-west to Cape Comorin in the distant south, and would make them think of India as a whole. Next he would identify them with the concept of India, taking advantage of the implicit and deep faith of the people in the sacredness of the motherland. As he approached a gathering, a great roar of welcome would greet him: *Bharat Mata Ki Jai*—'Victory to Mother India!' Unexpectedly, he would ask the people what they meant by that cry; who was the *Bharat Mata*, Mother India, whose victory they wanted. His question would amuse the people and surprise them, and then, not knowing exactly what to answer, they would look at each other and at him. But Nehru would persist in his questioning. At last someone would reply that it was the *dharti*, the good earth of India, that they meant. Wedded as the people were to the soil for immemorial generations, they could only reply in that manner. But Nehru would ask, 'What earth? Their particular village patch, or all the patches in the district or province, or in the whole of India?' And so the question and answer would go on, till he would explain that India was all that they had thought, but it was much more.

'The mountains and the rivers of India, and the forests and the broad fields, which gave us food, were all dear to us, but what counted ultimately were the people of India, people like them and me, who were spread out all over this vast land. *Bharat Mata*, Mother India, was essentially these millions of people, and victory to her meant victory to these people. You are parts of this *Bharat Mata*, I told them, you are in a manner yourselves *Bharat Mata*, and as this idea slowly soaked into their brains, their eyes would light up as if they had made a great discovery.'[1]

This attitude of mind had developed in him from an earlier period of his life. Of course, the land of India, with a continuity of life and culture from time immemorial, holds a greater signifi-

[1] *DI*, III, 44, and *Essays* III, 48-9.

cance than the people of India of any particular time. The depth of the soul of India seemed to Nehru difficult to fathom. 'India with all her infinite charm and variety began to grow upon me more and more, and yet the more I saw of her, the more I realized how very difficult it was for me or for anyone else to grasp the ideas she had embodied,' he wrote.[1] To him, she was like some ancient palimpsest on which layer upon layer of thought and reverie had been inscribed, and yet no succeeding layer had completely hidden or erased what had been written previously. India, to him, has been built up by countless generations of men. How can this complex and mysterious personality of India of many ages, therefore, be identified with the people of India of any given time? But what is India after all at any given time without her people? To Nehru, the spirit of the country lies in the conscious or subconscious selves of her people, though they may not be always aware of it. The people at any given time represent the entire spirit of the land they live in, and their objective existence makes the country what it is, or what it embodies.

But the people, identified with the land, are not converted into an ethereal, ethical or merely spiritual concept. That might mean the same thing as the land and nation in the idealist concept *par excellence*. To Nehru, therefore:

'I do not idealise the conception of the masses and, as far as possible, I try to avoid thinking of them as a theoretical abstraction. The people of India are very real to me in their great variety and, in spite of their vast numbers, I try to think of them as individuals rather than as vague groups.'[2]

In his voyage of discovery, Nehru thus looked at the land of India and the people of India in equal esteem, and felt that the spirit of the country had been impressed on 'all its children'. The idea of differentiating the greatness of the country from that of the people (at any given time) did not appeal to him.

The Essence of Democracy
This basic faith in the dignity of men, both in their totality and in their individuality, led Nehru to lay faith in the democratic

---

[1] *DI*, III, 42.
[2] *DI*, III, 41.

G

system of government. During the freedom movement, his aim was to win freedom for the entire people, in the real sense of the term. 'We wanted no change of masters from white to brown, but a real people's rule, by the people and for the people, and an ending of our poverty and misery.'[1] A few hours before India became independent, he said in the Constituent Assembly:

'To the people of India, whose representatives we are, we make an appeal to join us with faith and confidence in this great adventure. This is no time for petty and destructive criticism, no time for ill-will, or blaming others. We have to build the noble mansion of free India where all her children may dwell.'[2]

As Independent India began to follow the path of democracy, the desire to depend upon the people grew greater in Nehru's mind. The progress of a country is a complex phenomenon. Opinions are many, and ideas are diverse. How should democracy operate where differences exist? His reply is:

'One has to find an equilibrium among the various forces at work. In finding this equilibrium in a democratic country, one has to take the vast masses of the people into confidence. One has to produce a sensation in them that they are partners in the vast undertaking of running a nation, partners in government, partners in industry. That is the essence of democracy.'[3]

He regards the people as partners in everything, but democracy cancels itself out if people are regarded as partners in a totalitarian way. He does not want the people to constitute a bloc, and work with the government or industry in a regimented manner. People, to him, do not constitute this kind of phalanx. On the other hand, he means by the people individuals in their separate entity, united for the welfare of the state, which only means the welfare of the people. Once he was asked, 'What is your principal problem? How many problems have you got?' He replied, 'We have got 360 million problems in India,' referring roughly to the total population of the country. His answer amused people, but as he explains: 'It has an essential truth in it: that all our problems have to be viewed from the point of view of the 360 million

[1] *DI*, III, 49-50.
[2] *Speeches* I, 4.
[3] *Speeches* III, 60, December 14, 1953.

individuals, not some statistical mass which you see drawn in curves and graphs on paper ... we must think in terms of individuals, individual happiness and individual misery.'[1]

Democracy on Practical Lines

Did Nehru come under the influence of the Gandhian concept of democracy? It would appear that he is a practical democrat with faith in the democratic apparatus as necessary for the management of the state. 'The term Democracy,' described James Bryce, 'has in recent years been loosely used to denote sometimes a state of society, sometimes a state of mind, sometimes a quality in manners. It has become encrusted with all sorts of associations attractive or repulsive, ethical or poetical, or even religious. But Democracy really means nothing more nor less than the rule of the whole people expressing their sovereign will by their votes.'[2] Far from such definitions, Gandhi's conception of democracy was definitely a metaphysical one. It had hardly anything to do with numbers or majorities or representation in the ordinary sense. It was based on service and sacrifice, and it used moral pressure. Gandhi claimed himself to be a born democrat by completely indentifying himself with the poorest of mankind, longing to live no better than they, and making a corresponding conscious effort to approach that level to the best of his ability. Western democracy, to Gandhi, was on trial. As he explained:

'Corruption and hypocrisy ought not to be the inevitable products of democracy, as they undoubtedly are today. Nor is bulk a true test of democracy. True democracy is not inconsistent with a few persons representing the spirit, the hope and the aspirations of those whom they claim to represent. I hold that democracy cannot be evolved by forcible methods. The spirit of democracy cannot be imposed from without; it has to come from within.'[3]

Gandhi hoped for the evolution of a true science of democracy. To Nehru such Gandhian doctrines appeared highly problematical. Gandhi's theory that a few persons could represent the spirit, the hope and the aspirations of the people, made Nehru wonder if it

[1] *Speeches* III, 4.
[2] James Bryce, *Modern Democracies*, Preface, viii.
[3] Gandhi's statement, September 17, 1934, quoted in *AB*, XXXIV, 252-53.

was not similar to the authoritarian conception of democracy, where a few 'will claim to represent the real needs and desires of the masses, even though the latter may themselves be unaware of them. The mass will become a metaphysical conception with them, and it is this that they claim to represent.'[1] Of course, Gandhi was known to Nehru as being far from this kind of philosophy.

Certain other ideas of Gandhi created similar problems in the mind of Nehru. Once Gandhi surprised him about the future of the Congress Party after independence. According to him, the Party should continue, but on one condition—that none of its members should accept a paid position under the state, and, if one was accepted, the person in question would have to leave the Party. The whole idea underlying it was that 'the Congress by its detachment and having no axe to grind, could exercise tremendous moral pressure on the Executive as well as other departments of the Government, and thus keep them on the right track'. This was all to the good, but, as Nehru felt, was it not the very opposite of the modern idea of a party which is built up to seize state power in order to refashion the political and economic structure according to certain pre-conceived ideas? Thus, in spite of the Gandhian doctrines, Nehru's idea of democracy developed on practical Western lines.

A Tinge of Idealism

But it does not seem that he could entirely agree to look at democracy as nothing more than the rule of people expressing their sovereign will by their votes. Democracy to him is certainly this, but also something more. It is a state of society, a state of mind, as well as a quality in manners. The birth of modern Indian democracy took place as much under a political atmosphere as a moral one, the latter being mainly created by the Gandhian approach to the virtues of sacrifice and service. Nehru, while working with democracy in its practical aspects, took into account the moral values associated with it. Politics cannot be mean, nor can they stand on weak foundations. The politician, therefore, more so the democrat, should believe in the values of certain higher principles of life and society besides mere politics.*

* Aristotle did not separate the spheres of the statesman and the moralist.
[1] AB, XXXIV, 253.

'I would say that democracy is not only political, not only economic, but something of the mind, as everything is ultimately something of the mind. It involves equality of opportunity to all people, as far as possible, in the political and economic domain. It involves the freedom of the individual to grow and to make the best of his capacities and ability. It involves a certain tolerance of others and even of others' opinions when they differ from yours. It involves a certain contemplative tendency and a certain inquisitive search for truth—and for, let us say, the right thing.'[1]

If Gandhian metaphysics had any influence on Nehru with regard to his work as a democrat, it was to combine both the democrat and the moralist in him.

Influence of Humanitarianism

Nehru's attitude towards democracy has been greatly influenced by humanitarianism, the rise of socialism and working class movements. Both in theory and in practice, he was led to think in terms of amendments of democracy. As he saw, earlier democrats had laid greater emphasis on the notions of liberty and equality and the equal right of everyone to happiness. But new movements brought about new ideas that happiness did not come by merely making it a fundamental right. The idea of physical well-being came as a necessary part of democracy. To a starving man, democratic freedom meant nothing. So appeared the problem for democracy—a more equitable distribution of wealth, and material happiness among the people. Socialistic ideas became intimately connected with the idea of political democracy. To Nehru, it became not merely a question of intimate connection but, if possible, a necessary integration.

Opposition to Opponents of Democracy

In the world-wide conflict of ideas and politics which fascism and nazism caused, Nehru's faith in democracy became greatly strengthened. He was roused against fascism and the totalitarian state, as well as against those democrats who tried to compromise with the enemy at the cost of democratic ideals. During the post-Munich age, when the map of Europe changed from day to day,

[1] Talks, 19.

and 'barbarism and black reaction' triumphed, his mind was filled with horror. The 'murder of Spanish democracy', as he calls it, could lead him to say:

'It was not the rebels who killed Republican Spain, or traitors' hands that did it. Nor was it ultimately done to death by the Fascist Powers, much as they tried to do so. Britain and France must be held responsible for this, as for the betrayal of Czecho-slovakia, and history long ages hence will remember this infamy and will not forgive them. The infinite sadness in the looks of the Czechs and the Spaniards, whom they deserted and betrayed and, in the guise of friendship and impartiality, drove to death and slavery, will hunt them from generation to generation.'[1]

His opposition to illiberal views and autocratic systems has been developed on more pronounced lines. Even the heroes of history, if autocrats, fell away in his esteem. He wrote to Indira while speaking about Napoleon Bonaparte:

'I shall confess to you that all through my boyhood I had a soft corner in my heart for him. He was one of my heroes, though I knew little enough of him then. I know much more now and I am afraid he has shrunk in my mind and does not loom nearly so big as he used to long ago.'[2]

In the case of Napoleon he could not completely forget the picture of his boyhood days, or eradicate Napoleon's many failings. It is natural though strange that the impressions of one's childhood and boyhood persist through life. But towards the living Napoleons of his own time he had no sympathy whatever, political or personal, and at times his behaviour towards them was rather strange. One or two instances will illustrate it.

In the early months of 1936, when the great dictators of Europe had not made it clear how far they would really go, Nehru was with his ailing wife near Lausanne in Switzerland. On February 28th she passed away, and, broken in spirit, Nehru went with his daughter to Montreux to spend a few quiet days there. It was there that he had a visit from the Italian Consul at Lausanne, who came over especially to convey to him Signor Mussolini's deep sympathy at his loss. Some weeks earlier a friend in Rome had

[1] *Writings* II, 93, February 22, 1939.
[2] *WH*, Vol. I, 597, Nehru to Indira, November 4, 1932.

written to Nehru that Mussolini would like to meet him. Later, that message was repeated, and there was a touch of eagerness and insistence about it. 'Normally I might have got over my distaste for meeting him, for I was curious also to know what kind of man the Duce was. But the Abyssinian campaign was being carried on then and my meeting him would inevitably have led to all manner of inferences and would be used for fascist propaganda.' So he conveyed his regrets. After his wife's death, he sent another message that, even apart from other reasons, he was in no mood then for an interview with anyone.

After a few days at Montreux, Nehru proceeded to Geneva and Marseilles, where he boarded an airliner for the east. On arriving in Rome in the late afternoon, he was met by a high official who handed him a letter. The Duce, it stated, would be glad to meet Nehru and had fixed six o'clock that evening for the interview. 'I was surprised and reminded him of my previous messages. But he insisted that it had now all been fixed up and the arrangement could not be upset. Indeed if the interview did not take place there was every likelihood of his being dismissed from his office. I was assured that nothing would appear in the press, and that I need only see the Duce for a few minutes. All that he wanted to do was to shake hands with me and to convey personally his condolences at my wife's death. So we argued for a full hour with all courtesy on both sides but with increasing strain; it was a most exhausting hour for me and probably more so for the other party. The time fixed for the interview was at last upon us and I had my way. A telephone message was sent to the Duce's palace that I could not come.'[1]

Nehru refused to see Mussolini at a time when Britain's leading statesmen, according to him, 'referred to him tenderly and admiringly' and 'praised his regime and methods'.* Two years

* It is interesting to note also Gandhi's attitude to Fascism. In May, 1932, Sardar Vallabhbhai Patel showed Gandhi a picture of little boys of eight to ten years of age receiving military training in Mussolini's Italy, and said that when they grew up they would help him to destroy the world. Gandhi replied, 'You are right. I have seen all that with my own eyes. Fascist propaganda is being carried on even in England. There are some Fascists in Parliament and Winston Churchill is a great admirer of Mussolini's. Why, Baldwin told me there was no good in democracy. Macdonald's imperialism leads him to mock at Democracy. It all shows which way the wind is blowing. This is what we are fighting against. What powerful opponents have we got to resist? But resist we must till the end of time.' (*Diary of Mahadev Desai*, 131.)

[1] *DI*, II, 31.

later, in the summer before Munich, Nehru was invited, on behalf of the Nazi Government, to visit Germany. The nazis knew Nehru's opposition to nazism and yet they wanted him to see Germany for himself. It was suggested that Nehru could go there as their guest or privately, in his own name or incognito, as he desired, and he would have perfect freedom to go where he liked. 'Again I declined with thanks. Instead I went to Czechoslovakia, that "far-away country" about which England's then Prime Minister knew so little.'[1]

Such were Nehru's personal feelings against the fascists and nazis. Politically, he hated their ideals bitterly. Before the days of Munich he met some of the members of the British Cabinet and some prominent English politicans, and expressed his anti-fascist and anti-nazi views before them. But he found that his views were not welcomed and he was told that there were many other considerations to be borne in mind. During the Czechoslovak crisis, as he says, what he saw of Franco-British statesmanship in Prague and in the Sudetenland, in London and Paris, and in Geneva where the League Assembly was then sitting, amazed and disgusted him. 'Appeasement seemed to be a feeble word for it. There was behind it not only a fear of Hitler, but a sneaking admiration for him,' he felt.[2] The creeds of fascism and nazism were narrow and overbearing and were based on hatred and violence. He watched their growth and the fall in their respective countries, and came to the conclusion:

'They brought a certain prestige to their people for a while, but they also killed the spirit and destroyed all values and standards of thought and behaviour. They ended by ruining the nations they sought to exalt.'[3]

Opposition to Undemocratic Systems

In his struggle against the British, what he perhaps disliked most bitterly was the undemocratic set-up of their rule in India. Authority corrupts and absolute authority corrupts absolutely and, to Nehru, no man in the world had such absolute authority over such large numbers of people as the British Viceroy of India.

[1] *DI*, I, 4.
[2] *Ibid.*
[3] *Speeches* I, 116-17, December 13, 1947.

The Viceroy spoke in a manner such as no Prime Minister of England or President of the United States would adopt. 'The only possible parallel would be that of Hitler.'[1] Nehru refers to the attitude of the Viceroy, as he saw him, the British members of his Council, the Governors, and even the secretaries of departments, or magistrates, who speak 'from a noble and unattainable height, secure not only in the conviction that what they say and do is right, but that it will have to be accepted as right whatever lesser mortals may imagine, for theirs is the power and the glory'. This he resented.

In India, besides the British administrators, there was another class of people against whom Nehru felt hostile. They were the princes. There were about six hundred princely states—big, small, and insignificant ones which one could not even place on the map. 'This system has vanished from the rest of the world,' he said in 1939, 'and left to itself, it would have vanished from India also long ago.' But, as it appeared to him, in spite of its manifest decay and stagnation, it was propped up and artificially maintained by the British authorities. The system, as such, had no inherent importance or strength. It was in reality one of the facets of imperialism. 'Offspring of the British Power in India, suckled by imperialism for its own purposes, it has survived till today, though mighty revolutions have shaken the world and changed it, empires have collapsed, and crowds of princes and petty rulers have faded away.'[2] He declared himself the relentless opponent of this class.

Attitude towards Communism

What was his attitude towards communism, which had elements of totalitarianism in its actual practice? Between the two, fascism and communism, he was prepared to accept communism. He had developed a certain amount of goodwill towards communism from an early age, though it was not a doctrinal adherence of any kind. Certain aspects of communism attracted him. Communism to him was 'not hypocritical'. Moreover, the tremendous changes which took place in Russia attracted him greatly. But in spite of

[1] *DI*, VII, 271.
[2] *Writings* II, Part I, Ch. 2, 30-31.

all this, when the question of the basic values of human life came in for consideration, his mind revolted against communism. What irritated him about communism was the 'dictatorial ways' of the communists, their aggressive methods, and 'their habit of denouncing everybody who did not agree with them'.[1] These features were undemocratic. Otherwise, he was not averse to the praise of the achievements of communism in the field of material advancement.

In November, 1927, during the tenth anniversary celebrations of the Soviet Union, Nehru paid a brief visit to Moscow. He was favourably disposed towards the country, the people and the system. He was glad that he went, and even that glimpse of the Soviet Union was considered by him as worthwhile. 'It did not, and could not, teach us much about the new Russia, but it did give us a background for our reading,' he said.[2] He read about Marx, Lenin, Russia and communism. They impressed him, but without disturbing his democratic convictions. In later years he inclined to the belief that democracy and communism would have to co-exist in the twentieth century world. This realization led him to extend his friendly hands towards the communist governments, but he kept his feet stronger than ever on the ground of democracy. When he visited Moscow again in the summer of 1955, as the Prime Minister of India, he declared to the Soviet people:

'We believe in democracy, equality and removal of special privileges and we have set ourselves the goal of developing a socialistic pattern of society through peaceful methods.'[3]

Fundamental Faith in the Freedom of Man
It seems that it is Nehru's absolute faith in the freedom of man that makes him the staunch democrat that he is. In his study of the ancient past of India, her religion and philosophy, history and culture, he has tried to understand the real value of human life. Keeping that in mind he reacted against fascism, and had said:

'It was not merely the physical acts of aggression in which fascism and nazism indulged, not only the vulgarity and brutality that accompanied them, terrible as they were, that affected us, but

[1] *AB*, XXIII, 163.
[2] *AB*, XXIII, 164-65.
[3] *Biblio*, 349.

the principles on which they stood and which they proclaimed so loudly and blatantly, the theories of life on which they tried to fashion themselves; for these went counter to what we believed in the present, and what we had held from ages past. And even if our racial memory had forsaken us and we had lost our moorings, our own experiences, even though they came to us in different garb, and somewhat disguised for the sake of decency, were enough to teach us to what these nazi principles and theories of life and the state ultimately led.'[1]

In his study of the Indo-Aryan philosophy, he saw a kind of metaphysical democracy which formed the background to social existence. '*He who sees the one spirit in all, and all in the one spirit, henceforth can look with contempt on no creature*'. To Nehru, though such philosophy lay only in theory, yet there could be no doubt that it must have affected life and produced that atmosphere of tolerance and reasonableness, that acceptance of free-thought in matters of faith, that desire and capacity to live and let live, which, according to him, are the dominant features of Indian culture. 'There was no totalitarianism in religion or culture, and they indicate an old and wise civilization with inexhaustible mental reserves.'[2] He finds in the *Upanishads* of the Hindus a question: 'What is this universe? From what does it arise? Into what does it go?' And he finds the answer:

'In freedom it rises, in freedom it rests, and into freedom it melts away.'

In such ideas Nehru would discover how the sages of the past were passionately attached to the idea of freedom and wanted to see everything in terms of it. The urge of freedom, he would say, developed democratic ways of living and thinking in society from time immemorial. Within each group, whether village community, particular caste, or large joint family, there was a communal life shared together, a sense of equality, and democratic methods. This tradition continued. Nehru felt surprised to see the eagerness of a villager, sometimes illiterate, to serve on elected committees for political or other purposes.[3] Such individuals could be helpful members whenever any question relative to their

[1] *DI*, I, 4.
[2] *DI*, IV, 74.
[3] *DI*, VI, 233.

lives arose, and were not to be easily subdued. The democratic way was a common method of functioning in social life, in local government, trade-guilds, religious assemblies, etc. Even the caste system, with all its evils, kept up the democratic habit in each group. Nehru believes that Indian society could not have lasted so long without some such social virtues as these. And, he says:

'Behind it lay the philosophical ideal of Indian culture—the integration of man and the stress of goodness, beauty and truth rather than acquisitiveness. An attempt was made to prevent the joining together and concentration of honour, power, and wealth. The duties of the individual and the group were emphasized, not their rights.'[1]

His Idea of the 'Fullest Democracy'
Political liberty, equality, and progress through peaceful methods —they form Nehru's basic democratic ideals. These ideals are in no way new, but Nehru pleads for their unrestricted growth. He wants to have what he terms 'the fullest democracy'[2] since the days are gone when restricted democracy seemed desirable or practicable. The nineteenth century conception that each person should have a vote was good enough for those days, but it was incomplete, and so 'people think in terms of a larger and deeper democracy today'. After all, there is no equality between the pauper who has a vote and the millionaire who has a vote. 'There are a hundred ways of exercising influence for the millionaire which the pauper has not got.' Similarly, there is not equality between the person who has tremendous educational advantages and the person who has none at all. People will, he thinks, differ to some extent. All human beings are not equal in the sense of ability or capacity. But his whole point is that people should have equality of opportunity and that they should be able to go as far as they can go.[3] He said in December, 1946:

'Obviously, we are aiming at democracy and nothing less than a democracy. What form of democracy, what shape it may take is

[1] DI, VI, 234.
[2] Speeches I, 349, December 13, 1946.
[3] Debates C.A. (Legislative) 1948, Vol. IV, April 3, 1948.

another matter. The democracies of the present day, many of them in Europe and some elsewhere, have played a great part in the world's progress. Yet it may be doubtful if those democracies may not have to change their shape somewhat before long if they have to remain completely democratic.'[1]

Believing that the working democracies elsewhere required change, he did not want only to copy the democratic procedure or institutions of other countries. He wanted to discover avenues for improvement and, while thinking in those terms, he wanted to have such systems which would fit in with the temper of the people and be acceptable to them.*

The Extent of Political Liberty

How far can political liberty go in actual practice? In democracy, the role of popular franchise in the diffusion of political liberty has been immense, and the growth of democracy has been associated with the extension of franchise. European governments had been very cautious about the extension of the franchise, and till recent times universal adult suffrage continued to arouse suspicion even in Great Britain. Writing in the last quarter of the nineteenth century, Henry Maine said: 'But one of the strangest of vulgar ideas is that a very wide suffrage could or would promote progress, new ideas, new discoveries, new arts of life. . . . Universal suffrage which today excludes Free Trade from the United States, would certainly have prohibited the spinning-jenny and the power loom. It would certainly have forbidden the threshing machine. It would have prevented the adoption of the Gregorian Calendar; and it would have restored the Stuarts.'[2]

Maine believed that what was called universal suffrage had

* Nearly seven years after the independence of India, Eleanor Roosevelt wrote after a visit:—

'The democracy India is building probably will never be exactly like ours. There is no reason why it should be, for her history, cultural background and needs are completely different from those that dictated our forms of democracy and guided its development. What the leaders of India want and are determined to have is a democracy that is indigenous to their own country—not English or American or French or Russian—but one based on their own past and the character of their own people, and growing and taking from according to their own needs.' Eleanor Roosevelt, *India and the Awakening East*, 88-89.

[1] Speech moving the Objectives Resolutions at Constituent Assembly, New Delhi, on December 13, 1946.
[2] H. S. Maine, *Popular Government*, Essay I, 34-36.

greatly declined in the estimation not only of philosophers who followed Bentham, but of the *a priori* theorists who assumed that it was the inseparable accompaniment of a Republic, but who found that in practice it was the natural basis of tyranny. Views such as these could not, however, stand their ground, and universal suffrage held sway. But to many political thinkers, as well as democratic governments, it seemed a sound theory that the power to vote should be based on some qualifications such as property or education. It was believed that property brought responsibility to the voter, while education brought awareness or intelligence. Must it follow then that democracy should wait till all people acquire a reasonable amount of property or receive some kind of elementary education?

Nehru would argue from the other standpoint. The fullest democracy might be given to the people first, with universal adult suffrage, to be followed by education and a good standard of living. He remembered that even in England the franchise was strictly limited till recently. He wondered how, in quite advanced countries in the present-day world, women, who formed half the population, did not have the vote. 'Democracy in those countries is presumably "male democracy",' he says.[1] To him, at this period in the history of democracy, any talk of restricted franchise is out of the question, however illiterate or poor a people may be. When India became independent, universal adult suffrage was at once introduced; but long before that Nehru had advocated against the restricted franchise.

'My experience in this matter confirmed my faith in the widest possible franchise. I was prepared to trust that wide electorate far more than a restricted one, based on a property qualification or even an educational test. The property qualification was anyhow bad; as for education it was obviously desirable and necessary. But I have not discovered any special qualities in a literate or slightly educated person which would entitle his opinion to greater respect than that of a sturdy peasant, illiterate but full of a limited kind of common sense. . . . I am a convinced believer in adult franchise, for men and women, and though I realize the difficulties in the way, I am sure that the objections raised to its adoption

[1] *Speeches* III, February 25, 1956.

in India have no great force and are based on the fears of privileged classes and interests.'[1]

The Extent of Political Power

Universal franchise becomes the basis of democracy. But what is its purpose? Political liberty, said Hobbes, is political power. When a man yearns to be free, he is not longing for the 'desolate freedom of the wild ass'; what he wants is a share of political government. 'But,' says Maine, 'in wide democracies, political power is minced into morsels, and each man's portion of it is almost infinitesimally small.'[2] This is natural. Democracy keeps the door open for all, and those who can, enjoy political power. Those who can not, enjoy political liberty nevertheless.

Nehru more or less wants to co-ordinate political power and political liberty in a practical sense. People enjoying political liberty must also feel that they enjoy political power. The right to vote means a share in government. The government enjoying political power should necessarily feel that this power is after all the power of the people. It is in this process of co-ordination that the real self-government can work.

What is self-government? According to Nehru, parliament is sovereign, being elected by the people. It is obvious that the vast majority of measures considered and passed by parliament are in a way being considered by all the people in a country. 'If I may say so,' he says, 'the people's representatives tend to function on the basis of a feeling of the general pulse of the people. The latter have got the power to kick out a Government, or a Member, after a certain period of time, as it is important to keep the Government or Parliament in check. Again, there also exists a general feeling or awareness in the people that things are being done according to their wishes or in consultation with them; in fact, they have begun to feel that they are governing themselves.'[3]

Thus the political power of the people is exercised through the consciousness that they are governing themselves, that they can exercise a check on the government or parliament, and that they are being consulted. This consciousness is potential enough to

[1] *DI*, III, 48-9.
[2] H. S. Maine, *Popular Government*, Essay I, 29.
[3] *Speeches* III, 160, April 6, 1957.

keep the government in line with public opinion. By and large, a parliament or government does what it thinks reasonable without really referring to the people. But as Nehru would say: 'So long as it gives the impression that democracy has been preserved and that people are being consulted, that their wishes are being respected, all is well.'[1]

Then again, democracy does not merely mean that the government will be afraid of the people, and that the people will be jealous of their power. Since the government and the governed inseparably constitute a democratic state, the problems, like power, should be shared as common property. 'I do believe,' Nehru said while addressing the younger generation of India, 'in this country, if you have to get on in a democratic way and there is no other way of getting on—we must share our difficulties with one another, we must understand one another, we must give our ideas to one another and point out objections or difficulties to one another.'[2] In such ways governmental responsibilities become more or less responsibilities of the people.

Political Parties and Political Power

The government in a democracy, however, is a party government. Nehru advocates that parties outside the government also enjoy political power or responsibility. To some political thinkers it has appeared that party feeling is probably far more a survival of the primitive combativeness of mankind than a consequence of conscious intellectual differences between man and man. Or, that it is essentially the same sentiment which in certain states of society leads to civil, intertribal, or international war. So it may be, but parties have been indispensable with democracy, and Nehru finds in their rational working something even more than mere political results. He says:

'It is good to have various parties because when there are different approaches to a problem, more light is thrown upon it. I do not believe in all people being regimented to think in one way. I want free flow and free exchange of thought and out of that we sometimes find a bit of the truth.'[3]

[1] *Speeches* III, 160.
[2] *Speeches* I, 129-30.
[3] *Speeches* III, 36.

It is obvious that the negation or weakness of the party system has dangerous consequences for democracy, since that might lead to authoritarianism. Nehru objected to regimentation and authoritarianism, even though he was aware of the fact that in a country like India 'there is a variety of opinion over almost every subject'. Opinions differ, and parties, therefore, are inevitable. But for a smooth running of democracy he advocates:

'The democratic method inevitably implies trying to understand the other party's opinion, a certain give-and-take, and a certain adjustment to whatever the final decision might be. If this does not happen, we simply go to pieces.'[1]

This is in line with democracy and the party system, so far as they are indissolubly linked together. 'But democracy,' he goes on to say, 'while it ensures free expression, and freedom of thinking, also demands something else. It demands unified action afterwards. It demands acceptance of decisions taken. Otherwise, there is a break-up.'[2] In their respective spheres, party men, belonging to this or that group, should continue to act for their respective parties. Nevertheless, thinks Nehru, the time comes when people have to rise above party, and think of the nation, think sometimes of even the world at large of which the nation is a part.[3] What he eventually wants is a strong democratic government based on the political liberty and power of the people, as well as on the freedom and co-operation of political parties.* Moreover, it is the duty of the sovereign parliament to remember that eternal vigilance is the price of liberty, and every member of the house has the prime duty to watch the government in its work. In the Constituent (Legislative) Assembly of India, Nehru declared on March 8, 1949:

'. . . there is always a possible tendency for those in authority

---

* Harold J. Laski wrote on March 3, 1949:—

'One hope I strongly express, bold though the claim may be, is that he (Nehru) will be able, midst his special preoccupations to assist India to move from one party government to the normal representative system of bi-partisan government, in furtherance of my own belief that upon the existence of an opposition, with powers at once critical and constructive, rests the basis of good government. I am confident that Mr Nehru is also of this view, since it was his achievement as Leader of the Opposition to the British Government in India which gave him the high status he now enjoys among all who care for freedom and democracy.' *Birthday Book*, 21.

[1] *Speeches* III, 31.
[2] *Ibid.*
[3] *Debates* C.A., Vol. I, No. 5, December 13, 1946.

H

to become a little complacent. Therefore, I repeat, that for my part I welcome the vigilance of the Honourable Members of this House in drawing our attention to our failings or any error or delinquency on the part of the administration.'[1]

Preference for Parliamentary Democracy

India accepted the form of parliamentary democracy as a system of government. 'Why have we chosen parliamentary democracy?' Nehru would ask, and reply, 'Because we think that in the long run it produces the best results. If we come to the conclusion that it does not produce the best results, well, we change it, obviously because we want results. What are the results we are aiming at? National well-being, and the happiness of the millions and millions of our people.'[2] To him, parliamentary democracy demanded many virtues; it demanded ability and devotion to work. It also demanded a large measure of co-operation, of self-discipline, and of restraint. He is aware that it could not function without a spirit of co-operation and a large measure of restraint and self-discipline in each group. Parliamentary democracy to him was not something which could be created in a country by some magic wand. There were not many countries in the world where it functioned successfully. But he believed that it is only the spirit of democracy in the people which could make it function. It is in this kind of popular spirit that he laid great faith.

Principles of Change and Continuity

One of the reasons for Nehru's faith in parliamentary democracy appears to be the possibility of change and progress under that system. The keynote of human history is progress, and parliamentary democracy can best achieve it. In view of this, his preference for the supremacy of parliament and the flexibility of the constitution is obvious. The extreme rigidity of a constitution seems to him dangerous, as it might lead to the break-up of the constitution when it goes off at a tangent from reality. He regards life as a curve—'it is not a straight line'—and the life of a nation as even more of a curve. 'Logical and straight lines are tangents

---

[1] *Speeches* I, 229.
[2] *Speeches* III, 8, December 21, 1954.

which go off the curve,' he says, 'and if the tangent goes too far away from that curve of life and curve of growth of a nation, then there is conflict, an upheaval and after that upheaval, well, something new emerges. You come back, as you are forced to come back, to the line of life because you cannot depart too far from it. So if you are flexible in your action and Constitution, then you keep near that curving growth of the nation's life.'[1]

Even when the old order is good, he thinks, it has to yield place to the new. For countries like India, which remained more or less changeless for a long time on account of foreign domination or an antiquated social framework, 'change there must be, change there has to be'. Rather, rapid changes were needed in order to catch up. But Nehru is not a blind believer in change.

'. . . while change is necessary, there is another quality that is also necessary—a measure of continuity. There has always to be a balancing of change and continuity. Not one day is like another. We grow older each day. Yet, there is continuity in us, unbroken continuity in the life of a nation. It is in the measure that these processes of change and continuity are balanced that a country grows on solid foundations. If there is no change and only continuity, there is stagnation and decay. If there is change only and no continuity, that means uprooting, and no country and no people can survive for long if they are uprooted from the soil which has given them birth and nurtured them.'[2]

Thus the system of parliamentary democracy embodies the principles of change and continuity. Nehru pleads it before those who function in that system—members of parliament and numerous others—to increase the pace of change, to make it as fast as they like, subject to the principles of continuity. Progress invites problems, and problems require solution. Democracy has to face this in perpetuity. 'If there are no problems,' he says, 'that is a sign of death. Only the dead have no problems; the living have problems and they grow by fighting with problems and overcoming them.'[3] To him, the sign of the growth of a nation lies not only in solving problems, but in creating new problems to solve.

---

[1] *Debates* P.I., 1951, XII, Part II, May 29, 1951.
[2] *Speeches* III, 156-57, Speech in Loksabha, March 28, 1957.
[3] *Speeches* III, 157.

The Need for Re-orientation

With faith in political liberty through parliamentary democracy, Nehru thinks of what democracy ought to be at this period of history. He felt for long that democracy stood on the crossroads of time, requiring re-orientation. Every type of human association, political, social or economic, has some philosophy at the back of it. When these associations change, this philosophical foundation must also change. Usually the philosophy lags behind the course of events, and this lag creates all the trouble.

'Democracy and capitalism grew up together in the nineteenth century, but they were not mutually compatible. There was a basic contradiction between them, for democracy laid stress on the power of the many, while capitalism gave real power to the few. This ill-assorted pair carried on somehow because political parliamentary democracy was in itself a very limited kind of democracy and did not interfere much with the growth of monopoly and power concentration.

'Even so, as the spirit of democracy grew a divorce became inevitable, and the time for that has come now.'[1]

This is how he thought in 1934-35, when parliamentary democracy seemed to him to be in disrepute. It appeared then that the failure of parliamentary democracy was not that it had gone too far, but that it did not go far enough. 'It was not democratic enough because it did not provide for economic democracy, and its methods were slow and cumbrous and unsuited to a period of rapid change.'[2]

The Concept of Economic Democracy

So, what Nehru wanted was for democracy to become economic democracy. As time passed his emphasis on this aspect began to grow. He was not prepared to agree with those who confused democracy with capitalism. Simply because democracy had grown up in some capitalistic countries, it did not mean therefore that democracy was an essential part of capitalism. Some others went on to think that any kind of socialism necessarily meant authoritarianism. Nehru again did not entertain this kind of fear. He

---

[1] *AB*, LXII, 529.
[2] *AB*, LXII, 530.

thought in terms of amalgamating socialism with democracy. 'Democracy must mean removal of disparities,'[1] and this is what he wants to make clear.

Democracy has been regarded as a means towards an end. What is this end to Nehru? 'I do not know if everybody will agree with me,' he says, 'but I would say the end is the good life for the individual. What form it should take can be argued about, but the good life certainly must imply a certain satisfaction of the essential economic needs, which will release him from continuous oppression, and which will give him a chance to develop his creative faculties.'[2]

In elaborating this thesis he would say that in the past democracy has been taken chiefly to mean political democracy, roughly represented by the idea of every person having a vote. It is obvious that a vote by itself does not mean very much to a person who is down and out and starving. Such a person will be much more interested in food to eat than in a vote. 'Therefore,' says Nehru, 'political democracy by itself is not enough except that it may be used to obtain a gradually increasing measure of economic democracy.'[3] In his theory of economic democracy, the good things of life must become available to more and more people and gross inequalities must be removed. It is rather gratifying that this process has been going on for some time in countries where there is political democracy. 'Parliamentary democracy is inevitably going in the direction, everywhere, of what might be called economic democracy. It may take different forms, but only in the measure that it solves the economic problems does it succeed even in the political field. If the economic problems are not solved then the political structure tends to weaken and crack up.'[4]

Objectives by Consent not by Conflict

How should democracy, in fact, achieve the great objectives in view? That has been a major problem in Nehru's political thought. In the western countries, except perhaps Great Britain, democracy itself took birth in violent revolutions. In many places democratic

[1] *Speeches* III, 81-2.
[2] *Speeches* III, 138, February 25, 1956.
[3] *Ibid.*
[4] *Ibid*, 142.

rights were won by people through means other than peaceful. Since democracy is a dynamic system, and it calls for more and more change, should it mean that such new changes will come only through violence? If so, democracy will defeat its own purpose. He wants to establish, therefore, that democracy and peaceful ways of change are inseparable. His faith in peace, as a weapon to achieve great objectives, is unshakeable. After all, India could win independence through peaceful methods! After independence he declared:

'Democracy means tolerance, tolerance not merely of those who agree with us, but of those who do not agree with us. With the coming of freedom our patterns of behaviour must change also so as to fit in with this freedom.'[1]

Why should there be conflict, he would analyse, if democracy goes by consent. It may not be everybody's consent, but certainly it goes by the consent of the community as a whole. Conflict may arise on account of several factors. As he thinks of an economic democracy, it implies a conflict of economic interests. In society there are different classes, and economic democracy means more or less economic equality. This equality demands from the rich the sacrifice of their class interests. On the other hand, in their desire to bring equality by quicker means, the poor may think of violent methods. In fact, in some western countries economic changes have been brought about through class struggles. It may also be presumed that if political democracy could come through revolutions, economic democracy may also be brought in the same way, namely, through violent means. To Nehru, such fears will have no ground if democracy has reached its fullness.

'The problem that we really have to face is whether the changes we want to make in the economic domain can be effected peacefully by the democratic method or not. If democracy does not function in the political plane properly, then there is no way to bring about a change except by some kind of pressure, violence or revolution. But where this peaceful method is available, and where there is adult suffrage, there the question of trying to change things by violence is absurd and wholly wrong.'[2]

[1] *Speeches* I, 13, August 15, 1948.
[2] *Speeches* III, 287, February 25, 1955.

All Decisions Through Peace

It is not merely on the question of economic change that democracy and peace are linked together, but in other matters peaceful methods are the only methods. In democracy, it is not the decision itself, but how that decision is taken which carries greater significance. When people of varying opinions meet, how do they decide things? he would ask, and then reply: 'The method of democracy is discussion, argument, persuasion and ultimate decision and acceptance of that decision even though it might go against our grain. Otherwise the bigger *lathi* or the bigger bomb prevails and that is not the democratic method.'[1] Great or small, all violence is deplorable if democratic decisions are faced with them. To Nehru, the problem is the same whether atomic bombs are involved or street demonstrations. He does not object to demonstrations, because they are democratic ways of demonstrating popular feeling. But he objects to the violence of demonstrations. In this, he even goes to the extent of thinking that the atomic bomb, though it symbolizes tremendous violence, does not poison one's personal thinking so much as smaller violence does. 'When a man hates his neighbour, and cannot pull on with him, he is degraded as an individual.'[2]

Parliamentary democracy, thus, involves peaceful methods of action, peaceful acceptance of decisions taken, and attempts to change them through peaceful ways again. It is not parliamentary democracy otherwise. It is essential that those who talk and believe in the quest of peace should remember that the quest of peace and the quest of democracy can only be made through methods of peace and not through any other methods.[3] Further, peaceful methods are the right means to achieve ends. Since democracy stands on this principle, it removes the pressures which other forms of government may impose on the individual. It transforms the discipline which is imposed by authority largely into self-discipline. 'Self-discipline means that even people who do not agree—the minority—accept solutions because it is better to

[1] *Ibid*, 178, December 21, 1955.
[2] *Ibid*. In the Indian context he says: The hatred of an individual, group or community, the hatred of a Hindu for a Muslim or the hatred of a Muslim for a Hindu or a Sikh is much worse.
[3] *Speeches* III, 158, March 28, 1957.

accept them than to have conflict. It is better to accept them and
then change them, if necessary, by peaceful methods.'[1] Moreover,
democracy gives the individual an opportunity to develop, which
does not mean anarchy, where every individual does what he
likes. A social organization must have some disciplines to hold it
together. 'Those,' he says, 'can either be imposed from outside
or be in the nature of self-discipline. Imposition from outside may
take the form of one country governing another or of an
autocratic or authoritarian form of government. In a proper
democracy, discipline is self-imposed. There is no democracy if
there is no discipline.'[2]

Drawbacks of Democracy Considered

Solid though his faith in democracy is, Nehru does not shut his
eyes to the drawbacks of the system. This leads him to think of
its improvement all the time. In 1936-37 when he toured India in
connection with the general election, certain aspects of democracy
appeared to him as not very sound. Elections were an essential
and inseparable part of the democratic process, and there was no
way of abolishing them. 'Yet, often enough,' he wrote, 'elections
brought out the evil side of man, and it was obvious that they did
not always lead to the success of the better man. Sensitive persons
and those who were not prepared to adopt rough-and-ready
methods to push themselves forward, were at a disadvantage and
preferred to avoid these contests. Was democracy then to be a
close preserve of those possessing thick skins and loud voices
and accommodating consciences?'[3] He believed, however, that
such election evils were prevalent where electorates were small.
But under the widest possible franchise, such evils had the
tendency to vanish.

Having chosen a democratic system for India, Nehru was
convinced that it was good for his people in the ultimate analysis.
'Nevertheless,' he felt, 'it sometimes slows down the pace of
growth for we have to weigh the demands of tomorrow with the
needs of today in the building up of our country.'[4] This adjust-

[1] *Ibid*, 138, February 25, 1956.
[2] *Ibid*, 140.
[3] *DI*, III, 48.
[4] *Speeches* II, 252-53, February 18, 1953.

ment between today and tomorrow is a difficult problem. A country which is poor in resources does not have the means to invest for the future; and the country is pressed between the needs of today and the demands of tomorrow. If for adjustment the government wants a surplus, it has to be strict with itself in the present. And democracy does not usually like stinting itself in the present, though in times of great crisis it might. 'Democracy wants today the good things of today. That is the disadvantage of democracy.'[1]

Nehru has spoken much in favour of the fullest democracy. He thinks that in its present shape and form this kind of democracy is a relatively new concept. The old type of democracy was a limited one in many ways. With adult suffrage in India, Nehru possessed the biggest electorate in the world.* Of such developments he was proud, but at least on one occasion he proceeded to say:

'With all my admiration and love for democracy, I am not prepared to accept the statement that the largest number of people are always right.'[2]

He was aware of how people could be excited and their passions roused in a moment. In such cases, how can a parliament prepare itself to submit to the momentary passion of a democratic crowd? Democracy was functioning in India during the days of independence and partition, when people were killing one another and millions of them were migrating to escape from atrocities and horror. 'I do not blame those poor people,' he explains, 'but I do say that even democracy can go mad; democracy can be incited to do wrong. Democracy, in fact, is sometimes more warlike than individuals who at least have some training.'[3] Yet he declares his determination to build India according to democratic methods. 'We have decided to do so because we feel that democracy offers society something of the highest human values.'[4]

---

* In India's first general election, held during the winter of 1951-52, more than 176 million men and women were given power to vote. The vastness of the experiment appeared to Nehru as something 'yet unknown to history'. *Speeches* II, November 22, 1951.
[1] *Ibid.*
[2] *Speeches* II, 252-53, February 18, 1953.
[3] *Ibid.*
[4] *Ibid.*

The greatest danger to democracy is war. But to him it is worse if democracy itself prepares for war, because war puts an end to the very values that democracy cherishes. 'Democracy, in fact, is a casualty of war in the world today. It does not seem to function properly any more. That has been the tragedy of the last two world wars and something infinitely worse is likely to happen if there is another war.'[1]

Among other drawbacks of democracy Nehru finds wastage of time and energy. But this is something which he thinks can be avoided. Democracy is also slow. Men who work within the democratic framework work with a certain amount of freedom and individuality, which makes the system rather slow-moving. Totalitarian states have no such drawback where men work under a sense of fear, because failure or slackness are not lightly passed over. Democracy does not create this kind of fear complex in its own machinery. In Nehru's concept of democracy, this state of affairs should go.* 'To hell with the man who cannot walk fast,' he says. 'It serves him right if he gets out of the ranks and falls out. We want no sluggards.'[2] He wants 'work and work and work', and he wants achievement. 'I want men who work as crusaders. I want men who are going to fight for what they think is right and not submit humbly to wrong. . . . And let the weak and the slow and the lazy go to the wall. There should be no pity for them.'[3]

His Ultimate Optimism

In his quest for 'a full-fledged, full-blooded democracy, with adult suffrage', Nehru proceeds with optimism whatever the difficulty. He does not want democracy to be reduced to static theories incapable of change, but instead wants it to be the most dynamic of the arts of government. 'Many books have been written,' he once said, 'about parliamentary government. My

---

* India's Deputy Prime Minister, Sardar Vallabhbhai Patel, once said:—
'True, we have some outbursts of his temper, but with his passion for promptness and right and his impatience of wrong and delay, such outbursts have been an incentive to exertion and quick disposal. They have been the reserve forces which, when suddenly released, have at times conquered lethargy, delays, circumlocution and absence of will to act.' *Birthday Book*, xxix.
[1] *Ibid.*
[2] *Speeches* III, 6, October 13, 1954.
[3] *Ibid.*

knowledge is largely confined to English books, a few American books and a very few French books. When I read them, I get the feeling that they refer to developments in the nineteenth century and do not relate to today's problems.'[1] As a working democrat, he looks for new developments so that democracy can keep pace with time. And whatever the future may have in store, Nehru links democracy with the inner mind of a people, for its own success or failure.

'. . . all our institutions, including the parliamentary institutions, are ultimately the projections of a people's character, thinking and aims. They are strong and lasting in the measure that they are in accordance with the people's character and thinking. Otherwise, they tend to break up.'[2]

[1] *Ibid*, 140, February 25, 1956.
[2] *Ibid*, 144.

CHAPTER V

EXPERIMENT WITH SOCIALISM

Interest in Socialism

Jawaharlal Nehru became interested in socialism from an early period in his life. During and after his college days in England, he took to some general reading, and in course of this reading became 'vaguely attracted to the Fabians and socialistic ideas'.[1] On his return to India it was nationalism and patriotism which demanded his greater attention, his 'vague socialist ideas of college days having sunk into the background'.[2] And, 'Yet fresh reading was again stirring the embers of socialistic ideas in my head.'[3] Those were the years of World War I; also of his first contact with Indian politics, but his contact with the people had not yet begun. Ideas on socialism were formed mainly from books, and not from practical experience. As a result, 'They were vague ideas, more humanitarian and utopian than scientific'.[4] In later years, his study of socialistic theories as well as his observation of the real condition of the people, led him to develop some kind of concrete ideas on the subject.

It can be said that Nehru's ideas on socialism began to take shape more or less through his sympathies towards communism. His project of study was extensive, covering the problems of other countries, or, in brief, the world situation at large. To him, India, with her problems and struggles, became merely a part of a mighty world drama, of the great struggle of political and economic forces that was going on everywhere, nationally and inter-

[1] *AB*, IV, 25.
[2] *AB*, V, 35.
[3] *Ibid.*
[4] *Ibid.*

nationally. 'In that struggle,' he says, his 'own sympathies went increasingly towards the communist side.'[1]

New Russia had an appeal for him almost from the beginning, though he disliked much in the Soviet system, such as the ruthless suppression of all contrary opinion, the wholesale regimentation, and what seemed to him the unnecessary violence in carrying out various policies. The study of Russia, for better or for worse, led him to study the capitalist system as such. And he thought that in this world too there was no lack of violence.

'. . . I realized more and more how the very basis and foundation of our acquisitive society and property was violence. Without violence it could not continue for many days. A measure of political liberty meant little indeed when the fear of starvation was always compelling the vast majority of people everywhere to submit to the will of the few to the greater glory and advantage of the latter.'[2]

Violence was thus a common feature both in communism and capitalism. Rather, Nehru felt, the violence of the capitalist order was inherent in it, whereas the violence of Russia was a temporary phenomenon, aiming at a new order 'based on peace and co-operation and real freedom for the masses'. What in fact made Russia so appealing to Nehru was the progress which the Soviet regime was making even in the backward regions of the country. Russia and her achievements attracted him more and more towards the theory of communism, the latter appearing to him quite sound. The ruthlessness or other failings of the Bolsheviks could be safely separated from the theory of communism as such. If the theory was sound, there was no harm in applying it to other countries. He felt it absurd to copy blindly what had taken place in Russia, 'for its application depended on the particular conditions prevailing in the country in question and the stage of its historical development'. On the more practical side, Nehru thought in terms of radical results and revolutionary plans regarding land and industry. As for the theory:

'Russia apart, the theory and philosophy of Marxism lightened up many a dark corner of my mind. History came to have a new

[1] *AB*, XLVI, 361.
[2] *Ibid.*

meaning for me. The Marxist interpretation threw a flood of light on it, and it became an unfolding drama with some order and purpose, howsoever unconscious, behind it. In spite of the appalling waste and misery of the past and the present, the future was bright with hope, though many dangers intervened. It was the essential freedom from dogma and the scientific outlook of Marxism that appealed to me.'[1]

Thus while Marxism was rooted in Nehru's mind, the official communism in Russia or elsewhere appeared to him full of dogma and therefore deplorable. He was against any kind of dogma; and hence, even though accepting Marxism, he was not in a mood to be a thoroughgoing Marxist.

As contact with Marxist theories created socialistic ideas in his mind, so also his contact with some European countries in the late twenties of the century brought to him a more clear understanding of world affairs which also appeared to be pointing in a socialist direction. Vast political and economic changes were going on in Europe and America. Soviet Russia, despite its unpleasant aspects, held forth a message of hope. As he was returning from Europe at the end of 1927, he felt:

'My outlook was wider, and nationalism by itself seemed to me definitely a narrow and insufficient creed. Political freedom, independence, were no doubt essential, but they were steps only in the right direction; without social freedom and a socialistic structure of society and the State, neither the country nor the individual could develop much.'[2]

The Indian Background

The ideological conviction created in him some incentive to work. It was further developed by his observation of the Indian economic and social structure as it existed under the British rule.

To Nehru, many aspects of the British rule appeared appalling. 'Long subjection of a people and the denial of freedom bring many evils,' he would write, 'and perhaps the greatest of these lies in the spiritual sphere—demoralization and sapping of the spirit of the people. It is hard to measure this, though it may be

[1] Ibid, 362-63.
[2] AB, XXIV, 166.

obvious. It is easier to trace and measure the economic decay of a nation, and as we look back on British economic policy in India, it seems that the present poverty of the Indian people is the ineluctable consequence of it.'[1] India, during the British rule, besides being a political appendage of Britain, also became an economic appendage. Until the coming of British rule, according to Nehru, the village community in India was the basis of her economy. Those village communities were like little republics having nearly everything they wanted within themselves. All over India these communities had their village industries to supply the needs of the people. It is wrong to suppose that India was predominantly agricultural from the beginning; in fact, through her village industries, she was predominantly industrial as well. In the middle of the nineteenth century only about fifty-five per cent of the population is said to have been dependent on agriculture, though towards the end of British rule the percentage rose to seventy-four. What happened was that with the coming of the British the village community system disintegrated, losing its economic function. The village industries were destroyed, the balance between industry and agriculture was upset, and the traditional division of labour broke down. In early days of European contact with India, European merchants carried Indian manufactured goods and textiles etc. to European markets where there was a great demand for them. But with the developments in industrial techniques in England, a new class of industrial capitalists arose, and since India had been conquered by the British, this new class demanded a change in commercial policy. In course of time, Indian goods were excluded from Britain by legislation, whereas the Indian market was rapidly opened to British manufactures. By various other methods such as internal duties, which prevented the flow of Indian goods within India, the decay of village industries was gradually brought about. The Indian textile industry was brought to ruin in a systematic fashion and vast numbers of weavers and artisans were unemployed as a result. In 1834, Lord William Bentinck, the Governor General of India, had written, 'the misery hardly finds a parallel in the

[1] *DI*, VII, 280.

history of commerce. The bones of the cotton weavers are bleaching the plains of India.'[1] Other industries met the same fate sooner or later. England built up her colonial economy, 'India becoming an agricultural colony of industrial England, supplying raw materials and providing markets for England's industrial goods'.*

The dispossessed industrial population in villages fell upon land, which had no capacity to absorb them profitably. Consequently agriculture began to decline. The introduction of landlordism by the British on the other hand changed the whole conception of the ownership of the land. The village community which controlled the land lost that privilege. Instead, land became the private property of the landlord. As Nehru puts it, 'The introduction of this type of property in land was not only a great economic change, but it went deeper and struck at the whole Indian conception of a co-operative group social structure. A new class, the owners of land, appeared; a class created by, and therefore to a large extent identified with, the British Government.'[2]

These factors, and many more, as they operated through long years, resulted in the prodigal poverty of the Indian people. When Nehru for the first time saw the real people of India, far away in their villages, he got a true picture of them—naked,

---

* Speaking about the Indian village system and its destruction by the British, Karl Marx wrote the following:—

'The handloom and the spinning wheel, producing their regular myriads of spinners and weavers, were the pivots of the structure of that society. From immemorial times, Europe received the admirable textures of Indian labour, sending in return for them her precious metals, and furnishing thereby his material to the goldsmith, that indispensable member of Indian society, whose love of finery is so great that even the lowest class, those who go about nearly naked, have commonly a pair of golden earrings and a golden ornament of some kind hung round their necks. . . . It was the British intruder who broke up the Indian handloom and destroyed the spinning wheel. England began with driving the Indian cottons from the European markets; it then introduced twist into Hindostan, and in the end inundated the very mother country of cotton with cottons. From 1818 to 1836 the export of twist from Great Britain to India rose in the proportion of 1 to 5,200. In 1824 the export of British muslins to India hardly amounted to 6,000,000 yards, while in 1837 it surpassed 64,000,000 of yards. . . . British steam and science uprooted, over the whole surface of Hindostan, the union between agricultural and manufacturing industry.' To Marx, the Indian 'family communities were based on domestic industry, in that peculiar combination of hand-weaving, hand-spinning, and hand-tilling agriculture which gave them self-supporting power'. Karl Marx, *The British Rule in India*, London, June 10, 1853, *New York Daily Tribune*, June 25, 1853, Ed. B.P.L. & F. Bedi.

[1] *DI*, VII, 277, containing Bentinck's quotation.
[2] *DI*, VII, 282.

starving, crushed, and utterly miserable. He was frightened.*

'In 1920 I was totally ignorant,' he says, 'of labour conditions in factories or fields, and my political outlook was entirely bourgeois.'[1] But that year and thereafter, as he came to the villages and saw the people, he got a practical knowledge of the problems which faced India economically. His theoretical knowledge of socialism supplied a background to the practical problems which he faced. The national struggle absorbed his major attention, but he could nevertheless be known as a socialist, having the incentive to work in that direction.

Understanding of the Agrarian Problems and the Condition of the Industrial Proletariat

Before and during the nineteen-twenties, side by side with the national or political awakening, a new awareness was also taking place among the peasants and the industrial proletariat against their deep-rooted poverty as well as upper-class exploitation. Nehru came into close contact with the agrarian upheaval in the then United Provinces of India in 1920-21. Peasant movements were frequently taking place in various parts of the country and agrarian risings often resorted to violent means. But the government, the landlords, and the *taluqadars* were powerful enough to suppress them. The problems facing the agrarian population were numerous. As Nehru began to understand, the people had their innumerable tales of sorrow, their crushing and ever-growing burden of rent, illegal exactions, ejectments from land and mud hut, and beatings. They were 'surrounded on all sides by vultures who preyed on them'—*zamindar's* agents, money-lenders, and police. They toiled all day 'to find that what they produced was not theirs and their reward was kicks and curses and a hungry stomach'. Many were landless people who had been ejected by the landlords and had no land or hut to fall back upon. The burden on land was heavy, the holdings were small and there were too many people after them. 'Taking advantage of this land hunger

---

* 'Looking at them and their misery,' he writes in the *Autobiography*, 'I was filled with shame and sorrow, shame at my own easy-going and comfortable life and our petty politics of the city which ignored this vast multitude of semi-naked sons and daughters of India, sorrow at the degradation and overwhelming poverty of India.' *AB*, VIII, 52.

[1] *AB*, VIII, 49.

the landlords, unable under the law to enhance their rents beyond a certain percentage, charged huge illegal premiums. The tenant, knowing of no other alternative, borrowed money from the money-lender and paid the premium, and then, unable to pay his debt or even the rent, was ejected and lost all he had.' Nehru understood this kind of progressive pauperization of the peasants, and the various other evils associated with Indian land systems. The discontent among the peasants could be suppressed ruthlessly, but the flame could never be entirely extinguished.

In the meantime, with the coming of new industries, an industrial proletariat was growing up in India. The first Trade Union Congress was organized round about 1920. The workers were unorganized and helpless. In numbers they were very few. 'In the 'twenties the voice of industrial labour began to be heard, but it was feeble. It might have been ignored but for the fact that the Russian Revolution had forced people to attach importance to the industrial proletariat. Some big and well-organized strikes also compelled attention.'[1] The condition of the industrial workers in the 'twenties was miserable in the extreme. The profit from industries, such as the jute mills of Bengal and the cotton mills of Bombay, Ahmedabad and elsewhere, flowed to the owners of foreign capital in Dundee and London, and into the pockets of the Indian millionaires. The industrial capitalists did little to improve the living conditions of the workers, whose wages were extremely low. When Nehru visited some of the slums and hovels of industrial workers, he gasped for breath, and came out dazed and full of horror and anger. Going down a coal mine in Jharia he could see the conditions in which the womenfolk worked. 'I can never forget that picture or the shock that came to me that human beings should labour thus.'[2]

Work in a Socialist Direction
The poverty and misery everywhere, with which Nehru became thoroughly acquainted during the early twenties of the century, created in him a strong urge to work in a socialist direction. In the late twenties of the century he was seen busy in directing

[1] *DI*, VII, 331.
[2] *DI*, VIII, 335.

people's attention to social and economic changes. He travelled a great deal and addressed many gatherings. He not only talked to Congress people or at their conferences, but also to the youth and students of the country. From time to time he visited rural areas in the U.P. and occasionally addressed industrial workers. Everywhere he spoke on political independence and social freedom. 'I wanted to spread,' he says, 'the ideology of socialism especially among Congress workers and the intelligentsia, for these people, who were the backbone of the national movement, thought largely in terms of the narrowest nationalism.'[1]

Nehru saw that he was by no means a pioneer in the socialist field in India, there being others who had gone ahead with more radical views. The workers' trade union movement was based on socialist ideology, and the majority of the youth leagues were socialist. Earlier, many socialists thought along utopian lines, 'but Marxian theory was influencing them increasingly, and a few considered themselves as hundred per cent Marxists'. Whatever influence these individual socialists or socialist institutions could exercise, in his own case Nehru had some definite advantages in making his own influences felt. In the Congress hierarchy he was rapidly ascending to a position second only to that of Gandhi, and he held important Congress offices. In addition, the younger generation looked up to him as representing their aspirations. As a socialist worker, therefore, he could go forward with his task.

Like Nehru, some other prominent Congressmen also thought on socialist lines. As early as 1926, they together tried, in the U.P. Provincial Congress Committee, to draw up a mild socialist programme. U.P. was a *zamindari* and *taluqadari* province, and the main problem which they faced was that of the land. 'We declared that the existing land system must go and that there should be no intermediaries between the State and the cultivator. We had to proceed cautiously, as we were moving in an atmosphere which was, till then, unused to such ideas.'[2]

In 1929, the U.P. Congress Committee made some recommendations on socialist lines to the All India Congress Committee. The latter adopted the preamble of the U.P. Resolution and

[1] *AB*, XXVI, 182.
[2] *Ibid*, 183.

thus accepted the principle of socialism in outline.* During 1928-29, labour disputes and strikes took place at several places. There were strikes in the Bombay textile industry, the Bengal jute mills, and in the Iron and Tin Plate Works at Jamshedpur. 'The Labour Movement was becoming class-conscious, militant and dangerous, both in ideology and in organization.' The Government was also getting ready to strike, and it struck.

Towards the close of 1929, the Congress Session was going to sit at Lahore with Nehru as its President. A few weeks before that, he presided over the All-India Trade Union Congress at Nagpur. 'It was very unusual,' he wrote, 'for the same person to preside over both the National Congress and the Trade Union Congress within a few weeks of each other. I had hoped that I might be a link between the two and bring them closer to each other—the National Congress to become more socialistic, more proletarian, and organized Labour to join the national struggle.'[1]

It was a difficult task. The National Congress possessed a bourgeois outlook, though representing revolutionary force in the cause of nationalism. Nehru hoped to drive the Congress to a more radical ideology in facing social and economic issues. In December, 1929, in the Lahore Session of the National Congress, he took rather a bold step to declare:

'I must frankly confess that I am a socialist and a republican, and am no believer in kings and princes, or in the order which produces the modern kings of industry, who have greater power over the lives and fortunes of men than even the kings of old, and whose methods are as predatory as those of the old feudal aristocracy.'[2]

The leftist philosophy under Nehru's leadership began to grow within Congress. The Congress was fast moving on nationalist

---

* In 1929, according to Nehru, the All India Congress Committee, at a meeting held in Bombay, 'boldly faced the issue and gave an ideological lead to the country'. Its resolution ran thus:—

'In the opinion of this Committee, the great poverty and misery of the Indian people are due not only to the foreign exploitation of India but also to the economic structure of society, which the alien rulers support so that their exploitation may continue. In order therefore to remove this poverty and misery and to ameliorate the condition of the Indian masses, it is essential to make revolutionary changes in the present economic and social structure of society and to remove the gross inequalities.' *Essays* III, 34-5, 'Congress and Socialism', July 15, 1936.

[1] *AB*, XXVII, 197.
[2] *Essays* II, 27, 'Presidential Address', December, 1929.

lines with greater attention towards the peasant and the village. With regard to the industrial worker, it did not develop a detailed programme because the agrarian situation dominated the Indian scene.[1] In fact, the Congress avoided facing economic issues, except of course the programme for the encouragement of cottage industries and the *swadeshi*. However, the next significant step in a socialist direction was taken in 1931 at the Karachi session. A resolution on Fundamental Rights and Economic Policy was adopted, which, besides many other things, said, 'The State shall own or control key industries and services, mineral resources, railways, waterways, shipping and other means of public transport.'[2]

To Nehru, such developments were 'a very short step'. 'This was not socialism at all,' he said, 'and a capitalist state could easily accept almost everything contained in that resolution.'[3] Radical opinion began to grow among the left-wing element in the Congress, and before long a Socialist Party was shaped within the Congress itself, known as the Congress Socialist Party (CSP). It was 'designed as a cadre party, working within the Congress to keep it on the right line with regard to both the independence struggle and the subsequent establishment of a socialist society'. As its organization suggested, 'it owed much of its inspiration to Marxism or even to Marx-Leninism'.[4]

Nehru did not become a member of the CSP, though he continued to lead the Congress left wing. At times his radical outlook led others to think of him as being very near to Marxism. In December 1933 he declared:

'I dislike fascism intensely and indeed I do not think it is anything more than a crude and brutal effort of the present capitalist order to preserve itself at any cost. There is no middle road between fascism and communism. One has to choose between the two and I choose the communist ideal. In regard to the methods and approach to this ideal, I may not agree with everything that the orthodox communists have done. I think that these

[1] *Writings* II, Part II, Ch. 3, p. 72.
[2] Sitaramaya, *The History of the Indian National Congress, 1885-1935*, 782.
[3] *AB*, XXXV, 266.
[4] Narendra Deva, *Socialism and the National Revolution*, pp. 3 ff- quoted in Saul Rose, *Socialism in Southern Asia*, 17.

methods will have to adapt themselves to changing conditions and may vary in different countries. But I do think that the basic ideology of communism and its scientific interpretation of history is sound.'[1]

The CSP stood behind Nehru and vice versa. The former unanimously voted in his favour as the President of the Congress in 1936; and, when elected, he declared his socialist faith in his presidential address at the Lucknow Congress, and also appointed three CSP leaders* to his Working Committee.

Difficulties on the Way

To proceed with socialist activities was not all smooth sailing. The effect of Nehru's socialist propaganda upset many older Congressmen. 'I knew that some of my colleagues were no socialists,' he said, 'but I had always thought that, as a member of the Congress Executive I had perfect freedom to carry on socialist propaganda without committing the Congress to it. The realization that some members of the Working Committee did not think that I had that freedom came as a surprise.'[2] Whatever the feeling of the Congress high command, he decided not to give up what he considered the most important part of his work.

At times he felt irritated to see that the Congress came forward to pay only lip service to socialism, and, in so doing, changed its entire meaning. In August 1934, Nehru complained to Gandhi that the resolution of the Working Committee on the subject showed such an astounding ignorance of the elements of socialism that 'it was painful to read it and to realize that it might be read outside India'. It seemed to Nehru that the overmastering desire of the Committee was somehow to reassure various vested interests even at the risk of talking nonsense.

'A strange way of dealing with the subject of socialism is to use the word, which has a clearly defined meaning in the English language, in a totally different sense. For individuals to use words in a sense peculiar to themselves is not helpful in the commerce of ideas. A person who declares himself to be an engine-driver and

---

* Narendra Deva, Jay Prakash Narayan, and Achyut Patwardhan.
[1] Vide S. C. Bose, *The Indian Struggle*, 345-6.
[2] *AB*, LVII, 477.

then adds that his engine is of wood and is drawn by bullocks is misusing the word engine-driver.'[1]

There were some misgivings on the part of Gandhi, whose concept of ethical-spiritual socialism clashed with Nehru's idea of practical scientific socialism. Gandhi always considered himself 'a true servant of the peasants and of the workers'. He was firmly of the opinion that 'even a king can be a socialist by becoming a servant of the people'. 'Even when I die,' Gandhi said, 'you will have to admit that Gandhi was a true socialist.'[2]

Nehru thought of getting Gandhi around to his own way of thinking. Gandhi always listened patiently to whatever Nehru had to say, and made every effort to meet his wishes. 'This had, indeed, led me to think,' said Nehru, 'that perhaps some colleagues and I could influence him continuously in a socialist direction, and he had himself said that he was prepared to go step by step as he saw his way to do so.'[3] But differences on this issue were so great that there seemed no possibility of a compromise. Gandhi believed in a change of heart in men; to Nehru such ideals were incompatible with socialist objectives. 'How very different was his outlook from mine, I thought again, and I wondered how far I could co-operate with him in future.'[4]

While Nehru aimed at achieving through the political freedom of India real social change and economic freedom, Congress leadership in its bulk did not share the same views. The nationalist urge was so great that political freedom was considered by many as the supreme goal. The socialist leader, Jayaprakash Narayan, pointed out in 1935: 'The Congress at present is dominated by upper class interest and its leaders are uncompromisingly opposed to admitting into its objective any programme aimed at the economic emancipation of the masses.'[5] Of course, Jayaprakash admitted, within Congress there was a very large body of opinion which was prepared to welcome such a programme. What the Congress socialists wanted was to change the content and policy of the National Congress to make it truly representative of the

---

[1] Tendulkar, *Mahatma*, Vol. 3, Appendix, Nehru to Gandhi, August 13, 1934.
[2] *Ibid*, Vol. 8, pp. 40-1, July 2, 1947.
[3] *AB*, XXXIV, 255.
[4] *AB*, LVII, 478.
[5] Jayaprakash Narayan, *Towards Struggle*, 130.

masses, 'having the object of emancipating them both from the foreign power and the native system of exploitation.'[1] The old leadership believed that the socialist programme might weaken the national struggle by dividing the nationalist forces. In June 1936, several prominent leaders of the National Congress proceeded to remind Nehru, who was then Congress President, 'We feel that the preaching and emphasizing of socialism particularly at this stage by the President and other socialist members of the Working Committee while the Congress has not adopted it is prejudicial to the best interests of the country and to the success of the national struggle for freedom which we all hold to be the first and paramount concern of the country.'[2]

The forces of communalism also, during the thirties, attracted the attention of the masses towards a narrow type of religious programme and diverted their minds from greater visions of socialism, or new world orders. Nehru studied this situation and felt that the poor and illiterate mass of people should have been given a revolutionary outlook from the beginning of their struggle-consciousness in order to think not merely in terms of political independence but also in terms of revolutionary solutions of their economic problems. Referring to the growth of communalism, he said in 1934-35:

'The want of clear ideals and objectives in our struggle for freedom undoubtedly helped the spread of communalism. The masses saw no clear connection between their day-to-day sufferings and the fight for swaraj. They fought well enough at times by instinct, but that was a feeble weapon which could be easily blunted or even turned aside for other purposes. There was no reason behind it, and in periods of reaction it was not difficult for the communalists to play upon this feeling and exploit it in the name of religion. It is nevertheless extraordinary how the *bourgeois* classes, both among the Hindus and the Muslims, succeeded, in the sacred name of religion, in getting a measure of mass sympathy and support for programmes and demands which had absolutely nothing to do with the masses, or even the lower middle class.'[3]

[1] *Ibid.*
[2] *Letters*, 182, Letter to Nehru, June 29, 1936.
[3] *AB*, XIX, 137-38.

Nehru noted with surprise that Muslim communal leaders did not care at all for Indian nationalism or Indian freedom, whereas Hindu communal leaders, though always speaking apparently in the name of nationalism, had little to do with it in practice. 'Both agreed,' he saw, 'in condemning socialistic and such-like "subversive" movements; there was a touching unanimity in regard to any proposal affecting vested interests.'[1]

Attempt at Planning

In spite of the apparent difficulties Nehru had to carry on. In 1938, at the instance of Congress, a National Planning Committee was established. Industrialists, financiers, economists, professors, scientists, and representatives of the Trade Union Congress and the Village Industries Association were taken on to the Committee. The non-Congress Provincial Governments of Bengal, the Punjab, and Sind, as well as some of the major states like Hyderabad, Mysore, Baroda, Travancore, and Bhopal co-operated with this Committee. 'In a sense it was a remarkably representative Committee cutting across political boundaries as well as the high barrier between official and non-official India.' It was only the Government of India which did not co-operate. There were hard-headed big business, idealists and doctrinaires, socialists and near-communists, and experts and directors of industries. Nehru accepted the chairmanship of this 'strange assortment of different types', as he called it, because 'the work was after my own heart and I could not keep out of it'.[2]

As the fascination of this work grew on him, he came to realize the hard realities which faced planning in a country like India, with diverse interests and social diversities. Broadly he faced two problems: the socialist one aiming at the elimination of the profit motive and emphasizing the importance of equitable distribution; and Big Business striving to retain free enterprise and the profit motive as far as possible, and laying greater stress on production. There were other approaches as well. National self-sufficiency was taken, however, to be the objective for the country, and planning had to be thought of with that end in view. It is to the credit of

[1] *Ibid.*
[2] *DI*, VIII, 372.

Nehru that in that first attempt at comprehensive planning for India he could lead the Committee to think that the future of India lay in democratic socialism.

'Constituted as we were, not only in our Committee but in the larger field of India, we could not then plan for socialism as such. Yet it became clear to me that our plan, as it developed, was inevitably leading us towards establishing some of the fundamentals of the socialist structure. It was limiting the acquisitive factor in society, removing many of the barriers to growth, and thus leading to a rapidly expanding social structure. It was based on planning for the benefit of the common man, raising his standards greatly, giving him opportunities of growth, and releasing an enormous amount of latent talent and capacity. And all this was to be attempted in the context of democratic freedom and with a large measure of co-operation of some at least of the groups who were normally opposed to socialistic doctrine.'[1]

The Planning Committee ultimately disappeared as the War came, followed by Nehru's imprisonment, release, and the Revolution, and again imprisonment, etc. But the serious attention to planning which he had paid led him to form certain clear ideas as to the shape of things to come. He began to think whether, in bringing about socialism, class conflicts could be avoided. 'If conflict was inevitable, it had to be faced; but if it could be avoided or minimized that was an obvious gain.' Another idea that he formed was that if people adhered to the democratic state structure and encouraged co-operative enterprises, many of the dangers of regimentation and concentration of power might be avoided.

Why Socialism?

Through years of thought Nehru evolved his own ideas about socialism; and as he worked on, he wanted to give them a practical shape. Regarding the basis of his philosophy it may be said that he developed a deep faith in the ultimate success of socialism as the panacea of human ills. He saw no way of ending the poverty, the chronic unemployment, the degradation and the subjection of the people except through socialism. He declared in 1936:

[1] *Ibid*, 377.

'I am convinced that the only key to the solution of the world's problems and of India's problems lies in socialism, and when I use this word I do so not in a vague humanitarian way but in the scientific, economic sense. Socialism is, however, something even more than an economic doctrine; it is a philosophy of life and as such also it appeals to me.'[1]

Nehru saw through socialism the possibilities of vast and revolutionary changes in the political and social structure, the ending of vested interests in land and industry, as well as of the feudal and autocratic Indian States system. He also saw through socialism the ending of private property, except in a restricted sense, and the replacement of the profit system by a higher ideal of co-operative service. 'It means ultimately a change in our instincts and habits and desires. In short, it means a new civilization, radically different from the present capitalist order.'[2]

All socialists, utopian or scientific, would agree that socialism means a system of social reconstruction. Nehru starts from the same fundamental. Socialists differ to some extent when defining the exact nature of socialism in its working detail; and they differ widely on the method and tactics of changing capitalist society into a socialist one. As regards the main objective—social reconstruction—some think in terms of absolute change from old to new, while others think of modified change since society is based on a continuity of many systems, and a complete break with most things might lead to unforeseen risks. Nehru holds to the fundamental; but as he proceeds he finds his own way to working it out.

The Nature of Marxian Influence

As already discussed, Nehru had been drawn to the Marxist philosophy from an early age. Among many schools of socialist thought, Marxism not only stood pre-eminent, but it supplied a philosophy which could be worked into practical shape. The Marxist philosophy thus was the centre of modern socialist thought. Nehru's approach to history is, to some extent, Marxian. The long chain of history and of social development appeared to

[1] *Essays* II, 82-3, 'Presidential Address', April, 1936.
[2] *Ibid.*

him to have some meaning, some sequence; and the future lost some of its obscurity. He is too much of an individualist, and has great faith in personal freedom. But in his socialist thought, the Marxist-Leninist influence seems to have led him to doubt if socialism and unlimited freedom could go together. It appeared to him obvious that 'in a complex social structure individual freedom had to be limited, and perhaps the only way to read personal freedom was through some such limitation in the social sphere. The lesser liberties may often need limitation in the interest of the larger freedom.'[1]

Much of the Marxist philosophical outlook Nehru accepted without difficulty, such as its monism and non-duality of mind and matter, the dynamics of matter and the dialectic of continuous change by evolution as well as a leap, through action and inter-action, cause and effect, thesis, antithesis and synthesis. But Marxism did not satisfy him completely. He had a vague idealist approach of his own to various problems of life, and in his queries regarding many such problems Marxism could give no answer. Nehru came to the conclusion that, in questions regarding the betterment of human living and social organization, there remained vast possibilities of increasing human knowledge.

In his thought, Nehru laid complete faith in a scientific approach to social problems. In this respect he breaks with the concepts preached by religions and believed by society. To him individual and social problems should not lead to despair, inaction and triviality, nor should their solution be sought in dogmatic creeds. They should all be viewed through science. 'Social evils,' he says, 'most of which are certainly capable of removal, are attributed to original sin, to the unalterableness of human nature, or the social structure, or (in India) to the inevitable legacy of previous births. Thus one drifts away from even the attempt to think rationally and scientifically and takes refuge in irrationalism, superstition, and unreasonable and inequitable social prejudices and practices.'[2] Of course, even rational and scientific thought does not always take one as far as he would like to go, because there is an infinite number of factors and relations all of which

[1] DI, I, 14.
[2] Ibid, 15.

influence and determine events in varying degrees. 'It is impossible to grasp all of them, but we can try to pick out the dominating forces at work and by observing external material reality, and by experiment and practice, trial and error, grope our way to ever-widening knowledge and truth.'[1]

Marxist philosophy had suggested this kind of scientific approach to social problems. Since a scientific approach always means an ever-progressive search for truth, certain doctrines of Marx, by the Marxian interpretation itself, cannot belong to eternity. Nehru accepts certain principles of Marxism; but for the rest, says:

'Marx's general analysis of social development seems to have been remarkably correct, and yet many developments took place later which did not fit in with his outlook for the immediate future. Lenin successfully adapted the Marxian thesis to some of these subsequent developments, and again since then further remarkable changes have taken place—the rise of fascism and nazism and all that lay behind them. The very rapid growth of technology and the practical application of vast developments in scientific knowledge are now changing the world picture with an amazing rapidity, leading to new problems.'[2]

On the whole, the Marxian diagnosis of the ills of modern society made a deep impression on Nehru's socialistic ideas. He resolved the prophecies of Marx to understand more deeply the fundamental causes of the socio-economic conflicts which afflicted the world.*

---

* Speaking about socialism he once said:
'The socialist approach is the approach of Marxism. It is a way of looking at past and present history. The greatness of Marx none will deny today and yet few realize that his realistic interpretation of events, which has illumined the long and tortuous course of history, was not a sudden and brilliant innovation. It had deep roots in the past; it was known to the old Greeks and Romans as well as to European thinkers of the Renaissance and onwards. They conceived of history as a movement and a conflict of ideas and interests. Marx applied science to this old philosophy, developed it and made it the brilliant exposition that has so impressed the world. There may be lacunae in this exposition, over-emphasis here and there. We must not look upon it as a set of dogmas, but as a scientific way of looking at history and social changes. Much is made of the fact that Marx emphasized the economic side of life only. He did emphasize it because it is important and because there had been a tendency to ignore it. But he never ignored the other forces which have moved human beings and shaped events.' *Essays* III, 39-40, 'Congress and Socialism', July 15, 1936.
[1] *Ibid.*
[2] *Ibid.*

Concern over Social Issues

Marxism or not, Nehru's main concern has been over what he considered the real issues before him with regard to social reconstruction. The basic question is 'whether we must fight the evil effects that we see around us or seek the causes that underlie there'. To Nehru, those who concerned themselves with the effects only seldom went far. Fighting with effects, but not with the causes of those effects, meant merely retarding the downward movement, but not changing its direction; or, in other words, it was like applying palliatives, not curing the malady. 'That is the real problem—effects or causes. And if we seek for causes, as we must, the socialist analysis throws light on them.'[1]

Nehru believes in the adjustment between social problems and the forces of time by means of a scientific approach. Several vital issues are involved in this adjustment, but their proper assimilation makes the socialist objective sound. The real issues for him are the problems of individual and social life, of harmonious living, of a proper balancing of an individual's inner and outer life, of an adjustment of the relations between individuals and between groups, of a continuous effort to become something better and higher, of social development, and of the ceaseless adventure of man. In facing these problems he wants to follow the way of observation and precise knowledge and deliberate reasoning, according to the methods of science. In brief, in dealing with the day to day problems of life and the needs of men and women he wants to be intensely practical. 'A living philosophy must answer the problems of today.'[2]

Ideas on Inequality

It is said that the prime concern of the socialist in his programme of social reconstruction has been, through the ages, the removal of inequalities. This concern has inevitably led thinkers to examine the origin of inequality. Nehru has also examined the problem. While doing so, he has also analysed where wealth goes. Early man had a hard life even to find food. But the coming of agriculture made a vast difference to his life. In the later history of

[1] *Essays* III, 41, 'Congress and Socialism', July 15, 1936.
[2] *DI*, I, 16.

mankind, great changes were brought about by new ways of producing food and other commodities. Man began to require many other articles almost as much as food. 'So that any great change in the methods of production resulted in great changes in society.' New and quicker ways of producing food and other necessities were discovered in history from time to time. 'And you will of course think,' he says to his daughter Indira, 'that if better methods are used for production, much more will be produced, and the world will be richer and everyone will have more.'

'You will be partly correct and partly wrong. Better methods of production have certainly made the world richer. But which part of the world? It is obvious enough that there is great poverty and misery still in our country, of course, but even in a rich country like England. Why is this so? Where do the riches go to? It is a strange thing that in spite of more and more wealth being produced, the poor have remained poor.'[1]

He goes on to conclude that the wealth goes to those, usually the managers or organizers, who get the lion's share of everything good. What is still more strange, he finds, is that classes have grown up in society of people who do not even pretend to do any work, and yet who take this lion's share of the work of others. 'And—would you believe it?' he asks, 'these classes are honoured; and some foolish people imagine that it is degrading to have to work for one's living! Such is the topsy-turvy condition of our world.'[2]

In this there is nothing new or original since many thinkers in the past discovered in similar processes of history the origin of inequality *vis-à-vis* the accumulation of property and growth of poverty. Nehru described the above by way of a historical narration to his daughter. Nevertheless, by holding such views himself he more or less sided with many notable radical thinkers. Rousseau in a very radical way propounded doctrines on the origin and basis of inequality among men, maintaining that the progress of the sciences and arts had tended to degrade the morals of men. Proudhon traced the history of inequality and analysed *What is Property?* and declared 'Property is robbery'. Mahatma

[1] *WH*, Vol. I, 48-50, Nehru to Indira, January 18, 1931.
[2] *Ibid.*

Gandhi once said: 'To a people famishing and idle, the only acceptable form in which God dare appear is work and promise of food as wages. God created man to work for his food, and said that those who ate without work were thieves.' Nehru in his study of history understood the factors or forces which led to the origin and growth of inequality; and in so doing formed his views on its evil effects.

Nehru takes a critical view of the economic inequality in modern society. To him the whole of the nineteenth century civilization in Europe was based on the ideology of the French Revolution, which was again based on the idea of the sacredness of private property. This ideology, in its turn, derived from the ideas of Montesquieu, Voltaire, Rousseau and the Encyclopaedists, dated back to the period before the Industrial Revolution. This ideology, with its slogan of political liberty, equality and fraternity became completely out of date with the growth of industrial capitalism. 'It became evident, however, during the nineteenth century, that a theoretical equality before the law or the possession of a vote did not bring real equality. Economic inequality, the maldistribution of wealth, which capitalism progressively increased, made equality impossible of attainment and exploitation of man by man and group by group increased.'[1]

It was necessary, therefore, that economic equality should be aimed at; and in order to achieve this, the control of the means of production by society as a whole and the severe restriction of private property were necessary. In essence, all human beings should have equality of opportunity. To Nehru, the present capitalist system does not and can not in the nature of things provide this equality of opportunity.

'The famous nineteenth century saying about "government of the people, by the people and for the people" failed to materialize in practice because under the capitalist system the government was neither by the people nor for the people. It was a government by the possessing classes for their own benefit. The people, according to them were themselves: all others were in the outer darkness. A real government by the people and for the people can only be established when the masses hold power, that is under

[1] *Essays* I, 30-1, 'Some Criticisms Considered'.

socialism when all the people really share in the government and the wealth of the country.'[1]

Attitude to Poverty

Certainly, inequality arising from the exploitation of one class by another is a great social injustice. It leads to the poverty of the exploited. In Nehru's political thought the worst enemy of mankind is poverty. Poverty is abominable and therefore it must go. Whether poverty arises out of exploitation or otherwise, irrespective of the cause of its origin, its very existence must be challenged. In his ideas it is clearly noticed that he regards the removal of poverty as the prime objective of the socialist. Many a socialist might agree that since inequality is the root cause of poverty, removal of the former would bring about socialism. Nehru wants to fight inequality so far as it breeds poverty, but his greater emphasis is on the latter. His views tend to suggest at times that he would rather prefer inequality without poverty to equality with poverty. When he thinks of the equalization of wealth, mainly he means by it the equalization of plenty. As he explains:

'Socialism or communism might help you to divide your existing wealth, if you like, but in India, there is no existing wealth for you to divide; there is only poverty to divide. It is not a question of distributing the wealth of the few rich men here and there. That is not going to make any difference in our national income. We might adopt that course for the psychological good that might come out of it. But from the practical point of view, there is not much to divide in India because we are a poor country. We must produce wealth, and then divide it equitably. . . . Our economic policy must therefore aim at plenty. Until very recently economic policies have often been based on scarcity. But the economics of scarcity has no meaning in the world of today.'[2]

In his attitude towards poverty Nehru understands no compromise. Not even with Gandhi. Gandhi, in his work for the poor gave them a religious term *Daridranarayan.** Nehru could not for

---

* The Poor that is God, or God that resides in the Poor.
[1] *Ibid.*
[2] *Speeches* III, 17-8, January 22, 1955.

a moment appreciate such Gandhian terminology which appeared to him as the 'glorification of poverty', since God was especially thought to be the Lord of the poor and that the poor were His chosen people. 'That, I suppose,' he said, 'is the usual religious attitude everywhere. I could not appreciate it, for poverty seemed to me a hateful thing, to be fought and rooted out and not to be encouraged in any way. This inevitably led to an attack on a system which tolerated and produced poverty, and those who shrunk from this had of necessity to justify poverty in some way. They could only think in terms of scarcity and could not picture a world abundantly supplied with the necessaries of life; probably, according to them, the rich and the poor would always be with us.'[1]

Obviously Nehru had no liking for such tenets of religion or the commonplace faith that social inequalities are pre-ordained or predestined.* Whenever he had occasion, he discussed the above matter with Gandhi. Gandhi laid stress on his usual belief that the rich would treat their riches as a trust for the people. To Nehru, it was a viewpoint of considerable antiquity, and one comes across it frequently in India as well as in medieval Europe. 'I confess that I have always been wholly unable to understand how any person can reasonably expect this to happen, or imagine that therein lies the solution of the social problems.'[2]

Of course, Gandhi was never blind to the problem of poverty in India. He was, on the other hand, very much alive to it. The only difference between Nehru and himself was that while Nehru's outlook on life and society was very much more modern, Gandhi's was deeply religious. Nehru hated poverty, but preferred wealth, if not its concentration. Gandhi hated poverty as much as he hated the excess of wealth. To put it in Nehru's words: 'He (Gandhi) is not enamoured of ever-increasing standards of living and the growth of luxury at the cost of spiritual and moral values. He does not favour the soft life; for him the straight way is the

---

* Emperor Napoleon is reported to have once said:—
'Society cannot exist without inequality of property and the inequality not without religion. A man who is dying of hunger, next to one who has too much, could not possibly reconcile himself to it if it were not for a power which says to him: "It is the will of God that here on Earth there must be rich and poor, but yonder, in eternity, it will be different".'
[1] *AB*, XXVII, 192.
[2] *AB*, XXVII, 192.

hard way, and the love of luxury leads to crookedness and loss of virtue.'[1]

Gandhi was shocked at the vast gulf between the rich and the poor, and went over to the side of the latter. To him the abysmal poverty of India was due to the 'foreign rule and the exploitation that accompanied it, and the capitalist industrial civilization of the west as embodied in the big machine'. Gandhi reacted against both. He wanted the end of foreign rule; and as for an ideal society:

'He looked back with yearning to the days of the old autonomous and more-or-less self-contained village community where there had been an automatic balance between production, distribution, and consumption; where political or economic power was spread out and not concentrated as it is today; where a kind of simple democracy prevailed; where the gulf between the rich and the poor was not so marked; where the evils of great cities were absent and people lived in contact with the life-giving soil and breathed the pure air of the open spaces.'[2]

Through his spinning-wheel and the village industry, Gandhi aimed to give employment to millions and millions of the poor in order to raise their standard of living. Though he disliked the heavy industries of the west, yet his attitude towards them was not very hostile. Gandhi's economic views changed from time to time, keeping the moral foundation intact. With regard to the questions of poverty and wealth, he became more and more convinced that the millionaire's wealth should go to the community. In 1941, and again in 1945, Gandhi warned the Indian capitalists in the following terms:

'A non-violent system of government is clearly an impossibility so long as the wide gulf between the rich and the hungry millions persists. The contrast between the palaces of New Delhi and the miserable hovels of the poor labouring class nearby cannot last one day in a free India in which the poor will enjoy the same power as the richest in the land. A violent and bloody revolution is a certainty one day unless there is a voluntary abdication of riches

---

[1] *DI*, VIII, 381.
[2] *Ibid*, 381-82.

and the power that riches give, and sharing them for the common good.'[1]

Problem of Class Interests

What Nehru found in his reading of the problems of inequality and poverty was the growth of economic interests which ultimately shaped the political views of groups and classes. Those interests become vested interests, so much so that neither reason nor moral considerations can override them. Rare individuals may surrender their special privileges, but classes and groups do not do so. In Nehru's conclusion, 'The attempt to convert a governing and privileged class into forsaking power and giving up its unjust privileges has therefore always so far failed, and there seems to be no reason whatever to hold that it will succeed in the future.'[2]

The problem, therefore, is how to bring the class interests to an end so that a classless society can be formed. From a much earlier stage, Nehru began to look at the *zamindari* and *taluqadari* systems in India as semi-feudal, as out of date, and as a hindrance to production and general progress. He profoundly believed in the abolition of those interests. At one time he felt bitterly against the Gandhian approach to such problems when, for example, Gandhi said in July 1934 that 'better relations between landlords and tenants could be brought about by a change of hearts on both sides'.*

Gandhi disliked the socialism and communism of the west because, according to him, they believed in the essential selfishness of human nature. He, on the other hand, wanted to base his concept of socialism and communism on non-violence and on the harmonious co-operation of Labour and Capital, landlord and tenant. Nehru, however, did not know if there were differences in the basic conceptions of the East and West; but, if there were, they did not greatly matter to him. He saw in the Indian capitalist and the landlord no epitome of virtue, and prepared to agree to a

---

* Gandhi further told a deputation of landlords that 'I shall be no party to dispossessing propertied classes of their private property without just cause. My objective is to reach your hearts and convert you so that you may hold all your private property in trust for your tenants and use it primarily for their welfare.' Vide *AB*, LXII, 535.
[1] Louis Fischer, *Gandhi*, xx, 355.
[2] *AB*, LXIII, 544.

large extent with a western observer, H. N. Brailsford, that 'Indian usurers and landlords are the most rapacious parasites to be found in any contemporary social system'.[1]

On the whole, Nehru aimed at some practical ways to deal with class interests. The feudal states, the *zamindaris* and *taluqadaris*—the capitalist system in general, long appeared to him to be doomed, and therefore he thought of ways of extinguishing it. The Gandhian method and technique—in spite of the best intentions on the part of Gandhi and his undoubted and avowed mission for the emancipation of the poor—did not appear to Nehru sound. 'Is it reasonable to believe in the theory of trusteeship,' he asked, 'to give unchecked power and wealth to an individual and to expect him to use it entirely for the public good? Are the best of us so perfect as to be trusted in this way?'

'Even Plato's philosopher-kings could hardly have borne this burden worthily. And is it good for the others to have even these benevolent supermen over them? But there are no supermen or philosopher-kings; there are only frail human beings who cannot help thinking that their own personal good or the advancement of their own ideas is identical with the public good. The snobbery of birth, position, and economic power is perpetuated, and the consequences in many ways are disastrous.'[2]

The Question of Solution

So whither? What should be the method and technique? In the mid-thirties, when Nehru thought over the above problems, he had tried to avoid the question of how to effect the change, or how to get rid of the obstacles in the way, 'by compulsion or conversion, violence or non-violence'. But he could not long postpone finding out his own answers. Once he had recognized the necessity for change, it became almost imperative to find out the means. Gandhian means were not acceptable; should he therefore, turn to Marxist methods? Nehru understood the core of the class conflict. His battle was with a system and not with individuals. Of course, a system was always embodied to a great

---

[1] H. N. Brailsford, *Property or Peace?* Vide *AB*, LXII, 535.
[2] *AB*, LXII, 528.

extent in individuals and groups, and those individuals and groups had to be converted or combated. Transformation of society was taken for granted. Nehru hoped that this process of change would involve as little suffering as possible, but he felt that suffering and dislocation were inevitable. 'We cannot put up with a major evil for fear of a far lesser one, which in any event is beyond our power to remedy.'[1] Thus he thought of the inevitability of suffering and dislocation in the trek of socialism. In this he thought differently from the Marxist manner. He had to search for a different path.

As early as 1936, the Indian socialist leader Jayaprakash Narayan posed a question: 'Must Pandit Jawaharlal, supposing he became the Premier or President of Socialist India, line up the Taluqdars of the U.P. and have them blown up to bits? Must he seize the treasures of the *rajas* and the *mahajans* and distribute them to the people—equally, of course? Must he turn over the Tata Iron Works, for instance, to the workers employed there, and leave them to make as good or bad a business of it as they please? Must he split up all the land in the country, divide the total acreage by the total population, and hand over a little plot to each individual? Will that be socialism?

'No. Socialism is something more sensible, more scientific, more civilized than all that.

'What, then, must Pandit Jawaharlal do?'[2]

When Pandit Jawaharlal Nehru really became the Prime Minister of India eleven years later, and in fact engaged himself in laying the foundations of a socialist state, he certainly did not blow up the *taluqdars* with cannons, yet they disappeared for ever; he did not wage war against the *rajas* and *maharajas*, yet the entire princely class vanished from history; he did not turn over the Tata Iron Works to the workers to make a good or bad business of it, but yet inaugurated bigger iron works to be managed by the state; and he did not divide the total land by the total population, but yet attempted to solve the problem of land for the benefit of the tiller. And all this he tried to achieve in his own way.

[1] *Ibid*, 529.
[2] Jayaprakash Narayan, *Why Socialism?*, 4.

The Approach to 'Methods' and 'Tactics'

For long have world socialists thought over the problem of so-called methods and tactics of changing the old order into new. While the old schools of socialist thought suggested various methods, the Marxists brought forward their uncompromising thesis of revolution to establish the rule of the proletariat. Though the aim of socialism was to abolish class struggle and class rule, yet the Marxists wanted to organize the proletariat as a class to fight with the enemy and to effect revolution. According to their explanation, when after capturing power the proletariat, as the new political authority, has swept away by force the old conditions of production, there will no longer exist any basis for classes and class struggle.

The prime necessity to the socialist then appeared to be the capture and possession of power. Since socialism implied complete reorganization of the whole economic and social life of the country, it meant obviously that those who wanted to bring socialism about should have the power to do so. Conscious of this factor, Nehru had raised the question several years before the independence of India: 'In whose hands will power come when political freedom is achieved? For social change will depend on this, and if we want social change we must see that those who desire such change have the power to bring it about. If this is not what we are aiming at, then it means that all our struggle is meant to make India safe for vested interests who desire no change.'[1] Power in this context means the power of the state. When the state is in one's hands one can enforce one's will either through legislation or through force. The capture of the state is thus essential. This can be done in two ways; either by force and revolution or through the will of the electorate. Once the state was captured, its entire machinery could be employed to build up socialism.

In the nineteenth century when the electorate had not been enlarged even in many western countries, the masses of people had little opportunity to express their will. Since power remained in the hands of the upper classes, to the socialist revolution appeared as a logical and scientific weapon in the hands of the

[1] *Essays* III, 39, 'Congress and Socialism', July 15, 1936.

people in order to capture power. This theory continued into the twentieth century. In Russia, where the Tsarist regime was in possession of unlimited autocratic power, and there was no democratic franchise, revolution became the only method by which people could capture power. But as time advanced and democracy expanded to reach people, the capture of power through the electorate appeared to the socialist as more logical and more scientific than through revolution. Nehru realized that the concept of power through the electorate and socialism through the state was to be his main formula.

Towards Peaceful Technique

Violence, force and revolution as the means to socialism long appeared to Nehru as wrong. No doubt at times he was troubled as to whether socialism could be brought about by absolutely peaceful means. He thought that it was possible in theory to establish socialism by democratic means, provided the full democratic process was available. But he felt that in practice there were likely to be very great difficulties, because the opponents of socialism could reject the democratic method when they saw their power threatened. This once led him to say:

'The rejection of democracy does not or should not come from the socialist side but from the other. That of course is fascism. How is this to be avoided? The democratic method has many triumphs to its credit, but I do not know that it has yet succeeded in resolving a conflict about the very basic structure of the state or of society.'[1]

Such doubts, however, were only temporary. On a more permanent plane, he wanted to derive his strength from the people both for the capture of power and for achieving socialism. This strength was to be constitutional and not anything contrary. He discounted such feelings that a violent mentality increased the militancy of the masses and was therefore to be encouraged among the industrial workers and the kishans. To him, strength came not from occasional exhibitions of individual or group violence, but from mass organization and the capacity for mass

[1] Letters, 141, Nehru to Lord Lothian, January 17, 1936.

action, which should be peaceful action.[1] In February 1939, he declared:

'I have been and am a convinced socialist and a believer in democracy, and have at the same time accepted whole-heartedly the peaceful technique of non-violent action which Gandhiji* has practised so successfully during the past twenty years. I am convinced that strength can only come to us from the masses, but that strength either for struggle or for the great work of building a new world must be a disciplined and orderly strength. It is not out of chaos or the encouragement of chaotic forces that we can fashion the India of our dreams.'[2]

Through peaceful means India became independent, and power came into the hands of Nehru and his party. The Congress party was not socialist, but was prepared to some extent to bow before the inevitable. To Nehru, with his party in possession of the state, opportunities came to work in the direction of socialism. Since the capitalist and the bourgeois were required to surrender their privileges, conflict and coercion lay in the very nature of things. The state had two alternatives: either to exercise real force to put down resistance, or to create sufficient popular opinion to eliminate vested interests through peaceful coercion. To Nehru in power, the coercive powers of the state were based on public opinion, and therefore it was through public opinion and democratic legislation that he wanted to exercise the powers of the state against class interests.

The Necessity and Legality of Coercion

History, according to Nehru, shows that there is no instance of a privileged class or group or nation giving up its special privileges or interests willingly. Individuals have often done so, but not as a group. 'Always a measure of coercion has been applied, pressure has been brought to bear, or conditions have been created which make it impossible or unprofitable for vested interests to carry on.' And it is then that the enforced conversion takes place. The

---

* Gandhi suspected socialism of the west, and more particularly Marxism, because of their association with violence. The very words 'class war' breathed conflict and violence and were thus repugnant to him.

[1] *Writings* II, 120.
[2] *Writings* II, 134-35, February 22, 1939.

methods of this enforcement may be brutal or civilized; to Nehru the latter was the real method.

He had no doubt from the beginning that coercion or pressure was necessary to bring about political and social change in India. Indeed, according to him, the non-violent mass movements of the freedom struggle were powerful weapons to exercise this pressure. 'It is perfectly true,' he said, 'that this method of coercion is the most civilized and moral method and it avoids as far as possible the unpleasant reactions and consequences of violence. I think that it does offer a moral equivalent for violent warfare and, if civilization does not collapse, it will gradually adopt this peaceful method of settling its disputes.'[1]

Long before he came to power, Nehru had laid faith in the legality of the coercive powers of a democratic state. Since the very idea of private property was changing in the modern world, state coercion became apparent in dealing with it. At one time slaves were regarded as property, and so were women and children. Nehru wrote in 1934-35: 'As the conception of property changes, the State interferes more and more, public opinion demands, and the law enforces, a limitation of the anarchic rights of property-owners. All manner of heavy taxes, which are in the nature of confiscation, swallow up individual property rights for the public good. The public good becomes the basis of public policy, and a man may not act contrary to this public good even to protect his property rights.'[2] Covetousness, selfishness, acquisitiveness, the fierce conflicts of individuals for personal gain, the ruthless struggles of groups and classes, and the inhuman suppression and exploitation of one group by another, are all detestable, and if they are inherent in the acquisitive society of today, that society must undergo change. The time has gone when the strong preyed on the weak; and the old motto no longer applied that 'they shall take who have the power and they shall keep who can'. A modern state justified itself in its power to deal with such antiquated ideas.

Controlled production and distribution of wealth for the public good was the aim of a socialist state. If individuals or institutions

[1] *Essays* I, 35, 'Some Criticisms Considered'.
[2] *AB*, LXII, 521.

stood in the way of such change they would have to be removed. In brief, it was clear to Nehru that 'the good of a nation or of mankind must not be held up because some people who profit by the existing order object to the change'. It appeared quite moral to him that the state could pass laws of a coercive nature in order to take away some rights and privileges from various classes and groups. 'Democracy indeed means the coercion of the minority by the majority,' he said.

'If a law affecting property rights or abolishing them to a large extent is passed by a majority, is that to be objected to because it is coercion? Manifestly not, because the same procedure is followed in the adoption of all democratic laws. Objection, therefore, cannot be taken on the ground of coercion.'[1]

Nehru was told by some people that to attempt to nationalize private property, except with the consent of the owners, would be coercion, and as such opposed to non-violence. But his concept of non-violence did not extend so far as to entertain such ideas.

Coercion but no Class War

Though coercion was considered by Nehru natural and moral, yet did not rule out the possibility of conversion. Rather, at times he thought of large scale conversions. From earlier times he wanted to emphasize that world forces were moving in new directions calling for certain absolute changes. He only wished that every group or class studied the symptoms of the times in order to adjust themselves to changing circumstances without feeling any bitterness towards each other. The capitalist system of industry, he thought, was no longer suited to the present methods of production. Technical advance had gone far ahead of the existing social structure. He disliked the motive of those who were opposed to the idea of changing over to new systems because of their own vested interests in the old ones, even though the old systems were dying before their eyes. A proper understanding of affairs was necessary in order to avoid class conflicts. As early as 1933 he had said:

'It is not a question of blaming capitalism or cursing capitalists and the like. Capitalism has been of the greatest service to the

[1] *AB*, LXIII, 543.

world, and individual capitalists are but tiny wheels in the big machine. The question now is whether the capitalist system has not outlived its day and must now give place to a better and a saner ordering of human affairs, which is more in keeping with the progress of science and human knowledge.'[1]

Capitalism solved the problems of production, but in the new world it helplessly faced the allied problems of distribution and was unable to solve them. As Nehru believed, it was not in the nature of the capitalist system to deal satisfactorily with distribution; and production alone made the world top-heavy and unbalanced. To find a solution for distributing wealth and purchasing power evenly was to put an end to the basic inequalities of the capitalist system and to replace capitalism itself by a more scientific system.

In considering this kind of scientific system he imagined a classless society with equal economic justice and opportunity for all, a society organized on a planned basis for the raising of mankind to higher material and cultural levels, to a cultivation of spiritual values, of co-operation, unselfishness, the spirit of service, the desire to do right, goodwill and love—ultimately a world order. Such a system as he visualized could only be brought about by a process of compromise between compulsion and conversion. He said:

'Everything that comes in the way will have to be removed, gently if possible, forcibly if necessary. And there seems to be little doubt that coercion will often be necessary. But if force is used it should not be in the spirit of hatred or cruelty, but with the dispassionate desire to remove an obstruction.'[2]

Though this was difficult, Nehru with the assumption of power began to work out his theory with some degree of practical success. His coercion became more and more democratic and he did not forget to attempt conversion. In any case, violence was ruled out of the question of social reorganization. Before independence he was greatly apprehensive of the role which the Indian princes, who numbered more than six hundred, were supposed to play. A conflict between this class and the people

[1] *Essays* II, 50, '*Whither India?*', 1933.
[2] *AB*, LXIII, 552.

seemed evident. But that problem could be solved in a different way. Nehru in power appeared less aggressive, giving greater attention to peaceful technique. He did not feel inclined to hear what happened in the French Revolution or even in the recent Russian Revolution. To him, those revolutions had their lessons, but the conditions of France or Russia, America or China, were peculiarly suitable to themselves. Conditions in India were different. Rejecting the idea of class war, he said in December 1955:

'The communists tell us that the basis of society is class struggle and therefore the people must be trained for class struggle and for destroying the upper classes. I also want a classless society in India and the world. I do not want any privileged classes. I do not want a great deal of inequality among people. The point is how we are to proceed about it. Even recognizing the conflict between classes, the right way of liquidating that conflict is to put an end to it by peaceful methods.'[1]

Compromise and Conciliation in Social Relations

Apparently he wanted to bring about a human outlook for the adjustment of social relations. He did not want to proceed by the consent of the vested interests with regard to social legislation. He did not seek the consent of the landlords before he introduced land legislation. 'Nevertheless,' he prided himself, 'we have land legislation in a way so as not to throw the landlords to the wolves. That is, we try to fit them into our future structure.'[2] In fact, hundreds of thousands of landlords were badly hit by the land legislation, but they were not driven to become the enemies of the people. In industrial spheres, Nehru aimed at solving the problems of class conflict both by legislation and a normal change in the outlook of the opposing classes. Since a few private industries had necessarily to continue for some time longer, the relationship between the producer and labour needed orientation. He warned the capitalist:

'You talk of labour troubles and many other problems of yours. I think you are justified in complaining against them, more

[1] *Speeches* III, 136-37, December 26, 1955.
[2] *Ibid*, 13, December 21, 1954.

especially against the resort to violence. But how do you deal with it, apart from the governmental or the law-and-order point of view? You cannot deal with masses of people merely that way. You can only deal with them by the human approach, making them realize that they are not outside the pale, that they are not mere hewers of wood and drawers of water, but that they perform an essential function in this business, that in fact they are partners in a great undertaking.'[1]

The employer-worker relationship, thought Nehru, could be based on more judicious principles in modern times than hitherto. The conflict could be resolved through conciliation. He was in favour of trade unions and of labour's right to strike. With his background knowledge of the labour movement in England and Europe during the nineteenth and twentieth centuries, he wanted every employer to realize the terrible times labour had endured for generations, how they were crushed, how they were sent to Australia for the pettiest offence as life-term convicts, and how, slowly, by means of co-operative efforts, the trade unions gradually gained some normal human rights, if not privileges. That was why, according to Nehru, labour prized the right to strike jealously. But what worried him was the wastage involved in strikes and lock-outs. What he wants, therefore, is that there should be faith in mutual agreement, or, if that does not work, there should be faith in some third party in the shape of a conciliator, arbitrator or tribunal. 'A tribunal may not always decide rightly,' he says, 'from the point of the employer or of the workers. That argument could be advanced in the case of our normal judiciary, because one party or the other is bound to be dissatisfied. Are we then going to abolish the judiciary?'[2] He believed that if tribunals and conciliatory processes did not function rightly they could be improved. In any case, the tendency towards industrial conflict should be regarded as harmful to national growth.

As labour was required to move away from its tendency to strike, capital was required to give up 'the bullock-cart habit of mind' or even 'the nineteenth century or the early twentieth

---

[1] *Ibid*, 64, December 14, 1953.
[2] *Ibid*, 66.

century habit of mind'. 'I am not prepared to accept,' declared Nehru, 'that the only way for industry to flourish is to encourage acquisitiveness. You may call it by the name of the incentive of profit. I want you to have the incentive of profit, undoubtedly, but within limitations. But to believe that human beings are such that without this acquisitive instinct they cannot function properly is to do mankind a great injustice.'[1] He would point out that all the great things in this world had not been done through acquisitiveness but by the reverse of it. Great inventors, scientists, writers, musicians and engineers prospered and made the world advance because of other urges. A broader consideration of social relations and social interests was advocated by Nehru as the means towards social equality.

Main Objectives Before the State

Through peace and without conflict, Nehru proceeded to bring about socialism. As regards the main objectives, his mind was clear long before freedom came. These objectives could be modified when put into actual practice, if necessary. In 1933, he had written to Indira:

'Socialism, I have told you, is of many kinds. There is general agreement, however, that it aims at the control by the state of the means of production, that is land and mines and factories and the like, and the means of distribution, like railways, etc., and also banks and similar institutions. The idea is that individuals should not be allowed to exploit any of these methods or institutions, or the labour of others, to their own personal advantage.'[2]

Without this there was exploitation and therefore poverty. Also, the producers fought each other in cut-throat competition. There was wastage, and private war. Besides, there existed great inequalities in wealth between different classes and peoples. Socialism was required to deal with these.

There were other objectives as well. Again, before independence, Nehru had realized that the real problems of India, as of the rest of the world, were economic, and that they were so interrelated that it was hardly possible to tackle them separately.

[1] *Ibid*, 66-7.
[2] *WH*, Vol. II, 851-52, Nehru to Indira, February 16, 1933.

In the case of India, agriculture and the land system demanded revolutionary changes. Large-scale state and collective co-operative farms appeared to be the proper substitute for landlordism as well as for tiny, uneconomic and wasteful holdings which were too small for the application of scientific methods of agriculture. There was the problem of vast urban and rural unemployment. Keeping all this in view he had said in 1938: 'For that as well as for other obvious reasons we must push forward the industrialization of the country. This again requires the development of social services—education, sanitation, etc. And so the problem becomes a vast and many-sided one affecting land, industry and all developments of life, and we see that it can be tackled only on a nationally planned basis without vested interests to obstruct the planning.'[1]

Nehru was firmly convinced of the necessity of the industrialization of India both through small and heavy industries as one of the objectives of socialism. Gandhi considered it a sin and injustice to use machinery for the purpose of concentrating power and riches in the hands of the few. Otherwise he did not object to machinery as such. Nehru thought that political independence was a risk to industrially backward countries since economic control would tend to pass to others. Before freedom, therefore, he thought of state owned industries, especially heavy industries and large-scale key industries and public utilities. In 1944 he said:

'It can hardly be challenged that, in the context of the modern world, no country can be politically and economically independent, even within the framework of international interdependence, unless it is highly industrialized and has developed its power resources to the utmost. Nor can it achieve or maintain high standards of living and liquidate poverty without the aid of modern technology in almost every sphere of life.'[2]

He also believed in rapid industrialization of the country for relieving the pressure on land; and for defence, as well as for a variety of other purposes. He was equally convinced that the most careful planning and adjustment were necessary in order to

[1] *Writings* II, Part I, Ch. I, 21-22, January, 1938.
[2] *DI*, VIII, 384-85.

reap the full benefit of industrialization, and to avoid many of its dangers.

Socialism in What Form?

The objectives having been more or less determined previously, Nehru had to face actual problems while attempting to achieve socialism after independence. Socialism in what form, and how soon?—that became his immediate concern. One thing of which he was certain from an earlier period was that the mere emotional appeal of socialism was not enough; that had to be supplemented by an intellectual and reasoned understanding based on facts, arguments and detailed criticism. Moreover, he knew that if socialism was to be built up in India 'it will have to grow out of Indian conditions'.[1] In other words, he wanted socialism to be practical as well as indigenous.

In aiming at a socialistic pattern of society, which to Nehru was socialism itself, he made his position clear by saying: 'We have not approached this question in any doctrinaire way. And that is good, because doctrinaire thinking leads to rigidity and rigidity of outlook at a moment of great change in the world is bad, because it leaves us high and dry.'[2] Faith in the time factor, thus, leads him away from earlier socialist doctrines. In 1956 he said: 'Marx was a very great man and all of us can learn from Marx. But the point is that it is grossly unfair to ask Marx, who belonged to the middle of the nineteenth century, to tell you what to do in the middle of the twentieth century.'[3] India and the world, he thought, were destined to march in the direction of socialism, but that march might vary in different countries and the intermediate steps might not be the same everywhere.

Socialism and Individualism

Some people imagined that 'any kind of socialism necessarily means authoritarianism'. 'It does not,' said Nehru in 1956, 'at least in theory; in practice, I think it depends on how a country will develop.'[4] On this issue his mind was made up long since.

[1] *AB*, LXVII, 589.
[2] *Speeches* III, 85, April 14, 1956.
[3] *Ibid*, 84.
[4] *Ibid*, 82, January 7, 1956.

L

Democracy like socialism meant to him the removal of disparities. Therefore socialism could be democratic, and not authoritarian. For long he felt that it was necessary for any community to organize itself for the establishment of social and economic justice. This organization was possible on the fascist basis, but could not bring justice or equality, and was essentially unsound. The only other way was the socialist way. Liberty and democracy, thought Nehru, had no meaning without equality, and equality could not be established so long as the principal instruments of production were privately owned. Private ownership of the means of production thus came in the way of real democracy. It was the property relation which ultimately governed the social fabric and institutions and, according to Nehru, the essential contradiction between the existing property relation and the forces of production in the present-day world made it difficult for democracy to function. A transformation was thus necessary and while thinking on these lines he had said in March 1939:

'I do not see why under socialism there should not be a great deal of freedom for the individual; indeed, far greater freedom than the present system gives. He can have freedom of conscience and mind, freedom of enterprise, and even the possession of private property on a restricted scale. Above all, he will have the freedom which comes from economic security, which only a small number possess today.'[1]

Socialism and individualism do not seem to Nehru as inherently contradictory. Socialism is based upon the individual personality expressing itself in free labour. Distinctions between individuals are not destroyed by it. Nehru closely connects socialistic ideas with the idea of political democracy. 'Personally I am perfectly prepared to accept political democracy only in the hope that this will lead to social democracy.'[2] In the practical field, while he provided for the working of political democracy through the constitution and the law, he aimed at making socialism work through policy and actual governmental administration. The constitution establishes universal suffrage and political freedom, and through them the government derives its strength to

[1] *Writings* II, 117-18, March, 1939.
[2] *Letters*, 143, Nehru to Lord Lothian, January 17, 1936.

work for the social emancipation of the masses of the people.

The concept of social democracy does not conflict with the personal liberty of individuals. Even if state intervention is introduced, it is in the individual's own interest. In any case, the individuality of men is preserved in Nehru's socialism. Once Subhas Chandra Bose told Nehru: 'How a Socialist can be an individualist as you regard yourself, beats me. The one is the antithesis of the other. How Socialism can ever come into existence through individualism of your type is also an enigma to me.'[1] To this Nehru replied:

'Am I a socialist or an individualist? Is there a necessary contradiction in the two terms? Are we all such integrated human beings that we can define ourselves precisely in a word or a phrase? I suppose I am temperamentally and by training an individualist, and intellectually a socialist, whatever all this might mean. I hope that socialism does not kill or suppress individuality; indeed I am attracted to it because it will release innumerable individuals from economic and cultural bondage.'[2]

Democratic Collectivism

Nehru may be said to have leaned towards democratic collectivism, which to him did not mean a total abolition of private property, but did mean the public ownership of the basic and major industries. It meant also the co-operative or collective control of the land. Further, for India it meant co-operatively controlled small and village industries. Such a system of democratic collectivism required careful and continuous planning. 'The aim should be,' he said in 1944, 'the expansion of the productive capacity of the nation in every possible way, at the same time absorbing all the labour power of the nation in some activity or other and preventing unemployment. As far as possible there should be freedom to choose one's occupation. An equalization of income will not result from all this, but there will be far more equitable sharing and a progressive tendency towards equalization.'[3]

Nehru regarded it as one of the central problems of his time—

[1] *Ibid*, 328, Subhas Chandra Bose to Nehru, March 28, 1939.
[2] *Ibid*, 353, Nehru to Subhas Chandra Bose, April 3, 1939.
[3] *DI*, X, 497.

how to combine democracy with socialism; how to maintain individual freedom and initiative, and yet to have centralized social control and planning of the economic life of the people. As he worked for a solution, the hard realities faced him that for the success of such a system there had to be long processes of training for the people. It took time to build up a socialist society. It not only required a change of economic structure but also a change in the minds and hearts of men. For the Soviet Union and China, being authoritarian states, it also took time. Nehru said in January 1957, 'We must realize that the process of bringing socialism to India, especially in the way we are doing it, that is, the democratic way, will inevitably take time.'[1] His desire for democratic socialism is obvious. In the final analysis, he thought, democracy promoted the growth of human beings and of society. He believed in the production of material goods, and wanted high standards of living, but, as he said, 'not at the cost of man's creative spirit, his creative energy, his spirit of adventure; not at the cost of all those fine things of life which have ennobled man throughout the ages.'[2]

Towards a Socialist Pattern of Society

Nehru proceeded to work for a democratic socialist state. In this attempt he kept in view peaceful techniques, requirements of time and practical utilities. Hasty action seemed to him full of risks; moreover, where people had to be carried with the government, hasty action was not possible. He attached great importance to the public sector as against the private sector. But in the actual practice he had to realize that the biggest and the overwhelming part of the private sector was the private sector of the peasants in India. That in a sense was the real private sector in the country, and not the few factories which she possessed. This required therefore thoughtful consideration.

As regards the *zamindari* institution in India, that is, the big estate system, its abolition was effected as a matter of principle. In effecting this, no scope was left even for the judiciary to intervene. 'Within limits no judge and no Supreme Court can make

---

[1] *Speeches* III, 53, January 4, 1957.
[2] *Ibid.*

itself a third chamber. No Supreme Court and no judiciary can stand in judgement over the sovereign will of Parliament representing the will of the entire community,' declared Nehru in the Constituent Assembly.[1] In all other cases of the individual right to property, the broad principle of the authority of the sovereign legislature to effect necessary control was proclaimed. 'No individual can override ultimately the rights of the community at large. No community should injure and invade the rights of the individual unless it be for the most urgent and important reasons.'[2] The balancing authority, according to Nehru, was ultimately the parliament of the country. In the adjustment of the rights of the individual and the rights of the community, he wanted to pay utmost consideration to the practical aspect of every proposed action, before the step was taken. In his policy towards private industries he is rather cautious.

'I would beg of you not to imagine that because socialism conceives of nationalized industry, therefore you must have all industry nationalized. I think that as the socialist pattern grows, there is bound to be more and more nationalized industry, but what is important is not that there should be an attempt to nationalize everything, but that we should aim at the ultimate result, which is higher production and employment. If by taking any step you actually hinder the process of production and employment from growing, then that does not lead you to the socialistic pattern.'[3]

Cautious though his policy was, the goal before India was fixed. In December 1954, Nehru spoke to the Indian House of the People: 'The pattern of society that we look forward to is a socialist pattern of society which is classless, casteless.'[4] In January 1955, the 60th Session of the Indian National Congress at Avadi adopted the resolution aiming at a socialistic pattern of society. The principles involved were—work for substantially increasing production, for raising the standards of living and for having progressively fuller employment so as to achieve full employment. The machinery of the state was directed towards

[1] *Debates* C.A., Vol. IX, No. 31, September 10, 1949.
[2] *Ibid.*
[3] *Speeches* III, 12, December 21, 1954.
[4] *Ibid.*

implementing the above objectives. Some time later Nehru defined the 'socialist pattern of life' thus:

'We mean a society in which there is equality of opportunity and the possibility for everyone to live a good life. Obviously, this cannot be attained unless we produce the wherewithal to have the standards that a good life implies. We have, therefore, to lay great stress on equality, on the removal of disparities, and it has to be remembered always that socialism is not the spreading out of poverty. The essential thing is that there must be wealth and production.'[1]

Thus the primary function of a growing society was, according to him, the production of more wealth. 'Therefore, whether it is in industry or agriculture, the one and the primary test is whether you are adding to the wealth of the country by increasing the production of the country. If not you become stagnant in that field.'[2] He felt confident that some time or other society would reach the goal of equality, but he did not want the road followed to be artificial.

Looking at the entire question in a somewhat dynamic way, Nehru could not dissociate the objectives of socialism from the foreseen possibilities which the future held for mankind. To him, the world appeared to be at one of the major ages of transition, when completely new sources of power were being tapped, something in the nature of an industrial revolution or electrical revolution, but something even more far-reaching. The world was on the verge of a new industrial age which meant that many of the old methods of production would become completely out of date. This was the warning of the time. Nehru wanted to be wide awake about these changes, and to think in terms of the future rather than the past, because the past was dead and gone, and one could not go back to it, and even the present was a rapidly changing present. If one approached it in terms of the future, many of the present conflicts would seem out of place, and one could get out of the old mode of thinking. In the light of the above thought he would say:

'Speaking as a person who is a believer in the socialization of

[1] *Ibid*, 96, May 23, 1956.
[2] *Ibid*.

industry, I should like to say this, that far too much attention is often paid to acquiring existing industries than to the building of new industries by the State or under State control. In many cases, existing industries of the basic type may have to be acquired by the State and run by the State. But it seems to me a far better approach to the problem for the State to concentrate more and more on new industries of the latest type and to control them in a large measure, because then the resources of the State go towards further progress and controlled progress instead of merely trying to get hold of something which exists. Of course, one sometimes has to do that too.

'I say this because I am to some extent—if I may venture to say so—of a scientific bent of mind and I try to think more in dynamic terms than in static terms. The existing industry today that most people think of—capitalists, socialists or communists— is something of which they think in static terms, as if the thing must go on and on, while as a matter of fact the thing is completely out of date and most of it should be scrapped.'[1]

As he progressed with the aim that all individuals in India should have equal opportunities of growth, from birth upwards, and equal opportunities for work according to their capacity, the dimensions of the socialist objective began to grow greater in his thought, leading him to say:

'I look upon it (socialism) as a growing, dynamic conception, as something which is not rigid, as something which must fit in with the changing conditions of human life and activity in every country.'[2]

---

[1] *Speeches* I, 154-55, December 18, 1947.
[2] *Speeches* III, 52, January 4, 1957.

CHAPTER VI

THE STATE, GOVERNMENT, AND
THE INDIVIDUAL

A Realistic Approach

In his approach to subjects such as the State, Government, and
the Individual—both in their individual merit as well as in their
inter-relation—Nehru, as far as possible, tries to be practical-
minded. His political idealism is greatly circumscribed by his
practical politics; and when the above subjects come within his
consideration, his approach to them becomes critical. This in a
sense leads him to base his thoughts on experiment rather than on
dogma.

The State in the Past

According to Nehru, a State's obligations to the individual or the
individual's obligations to the State must necessarily have varied
during different periods of history. The original State, he says,
was a very, very simple state in which, practically speaking, all
that the State had to do was to protect the individual from a
foreign enemy or another tribe. From that developed the concept
of what might be called a police State. A State preserved law and
order, protected its citizens from foreign enemies, and took
taxes to carry on its business. For the rest, it was left to the
individual or the group. The present idea of the State, he con-
cludes, has grown far beyond that. A State is supposed to perform
much more.

The Modern State as a Socially Functioning Organism

With this supposition as the basis, Nehru finds it easy to assume that every state is trying to do very much more for the individual than has ever been attempted before.

'So the State becomes more and more of a socially functioning organism—for the good of society or the individual, as you like. And the more it becomes that, the more benefits it confers on the individual, the more, in a sense, the individual has obligations to that State. So the two things, the rights and the obligations, march together. If the State and individual are properly integrated and organized there is no conflict. Otherwise, if one side goes ahead of the other there is a lack of balance.'[1]

In illustrating his concept of the 'socially functioning organism', Nehru goes on to advocate that the State, apart from protecting the individual from foreign enemies or internal disorders, has the duty to undertake to provide him with opportunities of progress, of education, health, sanitation—generally, everything that would give him the opportunity of fitting himself for such work as he is capable of. This obviously leads the modern State to grow more and more centralized. But such a tendency appears to Nehru as a deep problem of the time. One cannot escape centralized authority, whether it is of the State, of the big corporation, of the trade union, or of any group. They all go on being centralized authorities. The difficulty which confronts Nehru is: all centralization is a slight encroachment on the freedom of the individual. He wants to preserve the freedom of the individual, but at the same time understands the impossibility of escaping centralization in modern society. How to balance the two is the real problem.

Nehru attempts to find an answer to the problem of the conflict between centralization and individual freedom. As for the State, he has no doubt that it cannot do without a large measure of centralization. But on behalf of the individual he feels it highly desirable that there should be some attempt to limit centralization, reducing it to a minimum; and so far as it is possible, to decentralize the rest.

Basic Functions of the State
In this light Nehru thinks of the basic functions of the State. First

[1] *Talks*, 23.

of all, the State has to try and function in such a way as to provide for the primary needs of the people, or, at any rate, to make such arrangements that people can obtain those primary needs. Next, there are the important secondary needs. As regards economic organization, Nehru believes in a flexible policy, especially with regard to his own country. Where private resources are not abundant, he says, any project should be a State project. Since schemes like river valley projects or similar large works cannot be undertaken by individuals, they must be State schemes if they are to be done at all. Certain other large projects can either be State projects or jointly owned by the State and private enterprise, with a measure of State control, but leaving a large field for private enterprise. 'Thus we get,' says Nehru, 'what I would call a public sector of our economy and a private sector and may be a sector where the two overlap, with part State control and largely a private sector managing under State control. So we have these three branches of our economy. There need not be any rigid lines between them, and we can see which functions better and more successfully and allow them to develop.'[1]

Nehru feels that as a State increases its centralization in certain sections of the national economy, it becomes all the more important to safeguard and increase the rights of the individual. So far as the political rights of the individual are concerned, he wants them to be safeguarded by the constitution of the State. 'So far as economic questions are concerned, it is a question of a State interfering to protect, rather than keeping away, because in rather undeveloped economies there is a tendency in certain groups of vested interests to override the interests of the large groups by whatever methods they have.'[2]

The State as a Means to an End

In thinking of the functions of the State, Nehru keeps it uppermost in his mind that the State exists to serve man. Political liberty, which a modern democratic State is proud to give to its people, is not an end in itself but is the means by which economic and social freedom may be attained. It is the function of the State to help develop all aspects of human happiness.

[1] *Ibid,* 24-25.
[2] *Ibid,* 25.

Development of man being the ultimate aim of the State, Nehru does not hesitate to place power in the hands of the people to judge the merit of the State and whether it functions in the right direction. He considers the Machiavellian concept of State in governing the people and keeping them down as absurd. A modern State cannot stand on such foundations as to support something believing it to be false, on pretensions, and on the sham appearance of virtues. While thinking of Machiavelli, Nehru also condemns the modern states if they still accept old Machiavellian statecraft.

'The greater the scoundrel, the better the prince! If this was the state of an average prince's mind in those days in Europe, it is not surprising that there was continuous trouble there. But why go so far back? Even today, the imperialist powers behave much like the Prince of Machiavelli. Beneath the appearance of virtue, there is greed and cruelty and unscrupulousness; beneath the kind gloves of civilization, there is the red claw of the beast.'[1]

This is what Nehru wrote as long ago as 1932. It was round about this time when he greatly disputed the British concept of an Imperial State that he came to understand the meaning of certain aspects of the nature of the State, which, however universal, provoked his serious thought. In other words, Nehru became fully aware of the evil though inevitable aspects of the State. Once, while a prisoner himself, he began to wonder, 'How important and essential is a prison to the modern State!' In that state of mind, the numerous administrative and other functions of the government appeared to him as almost superficial before the basic functions of the prison, the police, and the army.

'In prison one begins to appreciate the Marxian theory, that the State is really the coercive apparatus meant to enforce the will of a group that controls the government.'[2]

The State in Relation to Force and Violence
Nehru believes it as fundamentally true that civilization has been built up on co-operation and forbearance and mutual collaboration in a thousand ways. But when a crisis comes, so he thinks, and

---

[1] *WH*, Vol. I, 441, Nehru to Indira, August 5, 1932.
[2] *AB*, XXX, 225.

the State is afraid of some danger, then the superstructure goes, or, at any rate, is subordinated to the primary function of the State— self-protection by force and violence. The army, the police, and the prison come into greater prominence then, and of the three the prison is to Nehru perhaps the nakedest form of a State in miniature. Thus, the force, the compulsion, and the violence of the governing group constitute more or less the basic nature of the State. Nehru asks:

'Must the State always be based on force and violence, or will the day come when this element of compulsion is reduced to a minimum and almost fades away?'[1]

Not being a philosophical anarchist himself, he thinks that that day, if it ever comes, is still far off. Leaving that vision aside, he finds violence the dominating factor in the nature of the State. The violence of the governing group produces the violence of other groups that seek to oust it. It all appears to Nehru as a vicious circle, violence breeding violence, and on ethical grounds there is little to choose between the two. 'It always seems curious to me,' he says, 'how the governing group in a State, basing itself on an extremity of violence, objects on moral or ethical grounds to the force or violence of others. On practical grounds of self-protection they have reason to object, but why drag in morality and ethics?'[2]

However undesirable the violence of the State may seem, practical considerations lead him to believe that State violence is preferable to private violence in many ways, for one major violence is far better than numerous petty private violences. State violence is also likely to be a more or less ordered violence, and thus, according to Nehru, preferable to the disorderly violence of private groups and individuals, for even in violence order is better than disorder, except that this makes the State more efficient in its violence and powers of compulsion. 'But when a State goes off the rails completely and begins to indulge in disorderly violence, then indeed it is a terrible thing, and no private or individual effort can compete with it in horror and brutality.'[3]

---

[1] *Essays* II, 143-44, 'The Mind of a Judge', September, 1935.
[2] *Ibid.*
[3] *Ibid.*

Inevitability of State Coercion

To Nehru, in his scientific approach to the questions of force and violence, some kind of State coercion appears inevitable. In one sense or another all life, according to Nehru, is full of conflict and violence. To reject violence altogether leads to a wholly negative attitude, utterly out of touch with life itself.

'Violence is the very life-blood of the modern State and social system. Without the coercive apparatus of the State taxes would not be realized, landlords would not get their rents, and private property would disappear. The law, with the help of its armed forces, excludes others from the use of private property. The national State itself exists because of offensive and defensive violence.'[1]

Even if one assumes that the worst forms of violence will be gradually removed from the State, according to Nehru it is impossible to ignore the fact that both government and social life necessitate some coercion. 'Social life necessitates some form of government, and the men so placed in authority must curb and prevent all individual or group tendencies which are inherently selfish and likely to injure society.' Coercion on recalcitrant individuals as Nehru thinks will have to continue till such time when every human being in the State is perfect, wholly unselfish, and devoted to the common good. Similarly, the State will have to exercise coercion on outside groups who make predatory attacks in order to defend itself, meeting force with force, till such time when there is only a single World-State. Since the world is imperfect, everybody will admit that a National State will have to use force for self-defence. Of course, thinks Nehru, the State should allow an absolutely peaceful and friendly policy to its neighbour and other states, but nevertheless it is absurd to deny the possibility of attack. For internal purposes, laws of a coercive nature to take away some rights and privileges from various classes and groups and to restrict liberty of action, are necessary, and since 'all laws are to some extent coercive', coercion is almost indispensable with normal functions of the State.

[1] *AB*, LXIII, 540.

Coercion with Reason

Though coercion in some form or other lies in the very nature of the State, Nehru is prepared to accept it only on the basis of reason. He, according to himself, likes discipline in life, and dislikes anarchy and disorder and inefficiency. On account of this he is a firm believer in law and order which a State is required to preserve. But at times, more especially during his contest with the British in India, he became rather doubtful about the values of law and order which the states and governments impose on a people. It seemed to him that sometimes the price one pays for them is excessive, and the law is but the will of the dominant faction and the order is the reflex of an all-pervading fear. 'Sometimes, indeed,' he said, 'the so-called law and order might be more justly called the absence of law and order. Any achievement that is based on widespread fear can hardly be a desirable one, and an "order" that has for its basis the coercive apparatus of the State, and cannot exist without it, is more like a military occupation than civil rule.'[1]

He sought for an ideal as well as a practical basis for law and order and, for a moment while writing his *Autobiography*, went back to find them in the *Rajatarangini*, the thousand-year-old Indian historic epic of the poet Kalhana, which meant by law and order the duty of the ruler and the State to preserve *dharma* and *abhaya*—righteousness and absence of fear.

'Law was something more than mere law, and order was the fearlessness of the people. How much more desirable is this idea of inculcating fearlessness than of enforcing "order" on a frightened populace!'[2]

Government—its Defects

Towards the subject of government Nehru's attitude is a little more critical. During his fight against the British Government, he learnt to detest certain aspects of the government as a matter of conviction. Apart from that, in a general way also he could find certain things in the nature of governments which were not too desirable features. In the *Autobiography* he writes:

[1] *AB*, LVIII, 483.
[2] *Ibid.*

'Governments are notoriously based on violence, not only the open violence of the armed forces, but the far more dangerous violence, more subtly exercised, of spies, informers, *agents provocateurs*, false propaganda, direct and indirect through education, Press, etc., religious and other forms of fear, economic destitution and starvation. As between two governments it is taken for granted that every manner of falsehood and treachery is justified, provided it is not found out, even in peace-time and much more so in war-time.'[1]

He finds in modern times how ambassadors are supported by military, naval and commercial attachés whose chief function is to spy in the countries to which they are sent. Behind them, Nehru further observes, functions the vast network of the secret service, with its innumerable ramifications and webs of intrigue and deception, its spies and counter-spies, its connections with the underworld of crime, its bribery and degradation of human nature, its secret murders. Nehru regards all this as bad.

At one time Nehru proceeded to agree with a statement of George Washington who was reported to have said: 'Government is not reason, it is not eloquence—it is force! Like fire, it is a dangerous servant and a fearful master.'[2] During his struggle with the British, what he greatly disliked was the police conception of the State. The government's job, as it appeared to him then, was to protect the State and leave the rest to others. 'The very strength of a despotic government,' he considered, 'may become a greater burden for a people; and a police force, no doubt useful in many ways, can be, and has been often enough, turned against the very people it is supposed to protect.' He put forward an argument of Bertrand Russell, who, while comparing modern civilization with the ancient Greek, said: 'The only serious superiority of Greek civilization as compared to ours was the inefficiency of the police, which enabled a larger proportion of decent people to escape.'[3] Nehru was alive to yet another possible defect in the nature of governments—that power corrupts and absolute power corrupts absolutely.

[1] *AB*, LXIII, 540-41.
[2] *Essays* II, 143, 'The Mind of a Judge', September, 1935.
[3] *AB*, LIV, 435-36.

Good Government or Self-Government

Nehru's primary concern in these respects has been to understand the nature of good government. The efficiency of the coercive apparatus of the State does not establish a good government. Similarly a shiny administrative apparatus is not always the criterion of good government. A good government according to Nehru can be judged by greater efficiency in production, consumption, and the activities which go to raise the physical, the spiritual, and the cultural standards of the masses. His faith in good government is absolute, so much so that between good government and self-government he is even prepared to prefer the former.

'I believe that self-government is good for any country. But I am not prepared to accept even self-government at the cost of real good government. Self-government if it is to justify itself must stand ultimately for better government for the masses.'[1]

The Form and Approach of Government

Also allied to the concept of good government in the mind of Nehru there seem to lie ideas regarding the form of government. The form of government, according to Nehru, is after all a means to an end, the end being human well-being, human growth, the ending of poverty and disease and suffering, and the opportunity for everyone to live the good life. 'The long course of history shows us,' he says, 'a succession of different forms of government and changing economic forms of production and organization. The two fit in and shape and influence each other. When economic change goes ahead too fast and the forms of government remain more or less static, a hiatus occurs, which is usually bridged over by a sudden change called revolution. The tremendous importance of economic events in shaping history and forms of government is now almost universally admitted '[2] Besides economic improvement, Nehru also believes that national and individual freedom are other factors which influence the form of government. It seems that the outward form of government does not carry a great deal of meaning for him; but when the ends in view are

[1] *AB*, LVIII, 486.
[2] *Essays* II, 44, 'Whither India?', 1933.

properly served, the form, whatever it may be, is well justified. After all, 'the people get the government they deserve'[1] and therefore the elevation of the people becomes the main consideration.

While Nehru thinks about the general approach of a government to dealing with the governed, he seems to be mainly guided by his theory of good government, keeping certain practical aspects of the matter in view. In certain matters, what is good and what is evil may itself be a doubtful matter, and Nehru at one time felt that governments all over the world were not known to be particularly competent in giving such decisions. But yet he felt that the governments have to shoulder a heavy responsibility and they cannot discuss the philosophy of a question when action is demanded. 'In our imperfect world we have often to prefer a lesser evil to a greater one,' he said.[2] Knowing this, however, he advocated that a government's cannot merely be the policeman's approach, the method of force and violence and coercion. When in 1937 some power came into the hands of the Congress Party under the British made constitution of 1935, Nehru outlined in broad principles the approach to be followed by the Congress governments.

'Congress Ministers should avoid, as far as possible, all coercive processes and should try to win over their critics by their actions and, where possible, by personal contacts. Even if they fail in converting the critic or the opponent, they will make him innocuous, and the public sympathy, which almost invariably goes to a victim of official action, will no longer be his. They will win the public to their side and thus create an atmosphere which is not favourable to wrong action.'[3]

But in spite of this approach and the desire to avoid coercive action, occasions might arise when governments would find it difficult to avoid some such action. From practical considerations, therefore, he desired to say: 'No Government can tolerate the preaching of violence and communal strife, and if this unfortunately takes place, it has to be curbed by having recourse to the coercive processes of the ordinary law.' He believed that the

---

[1] *Talks*, 21.
[2] *Writings* II, Part II, Ch. 3, pp. 68-9.
[3] *Ibid*, August 30, 1937.

largest freedom should be given to the expression of opinions and ideas, and that bans and censorships must be got rid of and that governments should nurture the free soil from which the life of the intellect could grow and the creative faculties could take shape. But still, governments should be strong enough for exceptional situations to check violence, hatred and conflict. Nehru preferred to advise the adoption of a reformative approach towards evils by pointing out that violence is not killed by violence, but by a different approach and by removing the causes which lead to it.[1]

Governments often have to deal with wrongdoers and Nehru emphasizes a non-violent approach towards them, for violent suppression of wrongdoing does not end it. Accordingly, as far as a government possibly can, it must avoid the use of the coercive apparatus of the state. On the other hand, it should approach the wrongdoer and try to win him over and point out the evil conse- quences of his act. Even if this approach is not successful, coercive action should be avoided unless dangerous consequences are feared. The constant endeavour of governments should be to create an atmosphere which does not encourage a violent ap- proach to problems. 'Violent suppression of individuals or groups or ideas militates against this atmosphere, and so, though it might be momentarily successful, it adds to the difficulties.'[2]

The Purpose of Government

Nehru is no believer in the doctrine that that government is best which governs least and therefore an ideal government is one which governs not at all. On the other hand, he finds in govern- ments an extensive purpose. In the old days, as Nehru pointed out again and again, the state was looked upon almost as the private possession of the sovereign. His chief business was to tax his subjects and to protect them from external invasion and internal disorder from robbers and the like. Having given a certain measure of security to his people, his job was done. If he did this and did not impose too crushing a burden of taxation, he was looked upon as a good sovereign. Such days and such concepts of police duties by the government being out of date, modern

---

[1] *Ibid*, 70.
[2] *Ibid*, 84-5, November 4, 1937.

governments are faced with the multifarious activities of the modern State. Nehru, through his understanding of socialist doctrines, appears to have been influenced by the notion of 'the municipalization of the country' through governmental activities.

'The true civic ideal aims at common possession and common enjoyment of municipal amenities, and these amenities go on increasing till they comprise almost everything that a citizen requires. Roads, bridges, lighting, water-supply, sanitation, hospitals and medical relief, libraries, education, parks and recreation grounds, games, proper housing, museums, art galleries, theatres, music—are some of the activities that a modern up-to-date municipality should be interested in, and some of the amenities which it should provide free of cost to all its citizens.'[1]

Appreciating such a civic ideal he condemned the British Government in India for its negligible interest in such activities, and hoped to see the ideal materialize in the future. He saw in theory how the civic ideal gradually captured the State and with this how the activities of the State grew in all directions. The police State transformed itself into the modern State, 'a complex, paternal organism with a large number of departments and spheres of activities, and innumerable contacts with the individual citizen'.

'Not only did it give him security from external invasion and internal disorder, but it educated him, taught him industries, tried to raise his standard of living, gave him opportunities for the development of culture, provided him with insurance schemes to enable him to face an unforeseen contingency, gave him all manner of amenities, and made itself responsible for his work and food.'[2]

Difficulties and Responsibilities of Government
Finally, when Nehru acquired power and became the head of government, he began to realize the real difficulties and responsibilities which the governments of modern states were required to face. 'The problems of government have grown so enormously,'

---

[1] *Essays* I, 135-36, 'Civics and Politics', November 25, 1933.
[2] *Ibid*, 138, 'The Civic Ideal', December, 1933.

he once complained, 'that sometimes one begins to doubt whether the normal parliamentary procedures are adequate to deal with them.'[1] The nature of government, according to him, has progressively changed in every country, whether the structure of society there is capitalist or socialist or something in between. Even in countries supposed to be intensely capitalistic, the governments perform social functions to a large extent. To Nehru, the pressure of circumstances is such that the social sector of governments has grown even in countries which normally do not want it to grow. In other countries which deliberately aim at dealing with this sector governmentally, it will of course grow more. 'Thus, whatever the basic policy pursued by a country, it becomes inevitable for the governmental structure to become involved in social problems ever increasingly.'[2]

Government and People in the Welfare State

The burden of modern governments being so increasingly heavy, Nehru ultimately looks for the co-operation of the people for the success of governments. To him, freedom brings its own responsibilities and burdens, and they can only be shouldered in the spirit of a free people, self-disciplined, and determined to preserve and enlarge that freedom.[3] A government which deals with vital social problems has to function very differently from a government which is essentially a police state. In tackling intricate social and economic problems Nehru upholds the principle that there must be just laws and that the 'Government activity must be right and ought to be right', but activities should not end only within the orbit of governmental principles, because

'It is the activity of the people, it is the temper of the people, and the co-operation that the people in general give that will solve these problems this way or that. And I tell you that the best of our laws or activities of the Government can be, if not nullified, lessened greatly in effect if there is no will to work in the people or to co-operate to that end. And I tell you also that even an enfeebled government, even a bad political government

[1] *Speeches* III, 140, February 25, 1956.
[2] *Ibid*, 141.
[3] *Speeches* I, 7, August 15, 1947.

can yield greater results in the country if people co-operate to that end.'[1]

Nehru believes that ultimately all problems concerning human beings and their mutual relations depend on the character of human beings. The same type of governmental machinery or constitution might be totally unsuited to different conditions, to different backgrounds of people, although certain basic principles may be common.[2] He advocates complete co-ordination between administrative activities and the popular will together with co-operation in order that the purpose of the welfare state is served. It becomes all the more important, he feels, that the administrator has his finger on the pulse of the people all the time, and the people feel that he is one of them, that he is reflecting their wishes and will always continue to do so.[3] The administration not only has to be good but has also to be felt to be so by the people affected.

The Individual in the Modern State

It is not difficult to locate the place of the individual in the political philosophy of Nehru. At times he is confronted with the problem of a conflict between the State and the individual, but ultimately his sympathy goes back to the latter. He thinks that the growth of modern civilization with its magnificent achievements has led more and more to the centralization of authority and power, and encroachments continue to be made on the freedom of the individual. Perhaps, to some extent, this is inevitable, as the modern world cannot function without considerable centralization. But sometimes this process of centralized authority is carried to such an extreme that individual freedom almost vanishes.

'The State becomes supreme in everything or groups of individuals have so much concentrated power at their disposal that individual freedom tends to fade away. Different and some-times hostile ideologies, from their respective points of view, encourage this concentration of power in the State or the group. This must ultimately result not only in human unhappiness but also in a lessening of that creative genius which is so essential for the growth of humanity. We have to find some balance

[1] *Ibid*, 136, January 28, 1949.
[2] *Speeches* III, 142, February 25, 1956.
[3] *Ibid*, 161, April 6, 1957.

between the centralized authority of the State and the assurance of freedom and opportunity to each individual.'[1]

The Individual in the Past

Nehru believed that in the good old days in his own country the power of the State, however despotic in appearance, was curbed in a hundred ways by customary and constitutional restraints, and no ruler could easily interfere with the rights and privileges of the village communities, and those customary rights and privileges ensured a measure of freedom both for the community and the individual. An individual, in those days, was only considered as a member of a group and he could do anything he liked so long as he did not interfere with the functioning of the group. He had no right to upset that functioning, but if he were strong enough and could gather enough supporters it was open to him to form another group. If he could not fit in with a group, he could become a *sanyasi* who renounced caste, groups and the world of activity, and could wander about and do what he liked. Nehru further believed that while the Indian social tendency was to subordinate the individual to the claims of the group and society, religious thought and spiritual seeking always emphasized the individual.[2] He appreciated this kind of individualistic tendency, conditioned as it was by social structure and social activities; and upheld that this was better than the highly individualistic civilization of the modern west 'where personal ambition is encouraged and personal advantage is the almost universal aim, where all the plums go to the bright and pushing, and the weak, timid or second-rate go to the wall.'[3]

In India, comparatively up to the recent past, the people were far more interested in their local freedom and rights than in the machinery of government at the top. Kings changed, but the newcomers respected local rights and did not interfere with them. Because of this, felt Nehru, conflicts between kings and people did not take place as in Europe.[4]

[1] *Speeches* II, 421-22, October 31, 1949.
[2] *DI*, VI, 230.
[3] *Ibid*, 233.
[4] *Writings* II, Part I, Ch. I, p. 13, January, 1938.

Faith in the Ultimate Freedom of the Individual

Whatever might be the role of a modern state, Nehru does not believe in the sacrifice of the spirit of individual freedom. In a philosophical sense, he looks back and finds the long struggle of man against adverse surroundings in the face of innumerable difficulties. 'I see his repeated martyrdom and crucifixion but I see also the spirit of man rising again and again and triumphing over every adversity.' History shows him the eternal struggle of man for freedom, and Nehru feels that in spite of many failures on the part of man his achievements and success in this field have been remarkable. True freedom is not merely political but also economic and spiritual. Only then can man grow and fulfill his destiny. That freedom has also to be envisaged today not merely in terms of group freedom, often resulting in nations warring against one another, but as individual freedom within free national groups in the larger context of world freedom and order. However much the future might appear to be full of conflict and difficulty, Nehru has no doubt that the spirit of man, which has survived so much, will triumph again.[1]

From practical considerations, Nehru believes in various freedoms of man inside the State. For the better functioning of these freedoms he would rather allow a minor wrong to happen than suppress it, because if one attempts 'to suppress a wrong type of thing, a right type of thing may also be suppressed along with it, and it is bad to suppress a right thing'.

'Therefore, one tolerates a wrong thing, to some extent, so that the right may flourish, so that the right may ultimately overcome the wrong. So, one believes in the freedom of the press, freedom of expression and other freedoms which are very important. For my part, I do think that basically it is dangerous to suppress thought and the expression of thought in any way, because this may, besides suppressing a particular good thing, produce many kinds of evil which stunt the growth of a social group.'[2]

Freedom of the individual, however, should not be misapplied to affect society adversely. To Nehru, there is no such

[1] *Speeches* II, 422-23, October 31, 1949.
[2] *Ibid*, 468, September 17, 1952.

thing as one hundred per cent freedom for the individual to act as he likes in any social group. The idea of individual freedom arose in the days of autocracy in every country where an autocratic ruler or a group of rulers suppressed individual freedom. 'In a democratic society there is also that idea of individual freedom but always it has to be balanced with social freedom and the relations of the individual with the social group as well as other matters, as well as the individual not infringing on other individuals' freedom.'[1] It is necessary, in view of this, to define these balances; but 'the basic concept of individual freedom remains'.

Civil Liberty

For long during the struggle for freedom, Nehru laid repeated stress on Civil Liberty and on the right of free expression of opinion, free association and combination, a free press, and freedom of conscience and religion. Civil Liberty was not for him an airy doctrine or a pious wish, but something which he considered essential for the orderly development and progress of a nation. According to his interpretation, it is the civilized approach to a problem about which people differ, the non-violent way of dealing with it. To crush a contrary opinion forcibly and allow it no expression, because some people dislike it, is to Nehru essentially of the same genus as cracking the skull of an opponent because they disapprove of him. It does not even possess the virtue of success. The man with the cracked skull might collapse and die, but the suppressed opinion or idea has no such sudden end, and it survives and prospers the more it is sought to be crushed with force. History, he says, is full of such examples. Also,

'Long experience has taught us that it is dangerous in the interest of truth to suppress opinions and ideas; it has further taught us that it is foolish to imagine that we can do so. It is far easier to meet an evil in the open and to defeat it in fair combat in people's minds, than to drive it underground and have no hold on it or proper approach to it. Evil flourishes far more in the shadows than in the light of day.'[2]

[1] *Debates* P.I., 1951, Vol. XII, Part II, Constitution (First Amendment) Bill, May 18, 1951.
[2] *Essays* III, 307, 'The Right Perspective', August 30, 1937.

Law and Conscience; and Order

'No one can say that he will always and without fail act legally. Even in a democratic state occasions may arise when one's conscience compels one to act otherwise,'[1] wrote Nehru in the *Autobiography*. Of course, in a despotically or arbitrarily governed country such occasions are bound to be more frequent; and indeed, in such a State the law loses all moral justification. But what about a normally functioning democratic state? It will be perhaps difficult to estimate if Nehru would prefer conscience to law in a free democratic republic. Conscience being an individual concern, and all individuals not being competent enough to apply conscience in its proper meaning, statesmen would perhaps stand behind the law in order to preserve the State itself. Nehru's faith in individual freedom and civil liberty is fundamental, but when he speaks of them he does so in the context of a civilized orderly State. He is prepared to believe that there might be no law and order till freedom comes to a people; but once a people gains freedom, order becomes the foundation of society. He agrees with the French philosopher Proudhon who said: 'Liberty is not the daughter but the mother of order.'[2]

Freedom brings many opportunities. From a broader point of view, Nehru regards it as not merely a matter of political decisions or of new constitutions, not even a matter of what is more important, economic policy. 'It is of the mind and heart and if the mind narrows itself and is befogged and the heart is full of bitterness and hatred, then freedom is absent.'[3]

As the individual has to be protected in the State, so also the social organism has to be protected against the predatory individual. 'It is our duty,' he says, 'to protect the liberty of the individual, to see that there is no misuse of the law, to see that there is every safeguard that we can think of provided, but let us also at the same time remember that the major safeguard that we have to think of is the safety of the country and the community.'[4] Nehru keeps the individual uppermost in his mind; but he remembers

[1] *AB*, LII, 424.
[2] *Writings* I, 260, December 12, 1928.
[3] *Speeches* I, 10, August 15, 1948.
[4] *Debates* H.P., 1952, Vol. IV, Part II, Preventive Detention (Second Amendment) Bill, August 2, 1952.

well that in a social organism an individual cannot be separated from others. He believes, therefore, that 'The rights of the individual must be balanced by the obligations of the individual to the social organism. Without obligations there can be no real rights.'[1]

At times he expresses great concern over the individual in the twentieth century, because of the 'de-individualization and brutalization of individual man'. The individual is tortured by competing forces and pressures, and is subjected to all sorts of inner and outer tensions. What Nehru dislikes most is the individual giving way to the crowd. When the individual is by himself, he can be approached and he is responsive to reason. One can appeal to the good that is inherent in him; he also maintains a sense of responsibility. The individual's conscience, if not always in absolute control, is at least a factor in his decisions and notions. But when the individual is attracted to the crowd, strange things begin to happen. Nehru dislikes the crowd because it seldom places the reins on itself that the individual often feels compelled to do. The crowd dominates the individual but lacks a conscience of its own. Nehru is greatly disturbed that the individual should give himself over to the crowd or should be seized by it.[2] As he observes this tendency 'almost everywhere', his concern over the conditions required for individual creative development grows, which it is the purpose of society to provide.

Nehru, in actual administration, is a stern believer in the doctrine of discipline and order. Degradation of individuals or groups to the level of indiscipline or lack of understanding prompts him to justify firm actions. Use of violent methods on democratic issues is regarded by him as most dangerous, and he wants no government to take risks with it. '. . . one government may go and another government take its place, but if the government has violence done before its eyes, it must suppress that violence, and it will suppress it so long as that government has anything to do with administration.'[3]

He feels that unless the State is perfect and every individual is

[1] Talks, 22.
[2] Ibid, 6.
[3] Speeches I, 139-40, January 28, 1949.

perfect there is always some conflict between the freedom of the individual and the needs as well as the security of the State. Of course,

'You have extreme cases, as you have in some countries, of the State being put above everything, above every single individual freedom—the State becomes the God there. We have in great countries those cases—it is not for me to criticize them. For my part I cherish the freedom of the individual. I do not want even in the name of the State the freedom of the individual to be crushed. But undoubtedly the freedom of certain individuals has to be curbed for the safety of the State, if occasion arises.'[1]

On this essential question of conflict between the security of the State and the liberty of the individual, the line to be drawn appears to depend on circumstances. 'In war it goes far towards the State, in peace-time it should go far towards the individual, the State always being there—you cannot ignore the State or endanger the State.'[2]

With regard to the question of taking strong measures against individuals or groups, there is an obvious conflict in Nehru's mind. While as the head of a government he wants to protect the State against disorderly or violent activities, as an individual himself who suffered for a long part of his life from State coercion he personally hates the extreme measures of punishment. 'Ignorant people imagine,' he said at an earlier time, 'that if the punishment is not severe enough crimes will increase. As a matter of fact, the exact reverse is the truth.'[3] He hates 'long and barbarous sentences'. A century ago, he would point out, petty thieves were hung in England. When it was proposed to abolish the death penalty for thieves, there was a tremendous outcry and noble lords stated in the House of Lords that this would result in thieves and robbers seizing everything and creating a reign of terror. But in fact, he says, the reform had the opposite effect, and crime went down. When governing a State himself, circumstances demanded his government to resort to strong measures. In certain cases firings took place, or some people were shot down and killed, or

[1] *Debates* H.P., 1952, Vol. IV, Part II, Preventive Detention (Second Amendment) Bill, August 2, 1952.
[2] *Ibid.*
[3] *Essays* II, 123, 'Prison-Land', 1934.

were wounded. Referring to some such incidents Nehru once said:

'I do not think anyone in India can dislike this firing business as I do. I have a horror of it; I think it is a bad thing and I hope that it will be possible to put an end to it. My heart goes out in sympathy for those who may have suffered from it, specially if they are young people who are the hope of our nation.'[1]

The struggle between the head and the heart may go on. But the statesman in him would not confuse sentiment, however justified it may be, with higher political considerations of the nation's welfare. Order being essential for the growth of a nation, Nehru wants to face disorder, and at times rather he would like to face it in some novel way. He would think it better to appeal to the people to face the violent elements bent upon creating chaos in the country boldly, and not to remain passive spectators. Once he declared: 'Forces of chaos cannot be put down by the military and police alone. People have to co-operate with the Government in this task.'[2]

In the ultimate analysis, Nehru aims both at the growth of the individual as well as of the State. Freedom of the individual is as necessary as the freedom of the State for such growth. Finally, freedom itself leads to a higher ideal.

'Freedom for a nation and a people may be, and is, I believe, always good in the long run; but in the final analysis freedom itself is a means to an end, that end being the raising of the people in question to higher levels and hence the general advancement of humanity.'[3]

---

[1] *Speeches* III, 55, March 23, 1957.
[2] *Biblio*, 273, February 1, 1950.
[3] *Writings* II, Part I, Ch. 1, p. 11, January, 1938.

CHAPTER VII

INTERNATIONALISM

Nehru Against the Indian Background

Indian nationalism in the course of its own development was seen to be somehow moving towards the ideals of internationalism. In the liberal humanist tradition, the early internationalists felt that they had a message for the world. While inside India nationalism stood to mean the inviolable right of the Indian people 'to fully and freely live its own special life in its own way, following its own peculiar genius, and developing its specific culture to its highest perfection';[1] for the outside world it was felt to be the duty of nationalism 'to contribute what is highest and best in it'. Among the founders of the National Congress or the early pioneers of national awakening, there were a few people who thought that nationalism was not merely a political cry or principle, that it did not embody only the desire for the isolated independence and self-assertion of different national units, and that it did not stand to inspire an ambition for the exploitation of, or domination over, other weaker nationalities. On the contrary, nationalism had a broader significance, with a moral duty towards mankind.

The reputation of Jawaharlal Nehru as an internationalist grew while he was a thorough-going nationalist. It is rather interesting to note that as his role as a nationalist became more and more intensified, his faith in internationalism grew deeper and deeper. He could combine the philosophy of nationalism with that of cosmopolitanism or universalism. In India, as well as in the world at large, he held the above synthesis almost as a political doctrine of his own.

From his study of the Indian background to the growth of an

[1] Bepin Chandra Pal, *Indian Nationalism: Its Principles and Personalities*, 34.

international outlook, he traced the ideology of internationalism in three of the greatest Indians of recent times, Vivekananda, Tagore and Gandhi. Vivekananda was a religious man, but taking the world into consideration he believed that, even in politics and sociology, problems that were national some time ago could no longer be solved on national grounds only. They were assuming huge proportions, gigantic shapes, and they could only be solved when looked at from the broader view of international grounds. According to him international organizations, international combinations and international laws had become the cry of the day, and in science they were coming to a similar broad view every day. Further, this Indian saint believed that there could not be any progress without the whole world following in the wake, and that the solution of any problem could never be attained on racial, or national, or narrow grounds.* 'The fact of our isolation from all the other nations of the world is the cause of our degeneration and its only remedy is getting back into the current of the rest of the world. Motion is the sign of life,' said Vivekananda to his people.[1] Vivekananda died in 1902 when Indian nationalism was in the making. Nehru discovered in his preachings a new message for India.

In Rabindranath Tagore, the poet, who belonged to a later generation, Nehru saw another man who helped to bring into harmony the ideals of the east and the west and to broaden the bases of Indian nationalism. Tagore played a prominent part in the nationalist movement at the opening of the twentieth century, yet in spite of his strong nationalism he, as Nehru says, became India's internationalist *par excellence*, believing and working for international co-operation, taking India's message to other countries and bringing their message to his own people. It was Tagore's immense service to India, felt Nehru, that 'he forced the people in some measure out of their narrow grooves of thought and made them think of broader issues affecting humanity'.[2]

---

* Vivekananda also preached:—

'I am thoroughly convinced that no individual or nation can live by holding itself apart from the community of others, and wherever such an attempt has been made under false ideas of greatness, policy or holiness—the result has always been disastrous to the secluding one.'

[1] Vivekananda quoted in *DI*, VII, 316.

[2] *DI*, VII, 318.

Coming to Gandhi, Nehru saw the real synthesis between nationalism and internationalism and, that too, in its practical aspect. Gandhi, according to Nehru, was an intense nationalist, but the nationalist movement which he patterned was free from hatred. This gave Indian nationalism a new spirit; it could not be a narrowing creed. Moreover, Gandhi felt that he had a message not only for India but for the world, and that he ardently desired world peace. His nationalism, therefore, observed Nehru, carried a world outlook and was free from any aggressive intent. Gandhi's prime concern was to achieve the independence of India. But he came to believe that in the long run there would be a world federation of independent states which appeared to him as the only right goal. Gandhi's idealism was of a higher calibre. His patriotism included the good of mankind in general, and therefore his service to India included the service of humanity itself. He said:

'My idea of nationalism is that my country may become free, that if need be the whole of the country may die, so that the human race may live. There is no room for race hatred here. Let that be our nationalism.'[1]

Nehru also traced the growth of the ideal of internationalism in the National Congress of India. During the nineteen-twenties the Congress turned towards other countries, and gradually developed a foreign policy based on the principles of elimination of imperialism everywhere and the co-operation of free nations. While Nehru appreciated this tendency, he for his part, perhaps more than anyone else in the Congress circle, began to develop it as rapidly as possible. As early as 1929, he declared at the Lahore Congress:

'And if we use the word independence we do so in no sense hostile to the larger ideal. Independence for us means complete freedom from British domination and British imperialism. Having attained our freedom I have no doubt that India will welcome all attempts at world co-operation and federation, and will even agree to give up part of her own independence to a larger group of which she is an equal member.'[2]

[1] Gandhi quoted in *DI*, IX, 397.
[2] *Essays* II, 23, 'Presidential Address to the National Congress, Lahore', December, 1929.

It was an interesting development that by the thirties of the century those people who stood for national independence in India also stood for the widest internationalism. Nehru was a socialist and for him internationalism had a natural appeal, but he saw that even many of the non-socialists in the advanced ranks of Congress had become confirmed internationalists. In September 1933, Gandhi wrote to Nehru:

'Nor have I the slightest difficulty in agreeing with you that in these days of rapid intercommunication and a growing consciousness of the oneness of all mankind, we must recognize that our nationalism must not be inconsistent with progressive internationalism. India cannot stand in isolation and unaffected by what is going on in other parts of the world. I can, therefore, go the whole length with you and say that "we should range ourselves with the progressive forces of the world".'[1]

To Nehru, if the National Congress demanded independence it was not with a desire for isolation. On the contrary, he made it clear that it was willing to surrender part of that independence in common, of course, with other countries, to a real international order. To him any imperial system, by whatever high sounding name it might be called, was an enemy of such an order, and it was not through such a system that world co-operation or world peace could be reached.[2] It was seen that all over the world various imperialist systems were isolating themselves more and more by autarchy and economic imperialism. This was operating against the growth of internationalism. It produced greater co-operation within the area of autarchy, but it also meant isolation from the rest of the world. 'I do not believe,' said Nehru, 'in a narrow autarchy. But the internationalism that I look forward to is not one of common subjection, imposed from above, but a union and a co-operation of free nations for the common good. It is this kind of world order that will bring peace and progress to mankind.'[3] Not attracted towards narrow systems and policies, Nehru began to aim at wider international contacts. Even the very struggle for independence appeared to him as embodying some international significance. He had said in October 1933:

[1] Tendulkar, *Mahatma*, Vol. 3, Appendix I, Gandhi to Nehru, September 13, 1933.
[2] *AB*, LII, 420.
[3] *Essays* III, 184, 'Indian and Ceylonese in Malaya', June 2, 1937.

'The struggle for Indian freedom is essentially a part of the world struggle for the emancipation of the exploited everywhere and for the establishment of a new social order.'[1]

Internationalism not at the Cost of Nationalism

The growth of the idea of internationalism both in his own mind as well as in the country did not lead Nehru to reduce his faith in nationalism while India was dependent. 'In a contest between nationalism and internationalism,' he said, 'nationalism was bound to win. That had happened in every country and in every crisis; in a country under foreign domination, with bitter memories of continuous struggle and suffering, that was an inevitable and unavoidable consequence.'[2] While India was fighting for national independence she had a right to uphold nationalism strongly. But as Nehru saw, both before and during the war, even free nations and great countries betrayed the cause of internationalism for national gain. He saw England and France playing false to the republican Spain and Czechoslovakia, and thereby sacrificing internationalism for what they wrongly considered their own national interests. The United States of America, in spite of her sympathy towards England, France, and China, and hatred towards nazism and Japanese militarism, clung to isolationism out of national interest till Pearl Harbour forced her to fight. Even Soviet Russia by following strictly a national policy brought confusion to many who regarded her as an emblem of internationalism. From various other developments Nehru came to realize that 'Individuals and small groups may become internationally minded and may even be prepared to sacrifice personal and immediate national interests for a larger cause, but not so nations. It is only when international interests are believed to be in line with national interests that they arouse enthusiasm.'[3] While Nehru thought on such lines by observing world politics, there was nothing in his own country like an independent foreign policy for attempting a conciliation between national and international interests in order to make possible an effective internationalism. He felt:

[1] *Essays* I, 120, 'The Indian Struggle for Freedom', October, 1933.
[2] *DI*, IX, 395.
[3] *Ibid*, 396.

N

'Internationalism can indeed only develop in a free country, for all the thought and energy of a subject country are directed towards the achievement of its own freedom. That subject condition is like a cancerous growth inside the body, which not only prevents any limb from becoming healthy but is a constant irritant to the mind and colours all thought and action.'[1]

Yet it surprised Nehru that in spite of intense nationalism in India Congress became internationally minded. It appeared to him that no other nationalist movement of a subject country came anywhere near this, the general tendency in such countries being to make no international commitments. The Congress could succeed in creating a mass sentiment in favour of certain just and true aspects of internationalism.

Towards a Balance

Whether the idea of internationalism developed by itself or not, Nehru concerned himself with channelizing the spirit of nationalism in a proper direction. He was up against narrow nationalism. It was rather his understanding of the defects of nationalism which led him to understand more deeply the virtues of internationalism. In the nineteen-twenties, when he came into close contact with Congress workers and the intelligentsia who more or less constituted the backbone of the national movement, he saw them thinking largely in terms of the 'narrowest nationalism'. Their speeches laid stress on the glories of the past; the injuries, material and spiritual, caused by alien rule; the sufferings of the people; the indignity of foreign domination and how national honour demanded the necessity for sacrifice at the altar of the motherland. Those themes found an echo in every Indian heart and Nehru himself was moved by them. 'But,' he said, 'though the truth in them remained, they seemed to grow a little thin and threadbare with constant use, and their ceaseless repetition prevented the consideration of other problems and vital aspects of our struggle. They only fostered emotion and did not encourage thought.'[2]

Since those days he began to think of the national struggle in a

[1] *Ibid.*
[2] *AB*, XXVI, 182.

broader context of international issues. He was alive to the problems of India, of their difficulties and intricacies and could not run away from them to take shelter behind the wider problems which affected the world. 'But,' he would say, 'if we ignore the world we do so at our peril. Civilization today, such as it is, is not the creation or the monopoly of one people or nation. It is a composite fabric to which all countries have contributed and then have adapted to suit their particular needs.'[1] His study of world history, past and present, made him a convinced internationalist by and by. He began to realize more and more the futility of irrational or narrow nationalism. In August 1933, in a letter to his daughter, he explained:

'Our incursions in history have shown us how the world has grown more and more compact, how different parts have come together and become interdependent. The world has indeed become one single inseparable whole, each part influencing and being influenced by the other. It is quite impossible now to have a separate history of nations. We have outgrown that stage and only a single world history, connecting the different threads from all the nations, and seeking to find the real forces that move them, can now be written with any useful purpose.'[2]

Thus the history and life of a nation appeared to be a part of world history, influenced by world forces. In this kind of thought the idea of national seclusion or of national interest as an end in itself could not find enough space to grow. As time went by, and Nehru studied world problems more deeply, he began to wonder at the narrowing outlook which many countries possessed and showed. In 1944 he wrote: 'It is a curious and significant fact that, in spite of all modern scientific progress and talk of internationalism, racialism and other separating factors are at least as much in evidence to-day, if not more so, than at any previous time in history. There is something lacking in all this progress, which

---

[1] *Essays* II, 16, 'Presidential Address to the National Congress, Lahore', December, 1929.

[2] *WH*, Vol. II, 1494, Nehru to Indira, August 8, 1933. Nearly twenty years later, in 1952, Nehru expressed the same sentiment in a message to the International Buddhist Cultural Conference:—

'History today has ceased to be the history of this country or that. It has become the history of mankind because we are all tied up together in a common fate.' *Biblio*, 210, November 29, 1952.

can neither produce harmony between nations nor within the spirit of man.'[1]

Independence and Internationalism

After independence Nehru began to foster the spirit of internationalism among his people with a greater vigour. The narrowest type of nationalism, exhibiting itself through religion, resulted in the partition of India. That in itself was too much a proof of what narrow nationalism could do. Nehru had opposed religious fanaticism to the end, and had fought for the principle of a secular state based on broad nationalism. But what happened did so in spite of him. It is after independence that he found himself in a position to give a new turn to Indian nationalism. Within a few months of freedom and partition, he declared, from a place reputed for its communal background, the future nature of his country's nationalism thus:

'Whatever confusion the present may contain, in the future, India will be a land, as in the past, of many faiths equally honoured and respected, but of one national outlook, not, I hope, a narrow nationalism living in its own shell, but rather the tolerant creative nationalism which, believing in itself and the genius of its people, takes full part in the establishment of an international order.'[2]

India became independent after a long period of foreign domination. For more than half a century she was struggling for freedom while her nationalism was taking shape. At the achievement of that freedom the spirit of a triumphant nationalism dominated the minds of many Indians. India was predominantly a Hindu country at all times, and after her partition on the basis of religion, and after the Muslims had created the state of Pakistan, a spirit of militant revivalism among the Hindus was not an impossible thing. An aggressive Hinduism was likely to influence Indian nationalism in a different direction. With critical forces operating in the mind of a new nation, Nehru had to devote himself to directing Indian nationalism towards a more universal aspect. Within a short time a broader philosophy of nationalism triumphed over communalism and religious fanaticism; this in

---

[1] *DI*, X, 495.
[2] *Speeches* I, 123, Address at Aligarh, January 24, 1948.

turn was directed towards the concept of internationalism. Describing the failings of nationalism he said in April 1950:

'Nationalism, of course, is a curious phenomenon which at a certain stage in a country's history gives life, growth, strength and unity but, at the same time, it has a tendency to limit one, because one thinks of one's country as something different from the rest of the world. The perspective changes and one is continuously thinking of one's own struggles and virtues and failings to the exclusion of other thoughts. The result is that the same nationalism, which is the symbol of growth for a people, becomes a symbol of the cessation of that growth in the mind. Nationalism, when it becomes successful, sometimes goes on spreading in an aggressive way and becomes a danger internationally. Whatever line of thought you follow, you arrive at the conclusion that some kind of balance must be found.'[1]

Undesirability of National Isolation

A prominent defect of nationalism everywhere in the world, Nehru thought, was that almost every country believed that it had some special dispensation from Providence, that it was of the chosen people or race and that others, whether they were good or bad, were somewhat inferior. This feeling stood in the way of internationalism, and it was likely to be removed only by a proper understanding of other countries. For long he had believed in the merit of judging countries and peoples through personal contacts, because, 'If we do not personally know the people of a country we are apt to misjudge them even more than otherwise, and to consider them entirely alien and different.'[2]

Even personal contact among individuals of differing policies or principles was a desirable thing, especially when they belonged to rival or opposing countries. At a time in 1935 when Nehru's feeling ran high against certain British politicians so as to make him think that 'It is not easy to shake hands with a person who is endeavouring to strangle you', he wrote to one of them, Lord Lothian, that 'It is always a pleasure to meet people who open out new avenues of thought and help one to see a little more than the

[1] *Speeches* II, 361, April 9, 1950.
[2] *DI*, I, 21-2.

tiny corner of the world which is the average person's mental beat'. Though he could not think it possible at that time that conflicts could be charmed away or the prejudices and interests removed merely by friendly contact, yet he said: 'The pleasantest of smiles does not get over these ingrained prejudices and the varying world-outlooks that they produce. Still, the attempt must be made to cultivate friendly contacts for without them the world would be a drearier place even than it is.'[1]

Getting to know different peoples through personal contacts as well as trying to understand their viewpoints almost became a conviction with Nehru. This, among others, developed his faith in the cause of internationalism greatly. Referring to an earlier period, Vallabhbhai Patel, the deputy premier of India, said that Nehru's 'trip to foreign countries necessitated by the ailment of his wife raised his conception of Indian nationalism to an ethereal international plane. That was the beginning of that international phase of his life and character which has throughout been noticeable in his approach to internal and world problems. Ever since, Jawaharlal has never looked back.'[2]

Nehru thought that the isolation of any country was both undesirable and impossible. Force of circumstances made him in India act and think on the nationalist plane. This he felt was inevitable for all Indians wherever they lived. But at the same time he wanted them to develop 'the international habit of mind' as well as 'to develop contacts with other countries and peoples'. Thinking in terms of preparing for 'a big part to play in the future', Nehru declared in June 1937:

'Nationalist as I am in regard to Indian freedom, I do not look upon contacts with other peoples from a narrow nationalist viewpoint. My very nationalism is based on an internationalism, and I am very conscious of the fact that the modern world, with its science and world trade and swift methods of transport, is based on internationalism. No country or people can isolate themselves from the rest of the world, and if they attempt it, they do so at their peril and the attempt is bound to fail in the end.'[3]

The future of his own country that took shape in his mind

---

[1] *Letters*, 128, Nehru to Lord Lothian, December 9, 1935.
[2] *Birthday Book*, p. xxviii, Vallabhbhai Patel, October 14, 1949.
[3] *Essays* III, 184, 'Indians and Ceylonese in Malaya', June 2, 1937.

before independence was one of intimate co-operation, politically, economically, and culturally, between India and the other countries of the world. He believed that isolation meant backwardness and decay. Emerson, more than a hundred years ago, warned his countrymen in America not to imitate or depend too much culturally on Europe. He even said that it was for the want of self-culture that the superstition of travelling retained its fascination for educated Americans. To Nehru, the world of Emerson had changed and old barriers were breaking down; life was becoming more international. He therefore wanted his people to play their part in that coming internationalism and, for that purpose, to travel, meet others, learn from them and understand them. It was India's way in the past to welcome and absorb other cultures. 'That is much more necessary today,' wrote Nehru in the *Discovery*, 'for we march to the one world of tomorrow where national cultures will be intermingled with the international culture of the human race. We shall therefore seek wisdom and knowledge and friendship and comradeship wherever we can find them, and co-operate with others in common tasks, but we are no suppliants for others' favours and patronage. Thus we shall remain true Indians and Asiatics, and become at the same time good internationalists and world citizens.'[1]

The utility of outer contact seemed to him so apparent that not only he himself practised it when Prime Minister, but he wanted other leaders, and even people in general, to practise it as widely as possible. He felt that if a country was consumed with hatred and fear, its mind was clogged and naturally it could not think straight. This led him to advise even the biggest world powers to remove hatred and fear by mutual contact and understanding. In November 1956, he spoke in the Indian Parliament:

'I say with all respect that in the United States there is no clear thinking about Russia just as there is no clear thinking in Russia about the United States, because the minds of both are clogged with indignation, with fear and hatred of each other. I have not the shadow of a doubt that if they come to know each other more—it does not matter whether they agree or not and they probably will not agree about many things—hatred and

[1] *DI*, X, 540.

misconceptions will go and they will realize one thing more than anything else, namely, that the other country, whatever it is, however wrong it may be in its opinion, is a living entity, a growing entity, has something new and worthwhile that has to be studied.'[1]

Internationalism on a Practical Plane

No sooner was India independent than Nehru thought of putting his internationalism on a more practical plane. 'We may talk about international good will and mean what we talk. We may talk about peace and freedom and earnestly mean what we say. But in the ultimate analysis a government functions for the good of the country it governs and no government dare do anything which in the short or long run is manifestly to the disadvantage of that country.'[2] Whether a country was imperialistic or followed socialist or communist principles, its foreign minister had to think primarily of the interests of that country. Nehru does not doubt this. But keeping in mind the advantages of India, he wanted nevertheless to follow an enlightened policy. One could think of the interests of one's own country regardless of other consequences or take a short distance view. Others might think of a long term policy, considering the interests of another country as important as those of their own. To Nehru, it seemed: 'The interest of peace is more important because if war comes everyone suffers, so that in the long-distance view self-interest may itself demand a policy of co-operation with other nations, goodwill for other nations, as indeed it does demand.' Therefore

'Every intelligent person can see that if you have a narrow national policy it may enthuse the multitude for the moment . . . but it is bad for the nation and it is bad internationally because you lose sight of the ultimate good and thereby endanger your own good. Therefore we propose to look after India's interests in the context of world co-operation and world peace, in so far as world peace can be preserved.'[3]

Nehru enjoyed a few practical advantages in working out his internationalism. As he himself realized, a greater advantage lay

[1] *Speeches* III, 45, Lok Sabha, November 20, 1956.
[2] *Debates* C.A. (Legislative), 1947, Vol. II, December 4, 1947.
[3] *Ibid.*

in the fact that India was not fettered by the past, by old enmities, old ties, historic claims, or traditional rivalries. Even against her former rulers there was no bitterness left. Thus, India, according to Nehru, came into the family of nations with no prejudices or enmities, ready to welcome and be welcomed. Inevitably, of course, as we have seen, she had to consider her foreign policy in terms of enlightened self-interest, but, at the same time, she brought to it a touch of her own idealism. From the beginning the aim was to continue idealism together with national interest. Even while preparing a national flag for independent India, her philosophy of internationalism was kept uppermost in mind. Nehru reminded others to think that the Asokan period in the history of India was essentially an international period; it was a period when India's ambassadors went abroad to far countries, not in the way of an Empire and imperially, but as ambassadors of peace and culture and goodwill. The wheel of Asoka was designed on the flag, and in the Constituent Assembly of India Nehru said:

'Therefore this Flag that I have the honour to present to you is not, I hope and trust, a Flag of Empire, a Flag of Imperialism, a Flag of domination over anybody, but a Flag of freedom not only for ourselves, but a symbol of freedom to all people who may see it. And wherever it may go—and I hope it will go far—not only where Indians dwell as our ambassadors and ministers but across the far seas where it may be carried by Indian ships, wherever it may go it will bring a message, I hope, of freedom to those people, a message of comradeship, a message that India wants to be friends with every country of the world and India wants to help any people who seek freedom.'[1]

The main objectives of India's international policy according to Nehru became: the pursuit of peace, not through alignment with any major power or group of powers, but through an independent approach to each controversial or disputed issue; the liberation of subject people; the maintenance of freedom, both national and individual; the elimination of racial discrimination; and the elimination of want, disease and ignorance which afflict

---

[1] *Debates* C.A., Vol. IV, No. 7, July 22, 1947.

the greater part of the world's population.[1] The day that India became free, Nehru gave the following message: 'To the nations and peoples of the world we send greetings and pledge ourselves to co-operate with them in furthering peace, freedom and democracy.'[2]

Internationalism versus Alignment

From the beginning Nehru began to impress upon others that to lead his country into any power-bloc would mean working against the real spirit of internationalism. He was asked frequently why India did not align herself with a particular nation or group of nations, and was told that because he had refrained from doing so he was sitting on the fence. Such warnings appeared meaningless to him. The policy he sought to pursue was not a negative and neutral policy, but one that was positive and vital and should be clear. He did not want to keep anything secret. To the nations of the world he said: 'We have no quarrel with any of you, we seek only your friendly co-operation in the great task of ensuring freedom and well-being to all the peoples of the world; we seek no domination or advantage over others, but we shall guard our own freedom at all costs and with all the strength in us.'[3] At times he felt that his voice was feeble, but he gained confidence from the thought that the message it conveyed was no feeble message. It had the strength of truth in it and therefore it should prevail.

There was no desire on his part to interfere in world affairs. His main stake was peace, to see that there was racial equality and that people who were still subjugated should be free. He did not like the idea that other people should interfere in the affairs of his country. If there was interference, whether military, political or economic, he was determined to resist it. Keeping these objectives clear, he looked at the world with a friendly approach. But in doing so, he knew, he was often likely to be misunderstood, because, as he observed, 'passions have been roused all over the world and sometimes each country thinks that if you are not

[1] *Writings* I, 339-40.
[2] *Speeches* I, 6, August 15, 1947.
[3] *Ibid*, 39-40, January 30, 1949.

completely lined up with it you are its enemy or opponent'.[1] It was unfortunate that people thought so, but for Nehru, he just could not help it. As for India, whatever the feeling elsewhere against her policy of non-alignment, that policy was considered as fundamental. Nehru did not see why India should act in one way or another, or why she should become a part of the manoeuvring which went on in the world. 'We have to keep aloof from that and at the same time develop the closest relations with all those countries.'[2]

Against the Idea of Supernational States

Well before the independence of India, Nehru was conscious of the position which she occupied in the world. She was one of the very few countries which had the resources and capacity to stand on their own feet. While thinking of the emergence of India as a strong united state, Nehru was of the opinion that she would develop herself as the centre of economic and political activity in the Indian Ocean area, in south-east Asia and right up to the Middle East. Her position had an economic and strategic importance in a part of the world which was going to develop rapidly in the future. G. D. H. Cole considered India to be itself a supernational area, and thought that she was destined to be the centre of a mighty supernational state covering the whole of the Middle East. However attractive such considerations were, Nehru did not favour the growth of such powerful areas in view of the harm it could do to the cause of internationalism. 'For my part,' he said in 1944, 'I have no liking for a division of the world into a few huge supernational areas, unless these are tied together by some strong world bond. But if people are foolish enough to avoid world unity and some world organization, then these vast supernational regions, each functioning as one huge state but with local autonomy, are very likely to take shape. For the small national state is doomed. It may survive as a cultural autonomous area but not as an independent political unit.'[3]

---

[1] *Ibid*, 242, March 8, 1949.
[2] *Ibid*.
[3] *DI*, X, 511.

Desire for Responsibility but not Leadership

Similarly, for the cause of internationalism, Nehru does not believe in the theory of leadership by one country of others. When India became free, by virtue of her position and resources, she had to think of some neighbouring countries and their problems, and had to raise her voice for them, or on behalf of them. Because of various factors a certain special responsibility was cast on her which she had to shoulder. This responsibility, according to Nehru, was not necessarily for leadership, but for taking the initiative and helping others to co-operate. He pointed out: 'Some people talk rather loosely, and, if I may say so, rather foolishly, of India becoming the leader of this or the leader of that or the leader of Asia. Now, I do not like that at all. It is a bad approach, this business of leadership.'[1]

Foreign Policy on Broader Basis

Internationalism for its success demanded from all nations a foreign policy based on broader views. If countries thought only of their own interests and conducted their foreign relations in furthering that end, there was always a possibility of such interests clashing with world interests. Moreover, the days were over when the foreign policy of any country could be confined only to a few countries in close proximity or with which interests were closely connected. In view of this, Nehru did not want to relate the foreign policy of India merely to a few countries around her, but thought of practically every country in the world and took into consideration all possible areas of conflict, trade, and economic interest. Through the broader recognition of affairs he realized that if there was ever a conflict on a big scale anywhere in the world, it was apt to spread—'that war has become indivisible and, therefore, peace is indivisible'.[2] Considering world problems as something integrated, Nehru spoke to the Assembly of the United Nations in Paris, on November 3, 1948, thus:

'May I say, as a representative of Asia, that we honour Europe for her culture and for her advance in the civilization which it represents? May I say that we are equally interested in the solution

[1] *Speeches* I, 250, March 22, 1949.
[2] *Ibid*, 246.

of European problems; but may I also say that the world is some-what bigger than Europe, and you will not solve your problem by thinking that the problems of the world are mainly European problems. . . . It is a simple fact that we have to remember, because unless you have a full picture of the world before you, if you isolate any single problem in the world from the rest, you do not understand the world problem.'[1]

Nations and countries have their history, and history is most often a record of conflict, quarrel and war with others. If memories of wars and struggles are preserved by nations, international understanding becomes difficult. To Nehru, a country should not deny co-operation with another country simply because they had fought in the past, and thus carry the trail of its past action. Even while fighting with the British, when asked if he were anti-British he had said: 'We have grown beyond this anti-stage, I hope, and think of our national and international problems on broader and more fundamental lines. Why should I be anti-British, if by British is meant the British people? . . . But I am against im-perialism and empire, wherever they may exist, because I think they come in the way of the world's progress.'[2] With empire and imperialism gone from India, Nehru wanted to wash out the past with all its evils. He came forward to show a practical example of this by deciding to co-operate with the British in the develop-ment of Commonwealth relations. 'I wanted the world to see,' he said, 'that India did not lack faith in herself, and that India was prepared to co-operate even with those with whom she had been fighting in the past; provided the basis of co-operation today was honourable, that it was a free basis, a basis which would lead to the good not only of ourselves, but of the world also.'[3]

There was yet another difficulty in the way to co-operation among nations, arising out of ideological differences. The system of government was not the same everywhere, nor did all countries follow a uniform policy in the internal management of the life of their people. To assist the growth of internationalism Nehru believed in endeavouring to remove all walls and barriers of this kind which affected the mind and heart of nations. 'There is no

[1] *Birthday Book*, 10, Vide Anna Kamenky, March 6, 1949.
[2] *Essays* III, 182-83, 'A Question of Manners', June 1, 1937.
[3] *Speeches* I, 278, May 16, 1949.

reason why different countries having different political or social or economic systems should not co-operate in this way, provided there is no interference with one another and no imposition or attempt to dominate'—this is what Nehru emphasized to the Soviet people on a visit to Moscow.[1]

At times international affairs took a stronger turn with an element of dogmatic fervour—'something resembling that ordered division of "either you are with us, or you are against us".' To Nehru, this was a narrow approach which considered everything in terms of black and white, and which was somewhat like 'repeating that old, unfortunate bigoted approach of religion which brought about the wars of religion in the past, with not even the saving graces which religion sometimes had provided in the past'.[2] The entire attitude behind moralizing or crusading in relation to international problems appears to him as wrong. 'Why should I impose my view of religion or spirituality or anything else on the other person or on the other nation, except in so far as out of discussion, consultation, co-operation we adopt each other's ways?'[3]

The Danger of the Old Outlook

Believing in the widest international co-operation, Nehru advocated against the old outlook in politics which at one time dominated the policies of nations. On one occasion, during the debate on foreign affairs in the Indian Parliament, an honourable member quoted a dictum of Bismarck in support of his conclusion that India should consider her frontiers to be somewhere in East Africa, Malaya, Burma and various other distant places. To this Nehru replied that 'not only has Bismarck been long dead but his policies are still more dead'. He did not want nations to transport themselves to another century. If any country were to emulate Bismarck's policy, it was bound to fail. If India thought in terms of her frontiers extending thousands of miles away from India, other countries could equally think of their frontiers as existing in India, and immediately clashes were bound to occur. The nineteenth century outlook, according to Nehru, was the outlook of a

[1] *Speeches* III, 304, Statement at the Dynamo Stadium, Moscow, June 22, 1955.
[2] *Debates* H.P., 1953, Vol. VIII, Part II, September 17, 1953.
[3] *Talks*, 60.

few imperialist and expansionist European powers who were trying to spread over the world, in Africa, Asia, and elsewhere, sometimes coming into conflict with the peoples of those continents and at other times going to war with one another while trying to grab the world and divide it up among themselves. Those days were gone, and moreover there was no part of the world left at this time for any imperialist power to seize, though of course, according to Nehru, there still existed people with expansionist ambitions.[1] He laid emphasis on the factor of time and wanted to bear upon others that the foreign policy of nations was no longer like a game of chess played by superior statesmen sitting in their chancelleries; and it was no longer a matter, as in olden days, of siding with one power against another in return for some territorial possession or advantage.

Principles of International Behaviour
Nehru did not want to confine his internationalism merely to the sphere of idealism. He wanted to work it out in a practical field, devoting himself to influencing others towards his own line of thinking. In doing this he was conscious of various limiting factors. 'If a country talks bigger than it is, it brings little credit to itself.'[2] He advocated as much as he could practise, and instead of laying down maxims he concentrated on action. His faith in the cause was perhaps hardly doubted, and this was to an extent an advantage for him. As his reputation as a practical internationalist began to grow, he proceeded to lay down certain principles of international behaviour, calling upon others to adopt them. The 'Five Principles' which he put forward in recognition of the right of each country to fashion its own destiny were first accepted by the Government of China. The principles were: Respect for each other's territorial integrity and sovereignty; Non-aggression; Non-interference in each other's internal affairs; Equality and mutual benefit; and Peaceful co-existence. Subsequently these principles were accepted by Burma and Yugoslavia; and even the Soviet Union approved of them. They were further elaborated at the Bandung Conference and embodied

---

[1] *Speeches* II, 191-92, March 28, 1951.
[2] *Biblio*, 131, February 17, 1953.

in a declaration on world peace and co-operation. By 1955 more than thirty countries had accepted the principles in one form or another. 'I have no doubt,' said Nehru in 1955, 'that these principles of international behaviour, if accepted and acted upon by all countries of the world, would go a long way to put an end to the fears and apprehensions which cast dark shadows over the world.'[1] It was considered natural that while living in the gradually compressing world of today nations were likely at times to come into conflict of one kind or another. But what Nehru wanted was to spread the conception of a peaceful settlement of such disputes, and the idea of non-interference. There was nothing new about these ideas. 'No great truths may be new.' But, as he pointed out, it was true that an idea like non-interference required emphasis because there had been in the past a tendency for great countries to interfere with others, to bring pressure to bear, and to want these others to line up with them. 'I suppose that is a natural result of bigness,' he said. 'It has taken place throughout history.'[2]

The stress on non-interference of any kind, political, economic or ideological, according to Nehru, was an important factor, though he recognized the fact that it would not be wholly acted upon here and there. Any deviation from the principle, however, was considered by him as of little relevance because, in his analogy, if a law is made and it gradually influences the whole structure of life in a country, there may yet be some people who disobey it. But even those who do not accept it gradually come within its scope. What he wanted to advocate was the laying of faith in the ultimate objectives, no matter if petty and passing conflicts made their appearance.*

Ultimate Goal of Internationalism

Where should the philosophy of internationalism ultimately lead

---

* It is rather ironical that a few years later India and China, though they were the first to accept the Five Principles, faced each other on a border dispute of no small magnitude. Whatever the deeper significance of the dispute, it proved also to some extent the positive aspect of Nehru's internationalism. While the national temper in India rose very high, the Government while preparing for the eventualities did not rule out the possibility of peaceful negotiations. As for China, while initiating the dispute she professed again and again her faith in the spirit of the Five Principles.

[1] *Speeches* III, 303, Statement at Moscow, June 22, 1955.
[2] *Ibid*, 307, September 17, 1955.

nations? To Nehru the goal of internationalism is the world order at large. 'We have arrived at a stage in human affairs when the ideal of One World and some kind of a World Federation seem to be essential, though there are many dangers and obstacles in the way,' declared Nehru at the Asian Conference held in March 1947. He pleaded for that ideal and not for any grouping which came in the way of that larger world group.[1] The Asian nations were called upon by him to support the United Nations structure which was then painfully emerging from its infancy. It was only co-operation among nations which could make that larger ideal possible. People talked of the rights of individuals and nations; but Nehru reminded that every right carried an obligation. There had been far too much emphasis on rights and far too little on obligations; if obligations were undertaken, rights would naturally flow from them. With this in mind he proceeded to suggest a new approach to life, different from the competitive approach of the present time. In a broadcast speech to the United States of America from New Delhi in April 1948 he said:

'I have no doubt in my mind that World Government must and will come, for there is no other remedy for the world's sickness. The machinery for it is not difficult to devise. It can be an extension of the federal principle, a growth of the idea underlying the United Nations, giving each national unit freedom to fashion its destiny according to its genius, but subject always to the basic covenant of the World Government.'[2]

Nehru was troubled by prevailing fear everywhere. 'Today fear consumes us all—fear of the future, fear of war, fear of the people of nations we dislike and who dislike us.' That fear, he thought, might be justified to some extent. But fear was an ignoble emotion and led to blind strife. It was the duty of all thinking men to get rid of that fear, and to base their thoughts and actions on what was essentially right and moral, and it is only then that 'gradually the crisis of the spirit will be resolved, the dark clouds that surround us may lift and the way to the evolution of world order based on freedom will be clear'.[3]

[1] *Speeches* I, 299, Speech at Asian Conference, March 23, 1947.
[2] *Ibid*, 303, Broadcast to USA, April 3, 1948.
[3] *Ibid*.

O

Concern Over the Future of Humanity

Since the future of humanity depended on the success of internationalism, Nehru tried to evolve 'a sincere policy based essentially on goodwill and fellowship with other countries, with no ill will for any country'. 'I am quite convinced that in treatment of nations to one another, as in the case of individuals, only out of goodwill will you get goodwill and no amount of intrigues and cleverness will get you good results out of evil ways.'[1] In a systematic way he resolved the policy of his country in such a direction as to make her services available for decreasing international tension. 'But I do not go around offering them,' he said at Vienna in 1955. 'To do so would be undiplomatic. We help in an unobtrusive way wherever we can.'[2] His sincerity in the international cause was recognized by many small and big powers.* With a frank desire for friendship with all—'We are good friends of all, we have no enemies. If there are any we try to make friends'—Nehru worked with a feeling of sympathy for suffering people everywhere. 'Be it said to his credit,' said Gandhi at one time, 'that he (Jawaharlal) will consider it beneath his dignity to purchase freedom at the price of any other country. His nationalism is equal to his internationalism.'[3]

As Nehru began to pay more critical attention to world problems, his concern over the future of mankind grew deeper, and this in turn made his internationalism more avowed. In October 1951 he had declared:

'The world today is grim and cruel and the voice of calm and dispassionate reason has sunk to a whisper and is often drowned by strident and passionate cries. The proud culture and civilization, built up through ages of human effort, still endure in their outer semblance, but somehow they lose their inner content. Their values and standards fade away. The quest for truth and beauty and goodness gives place to a race for unabashed power. The tenderness and graciousness, the sanctity and dignity of

---

* In June, 1955, the University of Moscow paid the compliment that 'Mr Nehru has always spoken and continues to speak in defence of the principles of international law for the recognition of the sovereign right of large and small states for ceasing international tension of Asia and throughout the world.' *Biblio*, 333, June 22, 1955.

[1] *Debates* C.A., Vol. VIII, No. 1, May 16, 1949.
[2] *Biblio*, 319, June 27, 1955.
[3] *Birthday Book*, 127.

human life are replaced by callousness, vulgarity and naked force. Hate is propagated as a doctrine and politics and economics have assumed the form of dogmatic religion with all its fanaticism, which tolerates no heresies and persecutes those who differ from it.'[1]

This feeling being genuine, his service in the cause of internationalism tends to be realistic. To him, culture and civilization are not the monopoly of any one or more nations, and the hope of peace in the world is not just a pious aspiration but a vital necessity if civilized existence is to endure. And hence there should be faith in its triumph. It may be said that 'all this is impractical idealism, far removed from the cruel reality of today', but yet Nehru would believe in its ultimate success because, to him, 'it is the so-called reality that people talk about, that has brought great wars and might bring another and a greater one'.[2]

---

[1] Presidential Address, Indian National Congress, 57th Session, October 18, 1951.
[2] *Ibid.*

CHAPTER VIII

WAR AND PEACE

Nehru and his Time

'There is no peace for us in this turbulent twentieth century, a third of which has already passed with its full complement of war and revolution,'[1] wrote Nehru in 1933 when World War II was yet to come. World War II, like World War I, came and went, leaving behind grave problems. The horrors of two world wars and, even more so, the problems of peace that followed, left a deep impression on the mind of Nehru.

Nehru entered into active politics in the wake of World War I, and during the years which followed he studied the problems which faced the peacemakers. His writings and sayings during the late twenties and the early thirties strongly suggest his awareness of the period in which he lived; and from a much earlier time than the actual occurrence he anticipated the coming of World War II. As his understanding of international affairs grew deeper, he became more and more alive to the problems of peace which intervened between the two wars. Powerless during those years, he confined his feelings only to words, while resenting deeply his powerlessness to work. World War II rudely awakened him to the horrors of war but, being powerless, he became outspoken against those who could not save peace. After the war, when the problems of peace became more acute, Nehru found himself in a position, as Prime Minister of India, to exert himself for peace. It was Trotsky who had said, 'It is clear that the twentieth century is the most disturbed century within the memory of humanity. Any contemporary of ours who wants peace and comfort before everything else has chosen a bad time

[1] *WH*, Vol. II, 1495, Nehru to Indira, August 8, 1933.

to be born.'[1] Aware of such warnings, and conscious of world problems—of the shadow of war and revolution everywhere—Nehru decided to accept a philosophy of action in order to face these problems in a courageous manner, primarily in the cause of peace. Referring to the turbulent times in which he lived, he wrote in 1933:

'If we cannot escape from this inevitable destiny of ours, how shall we face it? Ostrich-like, shall we hide our heads from it? Or shall we play a brave part in the shaping of events and, facing risks and perils if need be, have the joy of great and noble adventure, and the feeling that our "steps are merging with those of history"?'[2]

With World War II coming to an end and India at the threshold of her independence, Nehru began to make a fresh appraisal of his time. 'We stand on the edge of a precipice,' he said in January 1947, 'and there are various forces which pull us on one side in favour of co-operation and peace, and on the other, push us towards the precipice of war and disintegration.'[3] Mindful of this he preferred to face his time as it was.

The Problems of Peace

It is only since 1947 that Nehru has found himself in a position to work for peace. But long before that he equipped himself with the knowledge of the probable dangers which threatened peace. The developments during the two wars served as good lessons. Well before the war, he came to regard the peace of the thirties as 'merely an interval between two wars', and this led him to apply himself to understand the real problems of peace. Peace could merely mean 'a preparation for war'; it could also mean to some extent 'a continuation of the conflict in economic and other spheres'. As he observed during the peace of the thirties, 'There is a continuous tug-of-war between the victors and the vanquished, between the imperialist powers and their colonial dependencies, between the privileged classes and the exploited classes. The war atmosphere, with all its accompaniments of violence and falsehood, continues in some measure therefore

[1] Trotsky quoted in *WH*, Vol. II, 1495.
[2] *WH*, Vol. II, 1495, Nehru to Indira, August 8, 1933.
[3] *Debates* C.A., Vol. II, No. 3, January 22, 1947.

even during so-called peacetime, and both the soldier and the civilian official are trained to meet this situation'.[1] He also saw during the period of peace how international law ceased to exist, how treaties and undertakings lost their value, and how gangster-ism prevailed unabashed among the nations.[2] These were the failings of peace which invited World War II, and when the war was about to be won, with the nazi power collapsing before the advancing armies in the east and west, Nehru in his prison began to wonder if the winning of war meant the winning of peace. He wrote in the *Discovery*:

'The problems of peace, more difficult than those of war, rise up to trouble men's minds and behind them lies the disturbing shadow of the great failure of the years that followed World War I. Never again, it is said. So they said also in 1918.'[3]

A Peep into the Future

For a moment, as Nehru thought of the prospects of peace while the war was ending, he felt somewhat pessimistic. He was still inside the prison, and the future of India was yet uncertain, as was also the future of most of Asia and Africa. What would the leaders of the victorious nations say, Nehru began to think, when they met together after their success in war? How was the future taking shape in their minds, and how far did they agree or differ among themselves? What other reactions would there be when the passion of war subsided and people tried to return to the 'scarce-remembered ways of peace'? Many problems and diffi-culties dominated his mind—the problems of a 'devastated and martyred Europe', and of Asia and Africa. 'What of all this and more? And what, above all, of the strange trick that fate so often plays, upsetting the well-laid schemes of our leaders?'[4]

He hoped the future to be different from the past, and feared that unless that was so fresh wars and disasters, on a more colossal scale, would follow World War II. But, as it appeared to him, those who had power and authority did not appear to be greatly

[1] *AB*, LXIII, 541.
[2] *Writings* II, Part I, Ch. 1, p. 25, January, 1938.
[3] *DI*, X, 511.
[4] *Ibid*, 512.

influenced by those considerations, or were themselves in the grip of forces beyond their control.

What surprised Nehru at the end of the war was the reversion to the old game of power politics on a gigantic scale in the biggest countries like America, Russia and England. That was considered by those countries as 'realism and practical politics'. But in this attitude Nehru saw the real danger to peace. He could not for a moment adjust himself to the idea that the statesmen of the world should conduct their foreign policy with the values of justice, fairness, and tolerance only to the extent that they contributed to, or did not interfere with, the power objective. The idea that the values of justice, fairness, and tolerance should be used instrumentally as moral justification for the quest of power, and that they should be discarded the moment their application brought weakness provoked him. Such strategy in world politics, the application of moral values to facilitate the attainment of power, the continuation of power politics on a vaster scale, and similar developments, made it difficult for Nehru to understand the real nature of the peace that was about to emerge from war. He did not dismiss the concept of 'realism' from political strategy 'for no nation can base its domestic or foreign policy on mere goodwill and flights of the imagination'. But 'realism' seemed strange to him when it ignored or refused to understand the hard facts of the present.

As the war was drawing to a close, Nehru perceived that threats to peace were also emerging from new developments. Before the war, Germany nursed the dream of world conquest, Russia feared a combination of her enemies, and England's national policy having been long based on a balance of power in Europe, was opposed to any dominating European power. There was always the fear of others, and that fear led to aggression and tortuous intrigues. The same kind of development in different forms seemed to have appeared while the war was ending. Nehru pointed out in 1944:

'An entirely new situation will arise after the present war, with two dominating world powers—the USA and the USSR—and the rest a good distance behind them, unless they form some kind of bloc.'[1]

[1] *Ibid*, 514.

The war came to an end, but the threats to peace became more apparent. Nehru began to draw world attention towards such threats.

To him it appeared that a major threat to peace came from the fear which nations entertained against each other, and which led to blind strife. Fear continued through the years, and as late as 1955 Nehru said, 'I believe that the vast majority of the people in every country hunger for peace, but fear of others often clouds their minds and makes them act in a different way. We must shed this fear and hatred, and try to cultivate the climate of peace. Out of war or threat of war or continuous preparation for war no peace can emerge.'[1]

The Crisis in the Spirit of Man

The years which followed the war were regarded by Nehru as representing an age of crisis. People lived continually in the midst of an international crisis; but perhaps a greater crisis confronted the world—the crisis in the spirit of man. Fascism and authoritarianism during the course of the war had greatly degraded man. The war was fought against this degradation of the spirit of man. To Nehru, the war was won, but the disease continued.[2] 'We have built up a great civilization,' he said in 1951, 'and its achievements are remarkable. It holds the promise of even greater achievements in the future. But while these material achievements are very great, somehow we appear to be slipping away from the very essence of civilization. Ultimately, culture and civilization rest in the mind and behaviour of man and not in the material evidence of it that we see around us. In times of war the civilizing process stops and we go back to some barbarous phase of the human mind. Are we speeding back to this barbarism of the mind?'[3]

This crisis of the mind always appeared as a potential threat to peace. Hatred, bitterness, and conflict, according to him, are almost more dangerous than active war. They are more dangerous because they degrade human beings, they make people frustrated and narrow-minded among other things. Basically, he believes that as in science every cause has its effect, so in human relations—

[1] *Speeches* III, 304, Statement at Moscow, June 22, 1955.
[2] Presidential Address, Indian National Congress, 57th session, October 18, 1951.
[3] *Speeches* II, 134, Broadcast from London, January 12, 1951.

whether national or international—every act one does, every
thought one thinks, has an effect. It may be very small. But if
the act or thought is evil it has a bad effect, whatever the motive
may be.

'Unfortunately, war, the fear of war, and the preparation for
war make one think almost a hundred per cent in an evil way;
full of hatred, of bitterness, of anger and in a spirit of destruction
which possibly harms the thinker more than the other side.'[1]

Ideologies and the Power Objective

Another grave threat to peace comes these days from the ideological conflict between nations or peoples. The two principal conflicting ideologies, one represented by communist Russia, and the
other by several of the western countries, presented problems;
though surely, according to Nehru, there is no justification for
saying that there can be only two ideologies in the world. However, as he points out, the above principal ideologies are, in a
sense, dominating the world today and are colliding with each
other. 'This is partly because behind these two ideologies there
is enormous military and economic power. But it is not the
ideology that dominates; but the power behind them.'[2]

The ideological conflict leading to the growth of a power cult
ultimately results in the production of nuclear and supernuclear
weapons. The piling up of armaments fosters a competitive
spirit among conflicting nations and consequently peace becomes
insecure. Further, ideological conflict divides the world into hostile camps pointing to unknown consequences. Nehru thinks that
it is the fear of so-called appeasement or the fear of appearing to
surrender to the ideology of the other that makes one speak in
terms of military power and to utter threats. The result is that
the other speaks in the same way. Thus a 'vicious circle' is created.

The Growth of Pacts and Alliances

A direct result of the ideological battle happens to be the forma-
tion of pacts and alliances. One hears frequently, Nehru says,
about pacts and military alliances in Europe, in the Middle East,

[1] *Conversations*, 103.
[2] *Ibid*, 74.

in South-East Asia and elsewhere. There are the two mighty powers, the United States of America and the Soviet Union; and some other powers such as the United Kingdom who are also big in varying degrees. Nehru understands, although he does not approve of, the military alliances between great powers. But he does not understand the 'military pacts and alliances between a huge giant of a power and a little pigmy of a country'. It does not have any meaning for him in a military sense. In this nuclear age the only countries that count, from the nuclear war point of view, are those countries which are in a position to use nuclear weapons. But an alliance with small countries means that the weak are becoming very much dependent on the strong. Nehru is sceptical towards the purpose and meaning of military alliances, and interprets them as threats to peace. 'There may be some individuals who might want war, but no country wants it. If that is so, what is the value of this policy of military alliances and armaments?'[1]

Pacts and alliances make governments military-minded, and the problems of the day are considered through military phraseology or military approaches. This tendency further makes the case of peace poorer. Besides, the judging of world affairs through the eyes and ears of soldiers is regarded by him as a dangerous thing. 'A soldier's idea of security may be one thing; a politician's or statesman's may be somewhat different. They have to be co-ordinated. When war comes, the soldier is supreme and his voice prevails almost, but not quite. But if the soldier's voice prevails in peacetime, it means that peace is likely to be converted into war.'[2]

Danger of the Cold War

The military approach leads people to think in terms of war, and the result is the so-called cold war. 'Well,' says Nehru, 'the cold war means thinking all the time in terms of war; in terms of preparation for war and the risk of having the hot war.'[3] The cold war approach seems to him utterly illogical, because a cold war has some meaning only as a prelude to a hot war. The cold war psychology has another danger. If the hot war is not to take place,

[1] *Speeches* III, 281, Speech in Lok Sabha, February 25, 1955.
[2] *Ibid*, 344, Lok Sabha, February 22, 1954.
[3] *Conversations*, 75.

some other methods have to be evolved. But the cold war approach prevents such methods being evolved. Speaking of the danger of the cold war, he goes on to say:

'The cold war creates a bigger mental barrier than brick walls or iron curtains do. It creates barriers of the mind which prevent the understanding of the other person's position, which divide the world into devils and angels.'[1]

Nehru wonders why there should be talk of cold war, rival camps and groupings, military blocs and alliances, all in the name of peace.[2] This is something contradictory, and to Nehru it means living in the dim twilight of the cold war, not knowing 'whether this will end in the black night of war or herald the dawn and sunlight of a fresh hope for humanity'.[3]

Faith of Powers in Strong Action

One more threat to peace arises from the idea of so-called strong action. The world is becoming enveloped by a mentality which might be called the military mentality. 'That is, statesmanship is taking a second place and is governed more by military factors than the normal factors which statesmen consider.'[4] Among many schools of thought and action in international affairs in recent times, Nehru discovered one which he terms the school of strong action. He criticizes it as 'a relic of the old days' when a warship or cruiser could be sent down to frighten into submission any small country which misbehaved. Ridiculing this idea in the present day, he points out that strong action might bring results when a very big country shows the mailed fist to a small country, but strong action does not go very far when the other country has also got a big fist. Equally, he ridicules the school which talks about 'negotiation through strength'. 'It is true that nobody will listen to you if you are weak. But as you develop your strength to negotiate, unfortunately the other party also goes on developing its strength.'[5]

---

[1] *Speeches* III, 45, Lok Sabha, November 20, 1956.
[2] *Ibid*, 310, November 20, 1955.
[3] Presidential Address, Indian National Congress, 59th Session, January 23, 1954.
[4] *Debates* H.P., 1953, Vol. I, Part II, February 18, 1953.
[5] *Speeches* III, 284, Lok Sabha, February 25, 1955.

Deeper Causes of War Analysed

While such were most of the immediate threats to peace which Nehru found operating after World War II, he also gave at different times serious thought to understanding some of the deeper causes which led to wars and conflicts. From his study of international affairs at an earlier period, he possessed a clear grasp of contemporary world events, and this understanding worked as a background to his analysis of the causes of wars. Outward or superficial causes leading to war might be many, and one can find in Nehru's writings and speeches of the pre-war years how he was aware of those developments which directly or indirectly paved the way for war. Keeping these apart, he also tried to analyse the more potential causes of war, as well as the deeper aspects of the human mind which brought about political conflicts in general.

Primitive Passion of the Individual Transferred to the Community

To Nehru, neither the growth of reason, nor the growth of a religious outlook, nor morality have checked in any way the human tendency to violence. No doubt, individuals have progressed and risen in the human scale, and probably there are far more of the higher-type individuals in the world today than at any previous period of history. Society as a whole has progressed. It has also begun to attempt the control of the primitive and barbarian instincts of men. 'But on the whole,' says Nehru, 'groups and communities have not improved greatly. The individual in becoming more civilized has passed on many of his primitive passions and vices to the community, and as violence always attracts the morally second-rate, the leaders of these communities are seldom their best men and women.'[1]

Thus, it is the rulers of states who, not being always the men in the highest plane of morality, incline towards actions which represent in a civilized form the primitive passions of men. In other words, Nehru would incline to trace the instinct for war in the very nature of human leadership.

Nehru's criticism is also focused towards the political 'realist' who does not understand that 'nothing is so changeable as human nature and society'. The realist's self-interest is far too limited

[1] *AB*, LXIII, 542.

by past myths and dogmas. Thus he too represents the same old passions, but of course in different forms. In the realist's mind, as Nehru would say:

'Religious forms and notions take permanent shape, social institutions become petrified, war is looked upon as a biological necessity, empire and expansion as the prerogatives of a dynamic and progressive people, the profit motive as the central fact dominating human relations, and ethnocentrism, a belief in racial superiority, becomes an article of faith and, even when not proclaimed, is taken for granted.'[1]

Cycle of Conflicts

National passions thus being more or less irrational, conflicts and violence operate as the deep-rooted factors of history. The most amazing thing which strikes Nehru is that, if one looks back the few decades which comprised the two wars, one finds the same cries—changing slightly with the changed situation—nevertheless, the same cries, the same approaches and the same arming on all sides and the like. One war may end, but the same conflicts continue and again the same preparation for war. Then comes another war. 'No body and no country wants war. As war becomes more and more terrible they want it still less. Yet some past evil or *karma* or some destiny goes on pushing people in a particular direction, towards the abyss and they go through the same arguments and they perform the same gestures like automatons.'[2]

The tendency to talk about war and of preparation for it goes on in a continuous process. Nehru wonders if men are fated to do this for all time. While addressing the General Assembly of the United Nations at Paris on November 3, 1948, he pointed out:

'The lesson of history, the long course of history, and more especially the lesson of the last two great wars which have devastated humanity, has been that out of hatred and violence only hatred and violence will come. We have got into a cycle of hatred and violence, and not the most brilliant debate will get you out of it, unless you look some other way and find some other means.'[3]

[1] *DI*, X, 515.
[2] *Speeches* I, 283, May 17, 1949.
[3] *Ibid*, 319, Address to United Nations General Assembly at Paris, November 3, 1948.

On occasions, Nehru would feel greatly disturbed by the complexity and irrationality of the age itself, and would regard the future as dark. A study of the times would sound in his mind notes of despair, and he would find events taking place one after another and the stream of events going on in an uninterrupted and unending manner. One seeks to understand a particular event by isolating it and looking at it by itself, as if it were the beginning and the end, the resultant of some cause immediately preceding it. Yet, to Nehru, it has no beginning and is but a link in an unending chain, caused by all that has preceded it, and resulting from the wills, urges, and desires of innumerable human beings coalescing and conflicting with each other, and producing something different from that which any single individual intended to happen. 'Those wills, urges, and desires are themselves largely conditioned by previous events and experiences, and the new event in its turn becomes another conditioning factor for the future. The man of destiny, the leader who influences the multitude, undoubtedly plays an important part in this process, and yet he himself is the product of past events and forces and his influence is conditioned by them.'[1]

Passion for Domination and Discrimination

There has always been a passion among nations to dominate others. This is a basically wrong approach and behind it lies the motive to arm. For while the nations pay homage to the goddess of peace in beautiful language, in reality they prepare for war. At a much earlier date Nehru declared, 'Peace can only come when the causes of war are removed. So long as there is the domination of one country over another, or the exploitation of one class by another, there will always be attempts to subvert the existing order, and no stable equilibrium can endure. Out of imperialism and capitalism peace can never come.'[2]

At one time he was surprised to hear from Lloyd George that there were 'Have-nots' amongst the great imperialist powers—'Have-nots' in the sense that they did not possess colonies to supply them with raw materials and provide sheltered markets

[1] *DI*, X, 456.
[2] *Essays* II, 24, 'Presidential Address to the National Congress, Lahore', December, 1929.

for their manufactured goods. Nehru saw in such a tendency 'the war-hunger' of the so-called 'Have-not' powers. He felt that whatever the immediate result of such tendencies might be, the ultimate result could hardly be doubted, which to him was the increase of rivalry between big powers leading to inevitable conflicts. This had been the history of the growth of modern imperialism, and as fresh colonial areas came under its domination, these conflicts increased. As he listened to Lloyd George, it struck him as very odd that Lloyd George should feel so keenly for the unhappy state of the 'Have-not' powers and yet ignore completely the colonial countries and their peoples. 'Have they no rights in the matter or no say in it? But even apart from the rights and the moralities, is it imagined that peace will be ensured and entrenched by a sharing of the booty by the imperialist Powers?'[1]

Nehru thought that so long as there were 'Haves' and 'Have-nots' frictions and conflicts were bound to continue. Moreover, it seemed to him a mockery to call powerful nations 'Have-nots' and ignore the real 'Have-not' countries and classes which were dominated and exploited. Nehru assailed those pacifists who desired ardently to prevent war by imagining that the way to bring it about was by satisfying the greed of certain big nations and by maintaining the *status quo*. These pacifists did not realize that it was that very *status quo* which produced ill will and conflict, and which was bound to lead to war. Struggle was inherent in the process where some classes were exploited for the benefit of the upper strata. 'The *status quo* has to go throughout the world before war goes and the causes of war.'[2]

In his own analysis Nehru regarded nazism and fascism as no sudden growths or accidents of history. They were interpreted as the natural developments of the past course of events, of empire and racial discrimination, of national struggles, of the growing concentration of power, of technological growth which found no scope for its fulfilment within the existing framework of society, and of the inherent conflict between the democratic ideal and a social structure opposed to it.[3] He saw in World War

[1] *Ibid*, 219, 'The Way to Peace', 1936.
[2] *Ibid*, 220.
[3] *DI*, X, 457.

II, which resulted from the above developments, nothing but an utter failure of human society.

Ignorance and Prejudice

Years after the war he came across instances when human dignity and freedom were outraged and the force of modern arms used to suppress peoples in order to gain political objectives. To him it appeared that the old colonial methods which belonged to a more unenlightened age were not dead, and could be revived and practised. In some parts of the world movements for freedom were crushed by superior might. The statesmen of the world used brave phrases to impress themselves and others, but their actions belied their noble sentiments, and so people lived in a world of unreality where profession had little to do with practice. That is why violence and hatred still dominated the world. The doctrine of the inequality of men and races was preached and practised. The democratic principles of dignity, equality and mutual respect were denied or ignored. To Nehru, the world war which devastated mankind was due to most of the above causes, but yet the causes continued even after the war. He ascribed this mostly to ignorance and prejudice.[1]

Futility of War

Aware of the causes of wars, Nehru was more conscious about the futility of wars. While describing the losses of World War I and the tremendous figures of human suffering in his letter to Indira in 1933, he pointed out the triumph of England, France, America, Italy and their smaller satellites by repeating the lines which the English poet Southey wrote on another and older victory:

> 'And everybody praised the Duke
> Who this great fight did win.
> But what good came of it at last?'
> Quoth little Peterkin.
> 'Why; that I cannot tell,' said he,
> 'But 't was a famous victory.'[2]

---

[1] *Speeches* III, 500-1, November 5, 1956.
[2] *WH*, Vol. II, 999, Nehru to Indira, April 1, 1933.

After World War II when he himself became greatly obsessed with the idea of peace, he came forward to lay greater stress on the futility of war. Some people thought that war was something which was unavoidable and, therefore, one should prepare for it not only in a military sense but also in a psychological sense. Nehru knew that no country dare take things for granted and not prepare for possible contingencies. He wanted every country to prepare for all possible dangers to its freedom and existence; what he denounced was the thinking in terms of the inevitability of war.

'It just does not matter who wins in the world war, because it will mean such utter catastrophe that for a generation or more everything that we stand for in the way of progress and advancement of humanity will be put an end to.'[1]

The futility of present-day wars became more real to Nehru when he keenly observed the consequences of some of the smaller wars, fought in more recent times. The Korean War, for example, was a glaring instance of such futility. 'After all the bloodshed and the suffering and the terrible destruction of Korea and her people,' said Nehru, 'it is a stalemate in Korea and neither side can say that it has won. That has a lesson for us. Wars nowadays tend to become stalemates—nobody wins . . . . a great war might go on indefinitely, with terrible destruction, no doubt, but with no ending and with nobody to end it.'[2]

Negative Aspects of War

The loss which wars cause to human life and to material prosperity is great. Even forgetting that, wars have certain negative aspects which affect humanity adversely. The world of today, according to Nehru, has achieved a great deal, but for all its declared love for humanity, it has based itself far more on hatred and violence than on the virtues that make man human. 'War is the negation of truth and humanity. War may be unavoidable sometimes, but its progeny are terrible to contemplate. Not mere killing, for man must die, but the deliberate and persistent propagation of hatred and falsehood, which gradually become the normal habits of the

[1] *Speeches* I, 243, Speech at Constituent (Legislative) Assembly, March 8, 1949.
[2] *Debates* H.P., 1954, Vol. II, Part II, March 23, 1954.

P

people. It is dangerous and harmful to be guided in our life's course by hatreds and aversions, for they are wasteful of energy and limit and twist the mind and prevent it from perceiving the truth.'[1]

The psychology of war consciously or unconsciously develops a brutal nature in man, about which Nehru feels much more worried. The nazi use of the word '*Brutalität*' and the idea behind it was something which it was difficult for him to conceive of. It was only the mentality of war or a preparation for it that could develop such feeling. Whether one was German, English or Indian, to Nehru the 'veneer of civilized conduct is thin enough, and when passions are aroused it rubs off and reveals something that is not good to look at'.[2] He pointed out how the Great War of 1914-18 brutalized humanity terribly, and how one saw the aftermath of that in the awful hunger blockade of Germany even after the Armistice.

War leads to a release from moral responsibility, and to the collapse of standards so laboriously built up by civilization. Successful war and aggression lead to a justification and continuance of such a tendency. 'Defeat results in frustration and the nursing of feelings of revenge. In either event, hatred and the habit of violence grow. There is ruthlessness and brutality, and a refusal even to try to understand the other's viewpoint. And thus the future is conditioned and more wars and conflicts follow with all their attendant consequences.'[3]

The leaders of men, who generally prepare for war, belong to an older generation, having already lived the greater part of their lives. To Nehru, it matters little what happens to a retiring generation, but it does matter a great deal what happens to hundreds of millions of others and to the world at large. More and more 'people in responsible positions' talk in terms of passion, revenge and retaliation; hundreds of millions all over the world are led to live under 'some kind of suspended sentence of death'.[4] Besides this, wars corrupt men, and by ever creating new problems, make the future ever more uncertain.[5]

[1] *DI*, X, 537-38.
[2] *AB*, L, 400.
[3] *DI*, X, 500.
[4] *Speeches* II, 133, January 12, 1951.
[5] *Ibid*, 165, October 3, 1950.

His Desire for Peace

Conscious of the dangers which wars brought upon mankind in the past, and of the possible consequences which a war may bring in the future, Nehru thought it better to devote himself to serving the cause of peace. In a single phrase he sums up the foremost issue in international affairs today—'peace or war'. If war comes, it will be an overwhelming and all-enveloping war, a war which will probably ruin the proud structure of modern civilization. His attitude towards the subject is 'one of earnestness and humility', though he finds no easy remedy. All he thinks he can do is to grope in the dim twilight for something that will, perhaps, prevent the twilight from becoming dark night. 'It is difficult to say whether or not we will succeed,' he says, 'but, in any event, it is our duty to try our utmost to avert a third World War.'[1] In this task of what he considers the preservation of peace and, indeed, of civilization itself, he calls upon other nations to lend their energies and find fellowship and strength in each other.[2]

Nehru remembers a point on which Gandhi laid stress always— the question of means and ends. Without entering into a metaphysical argument on the subject, he would say that 'surely if you demand peace, you must work for it peacefully'. Peace can be worked out only by peaceful means, but as he notes, 'quite a large number of countries, big and small, talk about peace in the most aggressive and warlike manner. . . . In fact, one might almost say that peace is now spelt WAR.'[3]

Peace has been said to be indivisible and to Nehru 'so also is disaster in this One World that can no longer be split into isolated fragments'.[4] If that is so he would not believe in sitting inactively or 'practising the policy of escapism'. 'You cannot escape. You have to face the problem and try to beat it and overcome it.'[5]

Certain Practical Considerations

While preparing himself for peace, Nehru does not want to

[1] *Biblio*, 211, Speech on Foreign Affairs in Parliament, December 6, 1950.
[2] *Ibid*, Broadcast from London, January 12, 1951.
[3] *Debates* H.P., 1953, Vol. I, Part II, February 18, 1953.
[4] *Debates* C.A., Vol. V, No. 1, August 14, 1947.
[5] *Ibid*, Vol. VIII, No. 2, May 17, 1949.

proceed very far in his idealism, leaving behind practical considerations for the defence of a country or the preparation for eventualities. One has to achieve freedom and to defend it. One has to meet aggression and to resist it, and the force employed must be adequate to the purpose. But even when preparing to resist aggression the ultimate objective of peace and reconciliation must never be lost sight of, and heart and mind must be attuned to this supreme aim, and not swayed or clouded by hatred or fear.[1]

Much as he hates war, if war comes in spite of one's own self, Nehru would like to face it in a determined manner. During World War II, when the prospect of a Japanese invasion of India became imminent, he felt in a sense attracted to the coming of war. For he wanted a tremendous shake-up, a personal experience for millions of people, 'which would drag them out of that peace of the grave that Britain had imposed'. This war was not of his seeking, but, as he said, 'since it had come, it could be made to harden the fibre of the nation and provide those vital experiences out of which a new life might blossom forth. Vast numbers would die, that was inevitable, but it is better to die than to live a miserable hopeless life. Out of death, life is born afresh, and individuals and nations who do not know how to die, do not know also how to live. "Only where there are graves are there resurrections".'[2]

Thus, Nehru's attitude to war is not purely negative. After the independence of India, he followed a policy which may be described as a policy of strength without offence. If war comes, it comes, and it has to be faced. To some extent it has to be provided for and all the consequences of war have to be accepted. His policy primarily aims at avoiding war or preventing war. Regarding this he said:

'The prevention of war may include providing for our own defence . . . but that should not include challenges, counter-challenges, mutual cursings, threats, etc. These certainly will not prevent war, but will only make it come nearer. . . .'[3]

[1] Biblio, 154, In United Nations World, 1951.
[2] DI, IX, 443-44.
[3] Speeches I, 255, March 22, 1949.

Pacifism Defined

Several times Nehru comes forward to define the pacifism of the type he believes and upholds. The people who think that his policy is 'a kind of passive negation or is an inane policy', appear to Nehru to be mistaken. He would argue that this has never been his idea on the subject, and that his is a positive and definite policy 'to strive to overcome the general trend towards war in people's minds'.[1] 'I am not a pacifist,' he declared in 1951. 'We have to protect ourselves and to prepare ourselves for every contingency. We have to meet aggression and evils of other kind. To surrender to evil is always bad. But in resisting evil, we must not allow ourselves to be swept away by our own passions and fears and act in a manner which is itself evil. Even in resisting evil and aggression, we have always to maintain the temper of peace and hold out the hand of friendship to those who, through fear or for other reasons, may be opposed to us.'[2]

Nehru had been asked, supposing an ideology became so aggressive that it foreshadowed physical aggression, what he would do. To this his answer was simple—resistance whatever the consequences. Referring to Hitler's invasion of Czechoslovakia, he once said: 'I happened to be in Czechoslovakia in 1938; just on the eve of Hitler's coming. I just could not reconcile myself to Czechoslovakia submitting to what happened.'[3] He recognized, of course, how very difficult it was for Czechoslovakia to resist Hitler's Germany. But, in any case, Nehru is not a pacifist in the sense that he would like to see any country coming under a demoralizing psychological atmosphere on account of the impending danger. He never rules out the possibility that 'under certain circumstances one has to fight'.*

'I can imagine conditions in India when we may have to fight. Why, after all, do we keep an Army, and Air Force and a Navy?

---

* Nehru points out that even Gandhi, who was a great pacifist, always said that it is better to fight than to be afraid. It is better to indulge in violence than to run away. He meant that one must not surrender to evil, to the basic evil, and that one must preferably fight in a peaceful way. If one cannot do that then one should fight in the military way. Nehru regards all this as theory, but believes that it does help to influence thought and action. Even the theory, he says, has to be adapted.

[1] *Debates* C.A., Vol. VIII, No. 2, May 17, 1949.

[2] *Speeches* II, 134-35, January 12, 1951.

[3] *Conversations*, 79.

. . . We keep them because there is an odd possibility of their being used.'[1]

But he would point out at the same time that when one thinks in terms of world conflict, and if one comes to the conclusion that conflict has become so dangerous for the world that it has to be ruled out, then one has to think of the alternative.

Nature of Neutralism

Like his pacifism, Nehru's neutralism is also based on practical considerations. He is not neutral in a passive or negative sense. He pleads for, and endeavours to practise, a binding faith in peace, and in order to ensure it he wants to co-ordinate his thought and action in that direction. But he makes it clear that he is neither blind to reality nor is he prepared to acquiesce in any challenge to the freedom of man from whatever quarter it may come. His policy is emphatic.

'Where freedom is menaced or justice threatened or where aggression takes place, we cannot be and shall not be neutral.'[2]

At times he argues that the word 'neutrality' is not a correct word with which to describe his policy. In his explanation, neutrality can normally only be used as opposed to belligerency in time of war. In time of peace the question does not arise—unless one is always thinking in terms of war. His policy he describes simply as this: 'We wish to judge every issue on its merits and the circumstances then prevailing, then decide what we consider best in terms of world peace or our other objectives. Repeatedly we have in the UN or elsewhere voted or encouraged a certain policy that was liked by some nations, disliked by others, and vice versa.'[3] He is not prepared to adopt a policy or oppose a country merely for the sake of being against that country. A policy is not formulated on presupposed notions against a particular country or group of countries, but on the judgement of the merits of any particular question.

In the present-day world, the classical forms of neutrality—

[1] Conversations, 80.
[2] Biblio, 149, An address to the East and West Association, the Foreign Policy Association, the India League of America and the Institute of Pacific Relations, New York, October 19, 1949.
[3] Talks, 52.

like Switzerland's—based on the guarantee of stronger powers, appears to Nehru as not very meaningful. 'In practice,' he says, 'there can be now no guarantee of the old type, unless it is a guarantee not to have war. A guarantee which says that there will be a war, except in your country, has no meaning today when war is world-wide.'[1] In view of this he pleads for the guarantee which should mean the avoidance of war, and of interference with any country. He lays special emphasis on the guarantee against 'interference', because interference might lead to war. When he speaks of interference he means also ideological interference. Neutrality should be viewed in the light of such matters, and not merely through guarantees.

'. . . if two powerful countries like the Soviet Union and the United States would just say that we guarantee the neutrality of India, or Burma . . . well, really it has no meaning to me in the present context. If there is no war, well and good. But if there is a war, no guarantee will remain effective. It is better to avoid war.'[2]

Positive Approach to Peace

Keeping the practical aspects of the world situation in mind, Nehru attempted a definite approach to the question of peace. Without claiming to influence world affairs greatly, nor having the desire to do so, he nevertheless feels that 'fate and circumstance have cast a certain responsibility' upon him to play some part in the whirlpool of world politics. 'We cannot easily escape this responsibility. The burden has to be shouldered to the best of our ability. In doing so, we have always to remember the main objectives for which we stand, and the principles that have governed our activities, whether in the past or in more recent times. It would be a misfortune indeed, if, either from passion or fear or for some temporary present advantage, we deviated from those principles and objectives and betrayed tomorrow for an uncertain today. Therefore, it is our firm intention to continue this policy which is the pursuit of peace and unfailing effort to maintain friendly relations with all other countries.'[3] Peace in

[1] *Conversations*, 81.
[2] *Ibid*, 81-2.
[3] *Debates P.I.*, 1951, Vol. VIII, Part II, February 12, 1951.

his view is not merely abstention from war but an active partici-
pation in international relations towards that objective. He
attempted simultaneously several methods of achieving his
purpose. Whatever the criticism against his policy or policies, he
followed certain principles consistently during the years following
his accession to power. After about eight years of an active approach, he could enumerate his work by saying that his policy
had been 'appreciated by many countries', and that some countries
of Asia, for their own reasons, had followed a similar policy.
'Even countries which have not followed it have begun to
appreciate our policy. We are following it because we are convinced that it is the right policy. We would follow it even if
there was no other country in the world that followed it.'[1] It was
not a question of balancing considerations and sitting on the fence,
so contradicting those who seemed to think that way, but it was a
positive policy and he followed it with conviction and faith.
Several fundamentals may be traced underlying this positive peace
policy of Nehru.

Lessening of Tension
The world at the present time is a changed world on account of
the progress of science and technology, and Nehru finds in its
wake the changing of the very thinking of men about themselves
and the world. 'Even conceptions of time and space have changed
and vast expanses open out for us to explore the mysteries of
nature and to apply our knowledge for the betterment of humanity.' Science and technology have further given men great power
which can be used for the good of all, or for self-destruction. In
such a changing world the question of peace becomes one of
paramount importance; and Nehru desires to achieve this through
the lessening of international tension. For this he advocates the
solution of problems by the methods of negotiation, and by
establishing a growing co-operation among nations in various
ways, such as cultural and scientific contacts, by an increase in
trade and commerce, and by the exchange of ideas, experience and
information. In brief, he pleads for the peaceful co-operation of

---

[1] *Speeches* III, 283, Lok Sabha, February 25, 1955.

different countries for the common good and elimination of war.[1]

Enlarging the Area of Peace

Nehru endeavoured to enlarge the area of peace in the face of rapidly expanding spheres of physical and ideological hostilities. '. . . India, in so far as it has a foreign policy, has declared that it wants to remain independent and free of all these blocs and that it wants to co-operate on equal terms with all countries. It is a difficult position because, when people are full of fear of each other, any person who tries to be neutral is suspected of sympathy with the other party.'[2] But when difficulties were balanced against considerations for peace, the former could be preferred even at risks.* Any kind of major aggression was likely to lead to a world war. Whether aggression took place in a small country or a big one, it was likely to upset the unstable balance in the world, and was therefore likely to lead to war. The real problem was that either of the major parties, communist and non-communist, were afraid that if any of the smaller or non-committed states linked up with, or were coerced into joining, one group, it would be to the disadvantage of the other. 'For instance,' said Nehru in 1955, 'suppose countries like Laos and Cambodia were overwhelmed and drawn into the sphere of China, the countries on the other side would naturally be frightened. On the other hand, if Laos and Cambodia became hostile to China and could be used as bases for an attack on China, naturally China would object to it very strongly.' Nehru tried to find a way out of such difficulties. 'Either you have war to decide who is stronger, or you place Laos, Cambodia and all the Indo-China States more or less outside the spheres of influence, outside the alignments, and outside the military pacts of the two groups, so that both could feel, at least to some extent, secure in the knowledge that these Indo-China States were not

* In December 1947 Nehru pointed out: 'We have sought to avoid these foreign entanglements and joining one bloc or the other. *The natural result has been that neither of these big blocs looks with favour on us.*' Debates C.A. (Legislative), 1947, Vol. II, December 4, 1947.
[1] *Ibid*, 303-4, June 22, 1955.
[2] *Debates* C.A., Vol. II, No. 3, January 22, 1947.

going to be used against them. There is no other way out.'[1]

Extending the above arguments Nehru went on to advocate that the only way to avoid conflicts was to accept things more or less as they were. No doubt many things required to be changed, but no one should think of changing them by war. He pleaded that by enlarging the area of peace, that is, of countries which are not aligned to this group or that, but which are friendly to both, the chances of war could be reduced. He had further explained:

'People talked about a third force and all that. I venture to point out that it has no meaning, and no logic, there is no force in it. You may have the third force or the fourth force, but it is no force, because it is all created out of nothing. But I do say, that it is desirable to have an area where peace might, perhaps, subsist, even if war was declared. That would be good, of course, to the countries there, but would be good for the world too, because that area would exercise some influence, when a crisis came, on avoidance of war. Also, if by some mischance, war came with all its terror, if a large area is outside the scope, it may play a useful role, even afterwards, in bringing about peace.'[2]

Against Armament

Future peace largely depends on the problem of armament, and Nehru hopes to perform 'a very important task' in that direction. According to him, the lessening of tension would lessen the burden of all the big countries, and relieve their taxpayers, and would result in the lessening of the burden of armaments.[3] In reality it is difficult—almost impossible—for any country to disarm unilaterally. But it should be bilateral, or multilateral.

'Everybody should disarm. That is the essence of the question of disarmament today; because if war is ruled out—as it apparently is—there is just no other way out—anyway, logically speaking. Ruling out war means settling a problem by means other than war. And if all the parties concerned disarm—proportionately, I mean—then one's fear of the other does not arise, because the situation remains much the same from the military point of view.'[4]

[1] *Speeches* III, 282-83, Lok Sabha, February 25, 1955.
[2] *Debates* H.P., 1953, Vol. X, Part II, December 23, 1953.
[3] *Conversations*, 84.
[4] *Ibid.*

He knows that this is difficult to arrive at, but yet wants to face the difficulties. Repeatedly he had been asked by others to pay greater attention to armaments in India. But, concentrating only on a stronger defence of his country, he had not gone as far as to join the race for armaments. 'The right approach to defence,' according to Nehru, 'is to avoid having unfriendly relations with other countries,'[1] and he has gone on to cultivate friendly relations with other countries by spreading the feeling that 'no quarrel is big enough for war to be required to settle it'. Off and on he made it clear to his neighbours that India shall use force only in her defence and that she should not provoke war, or start a war, or adopt any aggressive tactics in regard to a war.[2] Pointing to the dangers of armament Nehru once quoted an ancient saying before two of his distinguished foreign guests, Gamal Abdel Nasser and Sardar Muhammad Naim, that 'those who live by sword will perish by the sword'.[3]

Against Nuclear Weapons

With regard to nuclear weapons, Nehru's policy is firm. About two years after the independence of India, he was speaking in the Congress of the United States. 'As I said, we have no atom bomb. But, if I may say so, we rejoice in not having the atom bomb.'[4] A little while later he commented on President Truman's decision to make the hydrogen bomb by saying: 'If you have come to the conclusion that the world is a pretty bad show, then let the hydrogen bomb put an end to the hydrogen bomb.'[5]

To Nehru, the development of the thermonuclear bomb has changed the whole picture of fighting in modern times. To think of war, therefore, in this nuclear age 'is insanity'. He wants others to realize that a war is fought to achieve certain results, not to bring ruin on oneself. But war today will bring ruin to every country involved. It is irrelevant if one country has a few more bombs than the other because even the country that has less has reached saturation point; that is, it has enough with which to

[1] *Speeches* III, 41, Lok Sabha, March 21, 1956.
[2] *Ibid*, 382, Lok Sabha, July 26, 1955.
[3] *Biblio*, 330, April 15, 1955.
[4] *Speeches* II, 112, Washington D.C., October 13, 1949.
[5] *Biblio*, 141, February 13, 1950.

cause infinite damage to the other country. Saturation point is the stage of mutual extermination. Since that is so, 'the only way out is to prevent war, to avoid it'.[1]

The nuclear age, according to the interpretation of Nehru, has changed the entire world diplomacy. Alliances and pacts have little value in nuclear warfare. Threats through military pacts have become obsolete. With regard to peace, the significance of nuclear power has led him to think of the beginning of a new age in human history. Nuclear energy as a vast source of power is considered by him 'even more important than the coming in of wars and the like'. 'The wars may be forgotten. Even great world wars may come and go and bring enormous destruction in their wake. But we are on the verge, I think, of a tremendous development in some direction of the human race.'[2] He hopes for the utilization of this energy for peaceful purposes, for the development of human life and happiness and not for war and hatred.

Non-aggression and Non-interference

The dangers of war having grown stupendous, Nehru concerned himself with the preservation of peace by constantly advocating the policy of non-aggression and non-interference by one country in the affairs of another. He chose the path of non-alignment in any military or like pact or alliance. 'In our thoughts, in our proposals and our policies,' he claimed, 'we have endeavoured to adhere to a non-violent approach and our basic policy of non-alignment and non-partisanship.'[3] Upholding the principle that each country has the right not only to freedom but also to decide its own policy and way of life, he emphasized the necessity for the growth of tolerance and peaceful co-existence. Once it is recognized that war is no solution, 'then you have to co-exist, you have to understand, you have to be restrained and you have to deal with each other. If you reject co-existence, the alternative is war and mutual destruction.'[4]

It may be said that, in carrying out his policy of non-aggression, Nehru has rather gone to the extent of even sacrificing India's own

[1] *Speeches* III, 282, Lok Sabha, February 25, 1955.
[2] *Debates* C.A. (Legislative), 1948, Vol. V, April 6, 1948.
[3] Presidential Address, Indian National Congress, 59th Session, January 23, 1954.
[4] *Speeches* III, 273, Lok Sabha, September 29, 1954.

interests. Goa, although a part of India, continues to be under foreign domination. It has been pointed out by certain Indian leaders that the fight for Goa could be finished in a day or two, even perhaps in a few hours. Nehru himself knew that if there were a fight it would be over in two or three days, irrespective of the number of Portuguese troops. Pressure had been brought upon him that 'after all it will be a minor fight, and that since Goa is small, it will be a petty affair'. But Nehru continued to emphasize what he called 'a matter of principle'. Once, replying to a debate on the subject in the Indian Parliament in 1955, he said:

'If the points of the Opposition Members were conceded, it would boil down to this: that the big countries of the world have a right to bring the smaller countries under their sway. That is a wrong stand. Once we accept the position that we can use the Army for the solution of our problems, we cannot deny the same right to other countries. It is a question of principle.'[1]

In this connection it may also be pointed out that Nehru is opposed to the idea of a 'limited war' because it ignores the fact that the world is much more of a unit today, and is far more in favour of peace than it ever has been before. He does not say that it is impossible for any country to have a limited war. It may yield results; in essence a small war may not be the same as a big war. But yet he discounts it because 'a small war helps also to keep up the atmosphere which creates a big war'. Moreover, he would point out that formerly if evil triumphed it triumphed in a small corner of the world; today if it triumphs it might engulf the whole world. When he thought of the Korean struggle, he did not think of Korea so much as of the 'giant shadows' that fell over that unfortunate land. He thought of the possibilities of a world conflict and of the consequences that might ensue from it. 'As we face the world situation today,' he said in August 1950, 'it looks as though the fate of the world seems to hang in regard to war and peace by a thin thread which might be cut down by a sword or blown off by a gun.'[2] Similar apprehensions continued through subsequent years on account of other international developments.

[1] *Ibid*, 391, Lok Sabha, September 17, 1955.
[2] *Debates* P.I., 1950, Vol. V, Part II, August 3, 1950.

Quest for Balance in Favour of Peace

With a critical mind towards those who 'talk of security and behave in a way which is likely to put an end to all security', and who 'talk of peace and think and act in terms of war', Nehru posed the question: 'Are we so helpless that we cannot stop this drift towards catastrophe?', and answered:

'I am sure that we can, because vast masses of people in every country want peace. Why, then, should they be driven by forces apparently beyond their control in a contrary direction?'[1]

The idea that one could solve problems with 'hammers, bayonets and bombs' appeared as utterly wrong, and he became more convinced of this than of anything else, that 'no problem is solved by the bomb and the bayonet and tanks'.[2] A kind of intellectual determination is found in Nehru's thought inspiring him to evolve a new balance. 'We have had enough of war and hatred and violence,' he said in a message to the Mayor of Nagasaki on the anniversary of the dropping of the second atomic bomb on that city. 'Let us turn our minds to the ways of peace and co-operation.'[3] For long he wondered how people failed to learn the lesson of the last two great wars and started talking of a third world war. To him it is the question of having enough wisdom to prevent wars. There are rich stores of knowledge and there are all kinds of institutions for imparting that knowledge, but Nehru wonders whether the world is really growing in wisdom. In flights of fancy he would be reminded of what a great Greek poet said long ago:

'What else is Wisdom? What of man's endeavour,
Or God's high grace, so lovely and so great?
To stand from fear set free, to breathe and wait;
To hold a hand uplifted over Hate;
And shall not Loveliness be loved for ever?'[4]

On practical missions he tried to pitch the camp of peace and goodwill 'which should include as many countries as possible and

[1] *Speeches* II, 133, January 12, 1951.
[2] *Debates* P.I., 1950, Vol. V, Part II, August 4, 1950.
[3] *Biblio*, 328, August 9, 1955.
[4] *Speeches* II, 165, October 3, 1950.

which should be opposed to none'. The only alliance he sought 'is an alliance based on goodwill and co-operation'. 'If peace is sought after, it has to be by the methods of peace and the language of peace and goodwill.'[1] He requested the nations of the world to pay heed to the 'collapse of conscience and good morals' which could be seen all around, for unless heed was taken all the fine ideals of men would be shattered into nothingness.

As the danger of modern war became more and more evident, an ever increasing number of states decided to remain non-committed to the power-motives of the biggest powers. Few of the small countries wished to take risks with power-politics, thereby exposing themselves to nuclear war. An increasing tendency towards peaceful negotiation could also be noted in international politics. While helping to develop such trends, Nehru, to some extent, could think of an emerging force of peace. For example, in the Political Committee of the Asian-African Conference at Bandung, he exhorted the participants that it was within the power of Asian-African peoples to tilt the balance in favour of peace.[2]

Optimism for Triumph of Peace

On many occasions Nehru appears a pessimist when he thinks of war, but ultimately he emerges an optimist with hope for the triumph of peace. In the midst of World War II he hoped that out of the crucible, wherein so much was melting, something finer would emerge, something that would retain all the great achievements of humanity and add to them what they lacked. He was troubled that repeated and widespread wars damaged not only material resources and human lives, but the essential values that gave meaning to life. 'Was it that,' he thought, 'in spite of astonishing progress in numerous directions and the higher standards, undreamed of in previous ages, that came in its train, our modern highly industrialized civilization did not possess some essential ingredient, and that the seeds of self-destruction lay within it?'[3]

As he worked with hope, he evolved his own ideas regarding a

[1] *Speeches* III, 310, November 20, 1955.
[2] *Biblio*, 80, April 22, 1955.
[3] *DI*, IV, 64.

lasting peace. In this world of differing historical and racial backgrounds, cultural methods, ways of living, and economic conditions, he hoped for the growth of peace through freedom for each way of life to develop along its own lines. There should be help for this growth where possible without too much interference; and there should be an understanding of its ways, but no interfering with or allowing of it to interfere with others.[1] Through the principle of live and let live, but always with an evergrowing co-operation, he visualized a close but voluntary integration of the world.* He has no doubt that the United Nations—'with all its weaknesses in enforcing decisions'—has been a power for peace in the world, and it may grow along these lines.[2] The United Nations started at least with the assumption of universality, and countries entirely differing from each other in their structure of government, economic or political policy, all came together under this 'common umbrella'. 'So, one attribute of the United Nations—supposed attribute—was universality. The other, of course—the main objective—was the maintenance of peace, and the growth of co-operative effort among the nations, and the solution of disputes by peaceful means as far as possible.'[3] On occasions Nehru would think of some kind of close co-operation among autonomous nations for the preservation of world order, 'something even more than the United Nations represents today'. That 'one world' cannot be had suddenly or by a decree. One has to grow up to it. To Nehru, 'The United Nations—or rather the idea behind the United Nations—was a very big step towards that, and that idea is worth preserving and working for.'[4] And, obviously, one of the essential features of a world government through the United Nations, thinks Nehru, must be the prevention of aggression by one country against

---

* Speaking on the Resolution regarding 'Aims and Objects' in the Constituent Assembly, Nehru had said on January 22, 1947:—

'The only possible real objective that we, in common with other nations, can have is the objective of co-operating in building up some kind of world structure, call it "One World", call it what you like. The beginnings of this world structure have been laid down in the United Nations Organization. It is feeble yet; it has many defects; nevertheless, it is the beginning of the world structure. And India has pledged herself to co-operate in that work.' *Debates* C.A., Vol. II, No. 3, January 22, 1947.

[1] *Talks*, 58-9.
[2] *Conversations*, 87.
[3] *Debates* H.P., 1953, Vol. I, Part II, February 18, 1953.
[4] *Talks*, 40.

another. The world is torn by the conflict of different forces. In essence there is a conflict between two things, 'that atom bomb and what it represents and the spirit of humanity'. Finally, to Nehru, in this conflict, 'the human spirit will prevail over the atom bomb'.[1] Whatever the fear, the hope in peace is not lost.

'The danger of war is not past, and the future may hold fresh trials and tribulations for humanity. Yet the forces of peace are strong and the mind of humanity is awake. I believe that peace will triumph.'[2]

[1] *Debates* C.A., Vol. II, No. 3, January 22, 1947.
[2] *Speeches* III, 50, December 18, 1956.

Q

I. PRIMARY SOURCES

A. BASIC WRITINGS OF JAWAHARLAL NEHRU

Letters From A Father To His Daughter: Being a brief account of the Early Days of the World written for Children. (First published 1930) Allahabad, 1938 Ed.

Glimpses of World History: Being Further Letters to his daughter, written in prison, and containing a Rambling Account of History for young people. Two Vols. Allahabad, 1934-35.

Jawaharlal Nehru: An Autobiography: With Musings on Recent Events in India. (First published 1936) London, John Lane, 1958.

The Discovery of India. (First published 1946) London, Meridian Books, 1951.

Recent Essays and Writings. Allahabad, 1934.
Containing the following Essays:—Whither India?, Some Criticisms Considered, Further Criticisms, Hindu Mahasabha and Communalism, Hindu and Muslim Communalism, A Reply to Sir Mohammad Iqbal, Reality and Myth, A Window in Prison, Prison-land, The Andaman Prisoners, M. N. Roy, The Indian Struggle for Freedom, A Letter to England, Fascism and Communism, Labour and the Congress, Trade Union Congress, Indian States, Civics and Politics, The Civic Ideal, A Shadow Conference, A Message to the Prayag Mahila Vidyapitha.

India and the World: Essays. London, Allen & Unwin, 1936.
Containing the following Essays:—Presidential Address to the National Congress, 1929, Whither India, 1933, Presidential Address to the National Congress, 1936, Prison-Land, 1934, The Mind of a Judge, 1935, Quetta, 1935, First Letter to Indira, The Last Letter to Indira, Mahatma Gandhi, 1936, A Letter to an Englishman, India and the World, 1936, A Visit to England, 1936, The Way to Peace, 1936, Indian Problems, 1936.

Eighteen Months in India 1936-1937: Being Further Essays and Writings. Allahabad, 1938.

Containing the following Essays:—In a Train, Working Committee 1936, To my Friends and Critics, An Author Replies, The New Offensive, Congress and Socialism, Reality, A Roadside Interlude, This Touring Business, Students and Politics, A Pudukottah Reception, Farewell to Tamil Nad, Calcutta, Congress Presidentship, Presidential Address to the National Congress (Faizpur, December 1936), A Message to Socialists, A Note on the Tour, Election Messages, Presidential Address to the All-India Convention (Delhi, March 1937), Fascism and Empire, The Arabs and Jews in Palestine, Spain and Palestine, The Communal Award, The Congress and Muslims, Burma and Ceylon, India and China, Farewell to Burma, A Question of Manners, Indians and Ceylonese in Malaya, Indian Labour in Malaya, Farewell to Malaya, Back Home, The Princes and Federation, Bombing and Kidnapping on the Frontier, The Congress and Labour and Peasant Organizations, Note on the Constitutional Impasse, The Decision to Accept Office, Salaries of Public Servants, The Question of Language, Indian Troops to China, Zanzibar and the Boycott of Cloves, The Andamans' Hunger-strike, The Right Perspective.

B. SPEECHES, DEBATES, ADDRESSES AND LETTERS.

Independence and After: A Collection of the more important Speeches of Jawaharlal Nehru from September 1946 to May 1949. Ministry of Information and Broadcasting—Government of India, 1949.

Jawaharlal Nehru's Speeches 1949-1953. Ministry of Information and Broadcasting—Government of India, 1954.

Jawaharlal Nehru's Speeches: March 1953—August 1957. Ministry of Information and Broadcasting—Government of India, 1958.

Legislative Assembly Debates, 1946-1947.

Constituent Assembly Debates, 1946-1950.

Constituent Assembly of India (Legislative) Debates, 1947-1949.

Parliamentary Debates—Parliament of India, 1950-1952.

Parliamentary Debates—House of the People, 1952-1954.

Presidential Address, Indian National Congress, 57th Session. New Delhi, Thursday, October 18, 1951. Jawaharlal Nehru.

Presidential Address, Indian National Congress, 58th Session. Hyderabad —Deccan, Saturday, January 17, 1953. Jawaharlal Nehru.

Presidential Address, Indian National Congress, 59th Session. Kalyani, West Bengal, Saturday, January 23, 1954. Jawaharlal Nehru.

A Bunch of Old Letters: Written mostly to Jawaharlal Nehru and some written by him. Bombay, 1958.

C. MISCELLANEOUS.

The Life and Speeches of Pandit Jawaharlal Nehru. Edited by Dwivedi, R. Allahabad, 1929.

India on the March: Statements and Selected Quotations from the Writings of Jawaharlal Nehru . . . from 1916 to 1946. Edited by Bright, J. S. Lahore, 1946.

Selected Writings of Jawaharlal Nehru 1916-1950: Dealing with the Shape of Things to come in India and the World. Edited by Bright, J. S. New Delhi.

Before and After Independence: A Collection of the most important speeches delivered by Jawaharlal Nehru 1922-1950. Vols. I and II. Edited by Bright, J. S. New Delhi.

Jawaharlal Nehru: The Unity of India: Collected Writings 1937-1940. London, Drummond, 1948.

Nehru on Gandhi: A selection, arranged in the order of events, from the writings and speeches of Jawaharlal Nehru. New York, 1948.

The Question of Language by Jawaharlal Nehru. Allahabad, 1937.

Nehru-Jinnah Correspondence (Including Gandhi-Jinnah and Nehru-Nawab Ismail Correspondence). Allahabad, 1938.

Youth's Burden by Jawaharlal Nehru. Bombay, 1944.

Talks with Nehru: A discussion between Nehru and Norman Cousins. London, Gollancz, 1951.

Conversations with Mr Nehru: by Tibor Mende. London, Secker, 1956.
Jawaharlal Nehru, Press Conferences 1950, Press Conferences 1951, Press Conferences 1954. India Information Services, New Delhi.

Kashmir 1947-1956: Excerpts from Prime Minister Nehru's Speeches. Information Services of India, New Delhi, 1956.
(Several of the Speeches of Nehru as reported in various Newspapers of India have been consulted).

II. OTHER SOURCES

A. DOCUMENTARY (1)

Asian-African Conference, Bandung, Indonesia, April, 1955. Edited by Kahin, George McTurnan, New York, 1956.
Bande Mataram, Selections from the Articles published in the Calcutta Bande Mataram, I-III. Edited by Bhagavat, H. R. Poona, 1909.
Collected Works of Mahatma Gandhi. I. (1884-1896). Ministry of Information and Broadcasting, Government of India, Delhi, 1958.

Collected Works of Mahatma Gandhi. II. (1896-1897). Ministry of Information and Broadcasting, Government of India, Delhi, 1959.

Congress Presidential Addresses: From the Foundation to the Silver Jubilee. Containing full text of the Presidential Addresses from 1885 to 1910. First Series. Madras, 1937.

Congress Presidential Addresses: From the Silver to the Golden Jubilee. Containing full text of the Presidential Addresses from 1911 to 1934. Second Series. Madras, 1937.

Congress Resolutions Relating to the Legislatures, December 27, 1936 to August 17, 1937. A.I.C.C., Allahabad, 1937.

Delhi Diary: Prayer Speeches of M. K. Gandhi from September 10, 1947 to January 30, 1948. Ahmedabad, 1948.

First Five Year Plan. Ministry of Information and Broadcasting, Government of India, Delhi, 1953.

Gandhiji's Correspondence with the Government: 1944-1947. Ahmedabad, 1959.

India and the Aggressors: The Trend of Indian opinion between 1935-1940. Compiled by the Bureau of Public Information, Government of India, 1942.

India and the United Nations. New York, 1957.

Indian Communist Party Documents 1930-1956. Bombay, 1957.

Indian National Congress—Resolutions on Economic Policy and Programme 1924-54. A.I.C.C., New Delhi, 1954.

Indian National Congress, 1934-36: Being the resolutions passed by the Congress, the All India Congress Committee and the Working Committee during the period between May, 1934 and April, 1936. Allahabad, 1936.

Indian National Congress: February 1938 to January 1939: Being the resolutions passed by the Congress, the All India Congress Committee and the Working Committee. Allahabad, 1939.

Military Alliances 1947-57, Texts of Documents. New Delhi, 1957.

Nehru in Scandinavia. Information Service of India, Stockholm, 1958.

New India: Progress Through Democracy, Planning Commission, Government of India. New York, 1958.

Papers Relating to the Formulation of the Second Five Year Plan. Government of India, Planning Commission. New Delhi, 1955.

Report, National Planning Committee. Edited by Shah, K. T. Bombay, 1949.

Select Documents on Asian Affairs: India 1947-50. Two Vols. Edited by Poplai, S. L. London, 1959.

Young India, 1919-1922, Parts I and II. Madras, 1922.

A. DOCUMENTARY (2)

Besant, Annie. *Speeches and Writings of.* Madras, 1921.

Bose, Subhas Chandra. *On to Delhi: Speeches and Writings of.* Poona, 1946.

Bright, Esther. *Old Memories and Letters of Annie Besant.* London, Theos. Pub. House, 1936.

Campbell-Johnson, Alan. *Mission With Mountbatten.* London, Hale, 1951-2.

Das, Desabandhu. *Speeches of.* Madras, 1923.

Desai, V. G. (Ed.) *The Diary of Mahadev Desai.* Ahmedabad, 1953.

Duncan, Ronald. *Selected Writings of Mahatma Gandhi.* London, Faber, 1951.

Gandhi, M. K. *Speeches and Writings of.* Madras.

Jinnah, Mohd. Ali. *Speeches by Quaid-e-Azam.* Karachi, 1948.

Mavalankar, G. V. *Speeches and Writings.* New Delhi, 1957.

Mountbatten Earl. *Time only to Look Forward.* Speeches of Rear Admiral the Earl Mountbatten of Burma as Viceroy of India . . . 1947-48. (Including related addresses). London, Kaye, 1949.

Naoroji, Dadabhai. *Speeches and Writings of.* Madras, 1910.

Rajagopalachari, C. *Speeches of.* (*1948-50*). New Delhi, 1950.

Sharma, Jagdish Saran. *Mahatma Gandhi: A Descriptive Bibliography.* Delhi, 1955.

Sharma, Jagdish Saran. *Jawaharlal Nehru: A Descriptive Bibliography.* Delhi, 1955.

Sharma, Jagdish Saran. *Indian National Congress: A Descriptive Bibliography.* Delhi, 1959.

Sitaramayya, B. P. *The History of the Indian National Congress (1885-1935).* Madras, 1935.

Tilak, Bal Gangadhar. *Speeches of.* (*1889-1918*). Madras, 1918. (?)

B. BIOGRAPHICAL

Andrews, C. F. (Ed.) *Mahatma Gandhi: His Own Story.* London, Allen & Unwin, 1930.

Azad, Maulana Abul Kalam. *India Wins Freedom: An Autobiographical Narrative.* Bombay, 1959.

Besant, Annie. *An Autobiography.* Madras, 1939.

Bose, Subhas Chandra. *An Indian Pilgrim or Autobiography (1897-1920).* Calcutta, 1948.

Brecher, Michael. *Nehru: A Political Biography.* London, Oxford University Press, 1959.

Desai, Mahadev. *Maulana Abul Kalam Azad.* Agra, 1946.

Fischer, Louis. *The Life of Mahatma Gandhi.* London, Cape, 1951.

Gandhi, M. K. *An Autobiography: The Story of my Experiments with Truth.* London, Luzae: Probstharin, 1949.

Hutheesing, Krishna. *With No Regrets: An Autobiography.* Bombay, 1944.

Jack, Homer A. (Ed.) *The Gandhi Reader: A Source Book of His Life and Writings.* Bloomington, 1956.

Jayakar, M. R. *The Story of My Life.* Vols. I and II. Bombay, 1958-59.

Karmarkar, D. P. *Bal Gangadhar Tilak: A Study.* Bombay, 1956.
Khan, Aga. *The Memoirs of Aga Khan.* London, Cassell, 1954.
Masani, R. P. *Dadabhai Naoroji: The Grand Old Man of India.* London, Allen & Unwin, 1939.
Mody, H. P. *Sir Pherozeshah Mehta: A Political Biography.* Bombay, 1921.
Moraes, Frank, *Jawaharlal Nehru: A Biography.* New York, 1956.
Parikh, N. D. *Sardar Vallabhbhai Patel.* Ahmedabad, 1953.
Patel, G. I. *Vithalbhai Patel: Life and Times.* 2 Vols. Bombay.
Polak, H. S. L., Brailsford, H. N. and Pethick-Lawrence, Lord. *Mahatma Gandhi.* London, Odhams, 1949.
Polak, Millie Graham. *Mr Gandhi: The Man.* Bombay, 1949.
Prasad, Rajendra. *Autobiography.* Bombay, 1957.
Pyarelal. *Mahatma Gandhi: The Last Phase.* Vols. I and II. Ahmedabad, 1956-58.
Rolland, Romain. *Mahatma Gandhi.* London, Allen & Unwin, 1932.
Sahgal, Nayantara. *Prison and Chocolate Cake.* London, Gollanez, 1954.
Shukla, Chandrashanker (Ed.) *Incidents of Gandhiji's Life.* Bombay, 1949.
Tahmankar, D. V. *Lokamanya Tilak.* London, Murray, 1956.
Tendulkar, D. G. *Mahatma: Life of Mohandas Karamchand Gandhi.* In Eight Volumes. Bombay, 1951-54.
Toye, Hugh. *The Springing Tiger: A Study of a Revolutionary.* London, Cassell, 1959.
Wedderburn, William. *Allan Octavian Hume.* London, Fisher Unwin, 1913.

C. MISCELLANEOUS

Agarwal, Shriman Narayan. *Towards a Socialist Economy.* New Delhi, 1955.
Ali, Rahmat. *Pakistan.* (Great Britain), 1947.
Amery, L. S. *India and Freedom.* Oxford University Press, 1942.
Andrews, C. F. *Mahatma Gandhi's Ideas.* London, Allen & Unwin, 1949.
Ball, W. MacMahon. *Nationalism and Communism in East Asia.* Melbourne, 1956.
Benes, Eduard. *Democracy Today and Tomorrow.* London, Macmillan, 1939.
Besant, Annie. *India: A Nation.* London, Theos. Pub. House, 1930.
Besant, Annie. *India: Essays and Addresses.* London Theos. Pub. House, 1913.
Besant, Annie. *India and the Empire.* London, Theos. Pub. House, 1914.
Besant, Annie. *How India Wrought for Freedom.* Madras, 1915.
Besant, Annie. *The Future of Indian Politics.* London, Theos. Pub. House, 1922.
Besant, Annie. *India Bond or Free?* London, Theos. Pub. House, 1926.
Birla, G. D. *In the Shadow of the Mahatma.* Bombay, 1953.
Bolton, G. *The Tragedy of Gandhi.* London, Allen & Unwin, 1934.
Bose, Subhas Chandra. *The Indian Struggle: 1920-34.* London, Wishart, 1935.

Bose, Subhas Chandra. *The Indian Struggle: 1935-1942.* Calcutta, 1952.

Bryce, James. *Modern Democracies.* 2 Vols. London, Macmillan, 1921.

Buck, Pearl S. *Asia and Democracy.* London, 1943.

Callard, Keith. *Pakistan: A Political Study.* London, Allen & Unwin, 1957.

Carr, E. H. *The Twenty Years' Crisis 1919-1939.* London, Macmillan, 1939.

Chander, Jag Parvesh. *Teachings of Mahatma Gandhi.* Lahore, 1945.

Chander, Jag Parvesh. *India's Socialistic Pattern of Society.* Delhi, 1956.

Chintamani, C. Y. *Indian Politics since the Mutiny.* London, Allen & Unwin, 1940.

Churchill, Winston S. *The Sinews of Peace* (Post-war Speeches). London, Cassell, 1948.

Das, Taraknath. *Rabindranath Tagore: His Religious, Social and Political Ideals.* Calcutta, 1932.

Dayal, Shiv. *India's Role in the Korean Question.* Delhi, 1959.

De Mello, F. M. *The Indian National Congress: An Historical Sketch.* Oxford University Press, 1934.

Desai, A. R. *Social Background of Indian Nationalism.* Oxford University Press, 1948.

Deshpande, M. S. *Light of India: Message of Mahatmaji.* Saugli, 1950.

Dhawan, G. N. *The Political Philosophy of Mahatma Gandhi.* Bombay, 1946.

Duffett, W. E., Hicks, A. R., and Parkin, G. R. *India Today: The Background of Indian Nationalism.* New York, 1942.

Durai, J. Chinna. *The Choice Before India.* London, Cape, 1941.

Fifield, Russell H. *The Diplomacy of South-East Asia: 1945-1958.* New York, 1958.

Fisher, Margaret W. and Bondurant, Joan V. *Indian Approaches to a Socialist Society.* Berkeley, 1956.

Gandhi, M. K. *Satyagraha in South Africa.* Madras, 1928.

Gandhi, M. K. *Non-Violence in Peace and War.* Ahmedabad, 1942.

Gandhi, M. K. *To the Protagonists of Pakistan.* (Edited by Hingorani, A. T.). Karachi, 1947.

Ghosh, Aurobindo. *The Ideal of Human Unity.* Pondichery, 1950.

Gunther, John. *Inside Asia.* London, H. Hamilton, 1939.

Holmes, John Haynes. *My Gandhi.* London, Allen & Unwin, 1954.

Husain, S. Abid. *The Way of Gandhi and Nehru.* Bombay, 1959.

Iyengar, A. S. *All Through the Gandhian Era.* Bombay, 1950.

Kachroo, J. L. *India in the Commonwealth.* Delhi, 1959.

Khan, Shafa'at Ahmad. *The Indian in South Africa.* Allahabad, 1946.

Kothari, Shantilal. *India's Emerging Foreign Policies.* Bombay, 1951.

Kundra, J. C. *Indian Foreign Policy: 1947-1954.* New York, 1955.

Lal Bahadur. *The Muslim League.* Agra, 1954.

Levi, Werner. *Free India in Asia.* Minnesota, 1952.

Lovett, V. *A History of the Indian Nationalist Movement.* London, Murray, 1921.

Maine, H. S. *Popular Government.* London, Murray, 1886.

Marx, Karl. *Letters on India* (Edited by B.P.L. and Freda Bedi). Lahore, 1936.

Marx, Karl. *Articles on India*. Bombay, 1943.

Mashruwala, K. G. *Gandhi and Marx*. Ahmedabad, 1956.

Mellor, Andrew. *India Since Partition*. London, Turnstile Press, 1951.

Menon, V. P. *The Transfer of Power in India*. London, Longmans, 1957.

Morton, E. *Women Behind Mahatma Gandhi*. London, Reinhardt, 1954.

Narasimha Char, K. T. *A Day Book of Thoughts From Mahatma Gandhi*. Calcutta, 1951.

Narayan, Jayaprakas. *Why Socialism?* Benares, 1936.

Narayan, Jayaprakas. *Towards Struggle*. Bombay, 1946.

Narayan, Jayaprakas. *Towards A New Society*. New Delhi, 1958.

Nehru Abhinandan Granth Committee. *Nehru Abhinandan Granth: A Birthday Book*. New Delhi, 1949.

Nehru, Krishna. *Shadows on the Wall*. New York, 1948.

Nichols, Beverley. *Verdict on India*. London, Cape, 1944.

Pal, Bepin Chandra. *Indian Nationalism: Its Principles and Personalities*. Madras, 1918.

Pal, Bepin Chandra. *Swadeshi and Swaraj*. Calcutta, 1954.

Pandit, Vijaya Lakshmi. *The Evolution of India*. Oxford University Press, 1958.

Prasad, Rajendra. *India Divided*. Bombay, 1946.

Prasad, Rajendra. *Mahatma Gandhi and Bihar*. Bombay, 1949.

Prasad, Rajendra. *Satyagraha in Champaran*. Ahmedabad, 1949.

Prasad, Rajendra. *At the Feet of Mahatma Gandhi*. Bombay, 1955.

Pyarelal. *The Epic Fast*. Ahmedabad, 1932.

Pyarelal. *A Pilgrimage for Peace*. Ahmedabad, 1950.

Radha Krishnan, S. *Is This Peace?* Bombay, 1950.

Raman, T. A. *What Does Gandhi Want?* Oxford University Press, 1943.

Reddy, C. R. *Congress in Office*. Madras, 1940.

Reynolds, Reginald. *To Live in Mankind: A Quest for Gandhi*. London, Deutsch, 1951.

Reynolds, Reginald. *The True Book About Mahatma Gandhi*. London, Muller, 1959.

Rocker, Rudolf. *Nationalism and Culture*. California, 1937.

Romulo, Carlos P. *The Meaning of Bandung*. North Carolina, 1956.

Roosevelt, Eleanor. *India and the Awakening East*. London, Hutchinson, 1954.

Rose, Saul. *Socialism in Southern Asia*. Oxford University Press, 1959.

Roy, M. N. *Nationalism: An Antiquated Cult*. Bombay, 1943.

Roy, M. N. *New Humanism*. Calcutta, 1953.

Rushbrook Williams, L. F. *What About India?* London, Nelson, 1939.

Sahai, Govind. *'42 Rebellion*. Delhi, 1947.

Sarma, D. S. *The Father of the Nation*. Madras, 1956.

Satyapal and Probodh Chandra. *Sixty Years of Congress*. Lahore, 1946.

Schuster, George, and Wint, Guy. *India and Democracy*. London, Macmillan, 1941.

Sen, Ela. *Gandhi.* London, Allen & Unwin, 1948.

Shay, Theodore L. *The Legacy of the Lokamanya.* Oxford University Press, 1956.

Shridharani, Krishnalal. *The Mahatma and the World.* New York, 1946.

Smith, William Roy. *Nationalism and Reform in India.* Yale University Press, 1938.

Thomas, Lowell. *The Silent War in Tibet.* London, Secker & Warburg, 1960.

Townsend, Meredith. *Asia and Europe.* New York, 1907.

Trivedi, K. D. *Towards Red Ruin.* Lucknow, 1933.

Weiner, Myron. *Party Politics in India.* Oxford University Press, 1957.

INDEX

THE END